all my TOMORROWS

A Story of Tragedy, Transplant and Hope

ERIC GREGORY

Word Association Publishers
205 Fifth Avenue
Tarentum, Pennsylvania 15084
www.wordassociation.com
1.800.827.7903

Cover photograph by Grace M. Gregory

ISBN: 978-1-63385-213-6 [SOFTCOVER]
ISBN: 978-1-63385-220-4 [HARDBACK]

Library of Congress Control Number: 2017911297

For Grace

"I'd trade all my tomorrows for one single yesterday …"
—Kris Kristofferson
"Me and Bobby McGee"

prologue
MARCH 22, 2008

Plane tickets are cheap. That's one thing I learned the hard way. If a plane ride will put you next to someone you love, it doesn't matter how much it costs. Plane tickets are cheap.

In February, our entire family was in college. All of us. Grace, my wife, was working on a bachelor of science degree in nursing; she was finally pursuing her lifelong goal of becoming a nurse. Our oldest son, John, and I were working on master's degrees. Our middle son, Colin, and his little brother, Chris, were undergrads at Loyola University New Orleans. Do you have any idea how fast money burns through your pocket when the entire family is in college at the same time?

So when the idea of spending Easter break in Tucson with Grace's sister and her husband came up, my first reaction was, "No way." We simply couldn't afford the airfare. But in February, I had a change of heart. Maybe it was a moment of temporary insanity. I told Grace to buy the tickets. John couldn't make the trip, but Grace and I would fly to Tucson from Baltimore while Colin and Chris would fly from New Orleans. Our flights arrived within a few minutes of each other, just long enough for Grace and me to get a rental car and swing back to pick up the boys.

We saw them standing with their bags in front of the terminal. They were looking for us in every car that passed by. I slowed to a crawl as we passed them and started honking the horn and waving. But I didn't stop. I was kidding around a bit. We laughed as the boys picked up their duffle bags and started after us. Chris laughed as he ran beside us with his huge, oversize bag I'd given him for Christmas years before. He loved it and still used it despite its broken shoulder strap. Grinning from ear to ear, he chased us at a dead run through the traffic as we waved, honked, and kept rolling.

Two things made Chris Gregory rare in the world. He possessed no fashion sense whatsoever, a byproduct possibly of his color blindness. And he flat out didn't care about it. The combinations he put together were usually crosses between something he'd found in his grandfather's closet and whatever of yours he could steal.

So let's get the worst of Christopher's life out in the open now. He was an unrepentant clothes thief. He didn't even try to hide it. The more audacious the better. He would steal someone's shirt in the afternoon and wear it to a party that night with the shirt's owner in attendance. Chris didn't care.

As he ran after us laughing hysterically, he was in another of his trademark outfits— a blue, pinstriped dress shirt that hadn't seen an iron in months and the most hideous pair of green plaid Bermuda shorts. Man, he looked good!

That he could run at all was surprising because his shoes were as usual untied. At age nineteen, he wore size fourteens. He refused to wear sandals on planes.

Plane tickets are cheap. It was a great trip. One day, we visited Fort Huachuca, Tombstone, and Bisbee. It snowed that day. We were amazed that snow fell on the Sonoran Desert only a few miles from the Mexican border. It was magic.

At the Copper Queen Hotel in Bisbee, Grace stared across the table at lunch and asked Colin, "Are those hickeys on your neck?"

As Colin fumbled for an excuse (dirt, bruises, etc.), Chris burst out laughing. "Colin," he nearly shouted, "what were you thinking? How long did you think you would get away with it?" Much to Colin's chagrin, we all laughed. Not at Colin but with him. The laughter at lunch alone was worth the trip.

At dinner one night, our brother-in-law, Tom, said to me, "I've never seen a family have so much fun with each other. I've never seen a family laugh so much."

I was glad he made such an observation especially with Chris.

Chris was in his freshman year of college. I'd like to be able to say he made the most of his academic opportunities at Loyola, but I was told that on Halloween of his freshman year, he thought the campus library would make a fine place to carve a jack-o'-lantern from a huge pumpkin. I can only imagine the mess. When his grades arrived over Christmas break, we discovered he hadn't been devoting much energy to academics.

When the phone bill arrived, we discovered why. Chris had a girlfriend. Her name was Jenn. She was from Arizona. I was apoplectic. I screamed. I hollered. I told him he wasn't going back to Loyola. But there was a problem. Loyola was a Jesuit school, and Chris knew I wanted all the Gregory men to have Jesuit educations. It would be a common experience. Something that would make us even closer than we were. Chris was heartbroken when he didn't get into Gonzaga, the Jesuit high school his older brothers had attended. He worshiped his brothers and wanted to go to school with them. So going to Loyola was largely a way to make that right. I knew my gyrations and theatrics about the phone bill were largely for naught. In the end, we told Chris we hoped he'd learned a lesson. I'm glad we did. Still, Christmas was a little, shall we say, strained.

A month before our Arizona vacation, Chris sent me an e-mail after he received his itinerary. In between a running commentary on the subtropical weather in Louisiana, he reported that his test grades were much improved.

> I really want to thank you and mom for giving me the opportunity to come back here and give it another shot. I feel like I am really getting this college thing right finally. I could not be more thankful for how patient you and mom have been over the years, but I feel blessed that I had parents who believed in me even when I didn't believe in myself. Thank you so much for all of this, again. I will talk to you soon.

Plane tickets are cheap. It was a great week in Tucson. We laughed and joked. We ate dinner together every night. One night after dinner at Mary Lou's, Colin and I cleared the table and did the dishes while Chris, Grace, and Mary Lou stayed at the table and talked. The conversation turned to driver's licenses. Chris produced his, and it had a heart on it that identified him as an organ donor.

"So you're an organ donor?" Grace asked.

"Of course I am," he replied. "Why wouldn't I be? What am I going to do with my organs after I'm dead?"

Mary Lou was a nurse, and Grace was studying to be a nurse, so Chris's attitude met with their approval.

"And besides," Chris said with a huge grin, "who wouldn't want *this* body?"

I asked Chris if Jenn was in Arizona. It would have been nice to have met her. It turned out she was spending Easter in New Orleans, but I was glad I asked. It was my way of saying that the first semester had been forgotten, that he was loved unconditionally, that whatever anger I'd felt at Christmas was behind us.

That trip to Arizona allowed me to rebuild one of the most important relationships in my life. It gave me the chance to unload some baggage and focus on what's really important— just loving and enjoying one another. Christmas was over. Easter was upon us. It was spring. A time for new beginnings. It was so good to be with each other. I'm so happy we spent that time together.

Grace and I had an early flight back Saturday morning from Tucson. The boys' flight to New Orleans wasn't until late in the afternoon, so they were still awake watching TV in the predawn hours when we left. We hugged them and said our farewells. I stuffed three twenties in Christopher's shirt pocket and gave him a long hug. "I love you, son," I said as I kissed his cheek.

"I love you too, Pop."

Those were last words I would ever hear him say.

Time is precious. Plane tickets are cheap.

the meeting

JULY 9, 2009

No experience is worse than being a parent who has suffered the death of a child. It's so horrible that the English language doesn't have a word for it. Someone who loses his or her parents is an orphan. Someone who loses a spouse becomes a widow or widower. But losing a child is so wrong that there isn't even a word for it.

Throughout history, parents have suffered that awful fate. In earlier centuries, it happened with greater frequency than it does today, but that doesn't mean it had less of an impact on parents back then. The experience took a heavy emotional toll on Mary Todd Lincoln and Theodore Roosevelt. On the death of his five-year-old son in 1842, Ralph Waldo Emerson wrote,

> You can never sympathize with me; you can never know how much of me such a young child can take away. A few weeks ago I accounted myself a very rich man, and now the poorest of all.

But sometimes, life introduces circumstances that make things less wrong. Call it fate, or karma, or destiny. Sometimes, tragedy brings people into our lives who would not otherwise have been there. People who will always be part of our tragedy and be the vehicle of our healing and redemption. Sometimes, they appear when we least expect it. Sometimes, we don't understand it for what it is until we experience the moment of our rescue, our redemption. We didn't know it at the time, but we were about to experience such a moment.

BALTIMORE

The time on the dash read 4:40 p.m. as Grace and I pulled into a parking space at the Westin Hotel near BWI Airport. We were twenty minutes early. It was July. And it was hot. We sat in the car with the air conditioning running. There was no activity in the parking lot. Nobody coming or going. The sky was hazy and bright, and it wouldn't have been unusual for a thunderstorm to pop up. The radio was off. The silence was overpowering. We were very nervous but in a good way. Excited, not scared. Grace cleared her throat several times. That betrayed her anxiety. There we sat each of us deep in thought, each pondering what the next few minutes might bring. I broke the silence.

"You nervous?"

"A little. Aren't you?" Grace asked.

"Of course. But trust me, honey, these folks are a lot more nervous than we are."

And we were certain they were. They really had no idea what they would encounter. How do you say, "Thank you for saving my life? I'm thankful to be alive, and I'm sorry your son had to die for that to be possible"? We could have been bitter, angry people. We could have been filled with resentment that they were able to continue their happy lives while we cried ourselves to sleep every night.

We had somehow learned to exist in two states. On one level, we were normal, functioning human beings able to communicate with the world as mature adults. But always, just below the surface, lay another reality. That reality could surface with the recall of a memory, a song on the radio, the mention of his name, the discovery of an old photograph, or a note he'd written as a child. Like dropping an Alka-Seltzer in a glass of water, any of these could bring our emotions to the surface, overwhelming the normal people we pretended to be. Our visitors knew we were neither bitter nor angry. If they had, they wouldn't have made the trip. They had no desire to open old wounds. They came to help us heal.

They didn't owe us anything. They'd already paid their dues—years of making do with lungs that didn't function properly. Years of physical discomfort, always short of breath, and always worrying. All of that had grown worse as Jorge's health declined rapidly and the end drew near. It was a constant struggle between a flicker of life and the ever-present fear of imminent death. They really didn't owe anything to anyone.

Fifteen months earlier, we had buried Chris. Age nineteen. A freshman in college with his whole life in front of him. Then in an instant he was gone. Grace and I had flown home on a Saturday before the boys did from our spring break in Arizona. The following Monday, he suffered a brain aneurysm and collapsed at a friend's house. He was rushed to Tulane University Medical Center, where he was pronounced dead two days later. To our eternal gratitude and pride, Chris had registered as an organ donor.

For months, I prayed that God would give me a sign. That he would allow me to meet the people whose lives had become a continuation of Christopher's. That he might let me know that somehow Chris was okay.

The day after Chris died, Jorge Bacardi received a double lung transplant. A team of surgeons flew from the Mayo Clinic in Jacksonville, Florida, to New Orleans and removed Chris's lungs. The organs were flown back to Jacksonville only hours after Jorge and his wife, Leslie, had arrived from Nassau, Bahamas.

Before his transplant, he was very near death, but five days later, he walked out of the hospital with Christopher's lungs and a new lease on life. Life's funny. One day, some kid is a happy-go-lucky college freshman healthy as a horse and another guy is standing at death's door. And then in a matter of hours, they somehow trade places.

The Bacardis were making a special trip to Maryland to visit the family of the boy whose decision to be an organ donor had given Jorge a second chance at life. He'd already expressed his gratitude in letters and e-mails in beautiful ways. We were about to meet them. Some sentiments just can't be reduced to writing. Some things have to be said in person, face to face. Somehow, we had already learned to trust each other.

This meeting was the answer to countless prayers that had begun back in Christopher's hospital room. I prayed that some-day I might actually meet the people who would become the beneficiaries of my son's sacrifice. To speak to them. To hear their voices. To hold their hands. Maybe that would help me understand and accept what had happened. God had taken my son way too soon. Perhaps he would allow me the chance to just once more embrace some physical, living remnant of Chris's existence.

But it was really more than that. The spiritual and the physical had become one and the same in the five people who were Chris's organ recipients. Through these people, I was looking for some kind of sign that would let me know my son was somehow still okay.

A few weeks after Chris died, we received a letter from the Louisiana Organ Procurement Agency (LOPA). It identified the five recipients of his organs only by age, location, and the briefest description. This practice protects the identities of donors and recipients. Only the smallest doses of information are released to donor families.

It wasn't for some months that we learned any first names. We recalled a sixty-four-year-old woman who had received Christopher's liver. We knew she was in Shreveport because we'd been told that in the hospital. She had been on the transplant list for thirty-nine months. She was the oldest. The youngest recipient was forty-six. The recipients had been waiting for transplants from two months to more than three years. Disabled, retired, married, divorced, single, some with children, some without. All their lives changed for the better.

It was such an emotional relief to get news of that first match. It didn't necessarily make things any better, but for just a moment, it offered some glimmer of hope and stopped things from getting worse. That first match would become the initial thread of an emotional lifeline that along with the other recipients sustains us to this day.

Donors and recipients alike are warned not to expect to hear from each other for a long time if ever, but our hearts were aching for any news of Chris's organ recipients. We no longer had our Chris to hug, or call on the phone, or to swap e-mails with. All photographs of future family gatherings would forever be incomplete. We had a new reality. We were linked to people we didn't know through a miracle of science. I think donor parents have a special need to know about their children's organ recipients; it's a need that few outside that community can understand.

A longing is born from the loss of a child. A constant heartache whether the child was lost before birth or lived to maturity. For the parent of a deceased child of any age, the world no longer functions normally. The natural, linear progression of time, where children attend their grandparents' funerals, and then those of their parents, and then move on, no longer exists. The world is forever turned upside down. The grieving process becomes more complicated and severe when your child is gone.

And so news of a transplant recipient can be strangely comparable to a sign from the deceased child. Parents are looking for clues that maybe life doesn't end; perhaps it only changes. We are left with the hope we might see him again. Until then, we no longer had Chris, but we now had five new souls in our lives that hadn't been there a year earlier. And so, for a time, that longing, that desperation, was being answered.

"Perhaps we should go in," I suggested looking at the clock on the dashboard.

We stepped out of the car and into the heat. Slowly and deliberately, we walked to the entrance of the hotel. I reached out, and Grace took my hand. Her palms were moist. Meeting at their hotel was Jorge's idea. I'd seen these kinds of reunions on television—heartwarming images of families meeting for the first time. Lots of balloons and flowers and happy tears. Nothing wrong with that. But that just wasn't us. This seemed more appropriate. Subdued and dignified. Intensely personal and private. It would be just Grace, me, Jorge, and his lovely wife, Leslie. And by lovely I do mean lovely. As it turned out, finding each other was pretty easy. Except for the four of us, the hotel lobby was empty.

Walking through the door, I didn't know what to feel. I guess I went numb. I knew only that I wanted this moment to last a long time. We had shed too many tears not to savor this reunion. The moment we had dreamed of, for which I had prayed for so long, had finally arrived. Jorge and Leslie stood at the far side of the lobby opposite the entrance looking out the window.

"There they are," I whispered.

Time stood still for the briefest moment. Just as I had hoped. And then, very slowly, they turned toward the entrance. The Bacardis had been waiting in the lobby for as long as we had been sitting in the parking lot. Neither of us wanted to be late for this meeting. They had seen a dozen people come and go through the lobby. But when Grace and I walked through the door, they seemed to recognize us at once. We walked toward one another slowly at first. Then our paces quickened. Tears flowed before we even came together. Not a single word was spoken for the first few minutes. None of us would have known what to say anyway. It was as complete and honest a release of tension and emotion as one could ever hope to experience.

Jorge and Grace were crying in each other's arms before uttering even a hello. At some level, my mind's eye viewed the moment Grace finally reunited with her son. Grace hadn't touched Christopher's body since his funeral.

The four of us stood there for a moment laughing and crying. Finally, awkward and unnecessary introductions were made—formalities for people who had never met but were already close. And there we were. Four sets of watery eyes, four sets of trembling hands, four racing hearts brought together by the lungs of one very special young man.

Countless visits to our son's grave were nothing compared to the emotion we experienced holding a living, breathing part of Chris in our arms. It was a moment so surreal that after being through it the first time, I wondered if it could ever be repeated.

How did it happen? How was it that the five of us came together that July afternoon? Yes, five of us. Chris was there that day. With Jorge, Chris is never far away. From the very beginning, he always referred to Chris in the present tense.

What circumstances brought us together? Chris and Jorge are different in many ways but also much alike. Jorge Bacardi is the wealthy retired patriarch of the famous Cuban rum family, and Chris Gregory was a college freshman from an anonymous, middle-class community. One with the better part of his life already behind him, and the other with his entire life ahead. Both of them loyal, family-centered, and generous in their own ways.

The odds of them meeting one another under normal circumstances had been at least a million to one. And no one could have predicted that the Bacardi family and the Gregory family would grow as close as we have. But these were not normal circumstances by any stretch of the imagination. Their lives had indeed come together. More completely than anyone could comprehend.

But just how did it happen? And why? What miracles of science and faith allowed our broken hearts to begin to mend? Just as important was what transpired in the months after the meeting. To all of this, I am only a humble witness. What I have seen and been a part of since that meeting has left me dumbstruck. I will try to tell the story of how Christopher's death saved the lives of others, and in their gratitude, how they saved mine.

It's a story worth telling. I know I owe Chris that much. Perhaps it will offer some hope to another heartbroken parent. Maybe there's a guy out there not really looking forward to another Fathers' Day who will read this story and understand he's not alone. It might also help to clear up some common misconceptions about organ donation.

This is a story about relationships. About how friendships can result even from tragic circumstances. How difficult moments can bring out the best in people. How being a witness to something can have a tremendous and irreversible effect. It's also a story of how a seemingly small act at a particular moment can have a profound impact on someone else's life.

Most of all, I hope people will read these pages and remember Chris. Remember his sense of humor and the sincere soul he was. And maybe they'll read about what he did. He didn't save just one life. He saved five. And so many people who never knew him in life hold him in high esteem today. For all these reasons and some I have yet to understand, I think it's important that I tell this story. So I'll do my best.

To begin, we should go to Cuba and a little boy not unlike Chris.

jorge bacardi:

THE BENEFACTOR

Cuba is a tropical paradise unlike any other. It's an exotic mix of romance and danger and a tragic history of broken promises. It's the source of the finest tobacco and the sweetest fruit. Cuba is not one island but many; its coast is surrounded by hundreds of lesser islands and cays. The lush, green mountains of the Sierra Maestra are mysterious and have been the birthplace of insurrection. The waters that surround Cuba are so vibrant with greens and blues that they almost hurt the eyes. It's a land of white, sandy beaches and majestic palm trees.

The people who call themselves Cuban are the most passionate, warm, family-centered people one could ever wish to meet. Their passion for life is born of the violent and tragic history of the Cuban nation. Once they embrace you, they hold you in their arms and hearts forever. The history of Cuba is one of intrigue and romance in equal doses. Cuba produces the best cigars, musicians, and baseball players in the world. It's sad to be from such a place and not be able to call it home. It was here that Jorge Bacardi was born.

Jorge was the youngest of four children born to Joaquin Bacardi and Caridad Bolivar. Jorge's great-grandfather Facundo arrived from the Spanish town of Sitges in 1830. Facundo and his sons along with a French wine merchant purchased a rum distillery in 1862. One of Facundo's sons was Jose, Jorge Bacardi's grandfather. Over the years, the Bacardi family grew their rum into the largest and most famous brand in the world.

Because he's six years younger than his next-oldest sibling, Jorge sometimes refers to himself as the "mistake." Once one meets him, though, it quickly becomes obvious that nothing could be further from the truth. This guy is no mistake. Jorge is an intelligent, articulate gentleman and a well-read world traveler. Tio Jorge, or TJ, is loved and adored by all who know him. He's the kind of guy often found chatting up strangers on the dock of a marina. He's equally comfortable in a boardroom full of business executives or a high school auditorium filled with students. Jorge and his wife, Leslie, have a way of making lasting friendships. Once they draw you into their circle of friends, you're not leaving. You become a friend for life.

He was born in Santiago de Cuba, a city steeped in history. Jorge's birthplace is given away by the faint traces of a nasal Cuban accent. One thinks of Ricky Ricardo, and that's reasonable since Desi Arnaz is also from Santiago and a distant relative of Jorge's to boot. When they were children, their home life was normal, but his siblings were warned by their parents not to pick on Jorge since he was "not well." One suspects that he may have used that admonishment to perpetrate at least a little mischief as a child.

Sadly, neither he nor his siblings have set foot in Cuba since 1960. Like much of the Cuban diaspora after the Cuban revolution, Jorge's siblings and their offspring settled in different parts of the world. They're a tight-knit family in spite of the distances that separate them.

From birth, life was not easy for Jorge. He spent the first twenty days of his life in an oxygen tent. His health problems were originally misdiagnosed as cystic fibrosis. For a child in the 1940s, that was a death sentence, but it didn't seem to matter to young Jorge. As he grew older and became more aware of his medical condition, he figured as long as it wasn't cancer, he didn't care.

It wasn't as easy for his mother. Joaquin and Caridad were told he wouldn't live to age fourteen. At age fourteen, they were told he wouldn't live to twenty. He had the middle lobe of his right lung removed when he was ten. The bottom lobe of his left lung was removed when he was fourteen. In the early 1990s, his pulmonologist at Massachusetts General Hospital reviewing his lengthy medical records read one of the earliest notes. It noted that, "at 4 ½ years of age, the patient has had a long history of respiratory illness."

His parents were told to make the most of life with their son for however long they could. They shouldn't take unnecessary risks with the boy, their doctors advised. Don't allow him to get a cold or exercise too strenuously. Jorge was told to make the best of his condition. Jorge's mother was a saint, and the emotional toll Jorge's condition took on her was high. Described by family members as an intelligent, strong-willed, and loving mother, Caridad protected Jorge. She sometimes doted on the boy.

Prior generations of the Bacardi family have had family members die of pneumonia-type illnesses including an uncle of Jorge's. It would be years before Jorge would be properly diagnosed with primary ciliary dyskinesia (PCD). Because of the genetic nature of PCD, it's possible that some of these deaths may have been related to that condition before the disease was fully understood. So Jorge was protected by his mom, and his physical activity as a youngster was restricted.

However, Jorge loved playing soccer. That's a very anaerobic sport that requires more lung capacity than Jorge had, so he kept changing positions as they winded him beyond his ability to endure and ended up as goalie.

He committed himself at an early age to being the best he could be though at times that commitment often left him exhausted and out of breath. He found joy and therapy in water. The exercise he got from swimming and spearfishing necessarily required him to test the limits of his diminished lung capacity. The need to hold his breath underwater allowed his lungs to compensate for the void created by his surgeries. As it turned out, the water sports prolonged his life and kept him healthy enough to survive to adulthood.

Jorge attended the Jesuit-run Colegio de Dolores in Santiago de Cuba through second grade. For third grade, he joined his brothers Joaquin and Alberto at the Fessenden School in West Newton, Massachusetts, but he rarely saw them there. Two years later, his brothers were off at high school, and Jorge found himself all alone.

After grade school, Jorge's family sent him to the prestigious Tabor Academy in Sippican Harbor at Marion, Massachusetts. There, his love of the sea was nurtured and confirmed. Tabor, then as now, was a naval honor school in that it promoted the study of naval subjects at the secondary level and encouraged young men to apply to the nation's service academies.

While at Tabor, Jorge received a letter from his father. Conditions in Cuba had deteriorated. The company's property had been seized by the government. Jorge was told that he wouldn't return to Cuba after the school term ended. Instead, his father explained, the family would temporarily relocate to South Florida. So many other Cuban families who were planning on doing the same also thought it would be a temporary exile. Jorge hasn't set foot in Cuba since.

In 1962, he enrolled at Stanford University in California, where he majored in economics. Jorge was a founding member of a student-run *a cappella* vocal group, the Mendicants, a group of vocalists whose legacy has survived over fifty years. To this day, he enjoys serenading his wife and anyone else in earshot.

Jorge's father, Joaquin, was old-school Cuban. The Bacardi brothers were never raised to be playboys; they were expected to get an education and then get to work. No handouts. After graduation from Stanford, Jorge started working in the family business. Bacardi was then and still is a very paternal corporation due to its family-held nature. Young executives such as Jorge were often groomed for positions of greater responsibility in the organization. Their progress was closely monitored by senior management. Jorge's first "job" at Bacardi was not with Bacardi at all. The company wanted its management team to have outside experience, so Jorge spent 1967 in London working for the Royal Bank of Canada. The following year, he began his career at Bacardi as a shipping clerk and later posted as a salesman in the highly competitive Caribbean market. While the idea of island hopping throughout the Caribbean sounds like fun to most of us, for a white-knuckle flier like Jorge, it was sheer terror.

One trip required Jorge to charter a plane from Saint Eustatius to Saint Maarten. Jorge knew the flight was doomed once he learned that the French pilot would have to actually skip over a huge pothole on the runway at Saint Maarten, just part of the routine. After his meeting, Jorge climbed back into the prop-driven aircraft and repeated the pothole-skipping maneuver on takeoff. After achieving their desired elevation, the French-speaking pilot turned to Jorge and asked in broken English, "You smell smoke?" Jorge's eyes nearly bugged out of his head. He felt the blood drain from his face. His dread was replaced by absolute panic when the pilot told him, "Hold the wheel."

For the next several minutes, Jorge fought the urge to vomit and pee while the pilot climbed onto the floor of the aircraft and began looking under the instrument panel. After a few terror-filled minutes, the only worse possible thing that could happen did so. The pilot told Jorge, "We have to declare an emergency."

The pilot put the plane in a steep bank and headed back to Saint Maarten as he radioed his emergency to the airport. The cabin was filling with smoke. While still hundreds of feet over the Caribbean, the pilot had to actually open the window to see out of the aircraft. The two men gazed out their windows fighting the stinging in their eyes and trying to spot the runway. They made their final approach, and Jorge's relief at seeing the fire truck below turned to disgust and resignation at what seemed to be his cruel fate. The fire truck was speeding down the potholed runway in the wrong direction.

Another memorable time, Jorge was waiting to board a flight from Puerto Rico to Miami when an attractive blonde caught his eye. She was wearing the uniform of a Pan Am flight attendant. It fit her well, he observed. *Very well indeed. I hope she's on my flight*, Jorge thought.

Leslie Folk was still a relatively new flight attendant when she realized the handsome Cuban in the boarding area was staring at her. She turned to a coworker and whispered, "Goodness. I hope he's on our flight."

What happened next is still a matter of dispute. Depending on whom you believe, a terrified passenger asked the flight attendant to hold his hand during landing, or a flirtatious airline stewardess presented a specific passenger with not one but two sets of children's wings to get his attention. But this much is not in dispute: Leslie eventually asked Jorge what he did for a living. Jorge replied that he worked for a large rum distiller. Leslie, having been raised by her father to handle her drinking before she left for college, mentioned that she was indeed a rum drinker herself.

"What brand do you prefer?" he asked her.

"Why Bacardi of course!" she said.

Jorge replied, "I think I'm in love. Will you marry me?"

And the rest, as they say, is history.

Leslie was based in Miami, and Jorge was about to start engineering school at the University of Miami when they met. When Leslie was transferred to Los Angeles, they conducted their relationship long distance. Actually, Jorge pursued Leslie around the western hemisphere and would catch up with her in Colombia, Panama, and Guatemala. He once flew from Miami to Hawaii to spend just two days with her. Leslie once flew from London to Los Angeles, took a shower and then an immediate red-eye to Miami to be with Jorge. At one point, Jorge finally decided, *It'll be cheaper to marry her.*

And so after his graduation, Jorge and Leslie married in Nassau in December 1973. The ceremony was an intimate affair conducted in a park alive with the purples, reds, yellows, and greens of tropical flowers that created an Eden for the young lovers.

They set up a home in the Bahamas, and Jorge returned to work for Bacardi. Jorge's work took them around the world. In the 1970s, they lived for a time in London. This was during the Troubles, when IRA bombers made life in the UK uneasy. Compounding their anxiety was Jorge's inability to be on the water, where he felt so much at home. He bought a car just so he could enjoy trips to the coast to see the ocean and ships coming in.

Despite his illness, Jorge continued to exceed his doctors' expectations about his life expectancy. He had lived past the supposedly terminal ages of fourteen and twenty and was well into his thirties.

Jorge and Leslie traveled the world with his job at Bacardi. Theirs was a magical life—they visited exotic locations and met interesting people. From castles in Great Britain to manor houses in France. By the time Jorge retired from the company, he was a vice president of Bacardi & Company in Nassau and was on the boards of Bacardi & Company and Bacardi International.

Since he and Leslie lived in Nassau and he loved the ocean, it only made sense then that he get his own fishing boat. Weekends and vacations were spent cruising and fishing around the Bahamas. The Exumas, in particular, became a favorite spot. That exotic archipelago lies forty miles east of Nassau and is home to some of the most beautiful beaches and abundant fishing in the Atlantic.

But in the late 1970s and early 1980s, it was also a very dangerous place. Jorge set anchor one afternoon at the southern tip of Norman's Cay. Leslie began preparing dinner in the galley, and they intended to spend the night sheltered from the weather. From the scrub and palms beyond the beach emerged an equally scrubby-looking young man carrying an automatic assault rifle. Norman's Cay had recently been taken over by the Carlos Lehder organization and was rapidly becoming a transshipment point for illegal drugs being smuggled into the United States. Nervously, Jorge and the man on the beach eyed one another. And then slowly, Jorge raised the anchor and departed.

As dangerous as the Exumas could be, they also provided a playground where Jorge and Leslie vacationed with their family. Unable to have children of their own, Jorge and Leslie became surrogate parents to their many nieces and nephews. The closest bond was formed with his brother's son, Joaquincito. Despite his considerable wealth, Jorge didn't spoil his nieces and nephews. His treasure was his time. And if they were willing to make the time to come to Nassau, Jorge would make the arrangements. They would spend days cruising, fishing, and swimming in the tropical paradise. Joaquincito took full advantage of his uncle's offer, and the two grew exceptionally close over the years.

Jorge and the younger Joaquin became kindred spirits. Joaquincito was very close to his own father and benefited from his uncle's love. The younger Bacardi could tolerate his uncle's sometimes cantankerous nature. Sam Breakstone they called him. The two men shared similar personalities, values, and politics. They became close enough that when Joaquin married Sonia, Sonia would call Leslie and the two would commiserate about their husbands. With Joaquincito, Jorge shared some of his deepest feelings about God, about his health, and about the moral concerns he would face in the years to come.

Such discussions often left Joaquincito frustrated. "How can you say there's no God, no heaven?" he would ask. "You were raised Catholic for crying out loud." But Jorge would just scoff. It wasn't God or even the church Jorge had difficulty with. And he certainly never doubted the existence of heaven. But he thought too much time and effort were expended on out-ward symbols of piety—incense and rituals—and not enough on what mattered—treating people with love and respect. "God is in my house," Jorge countered. "God is everywhere." Jorge believed. He prayed. He didn't need the smells and bells.

His illness left him unable to have children; maybe that was why Jorge had a sharp edge to his personality. Perhaps his upbringing made him who he was. Like his father, Jorge became stubborn and hardheaded. The elder Joaquin had certain standards of conduct and behavior and could be a difficult man to be around when those standards weren't met. Perhaps Jorge's illness left him resentful and bitter. But the younger Joaquin was hardheaded as well, and despite their disagreement on religion, he loved his uncle and cherished their time together.

It wasn't until 2005 that doctors at Massachusetts General Hospital discovered Jorge didn't suffer from cystic fibrosis but from primary ciliary dyskinesia (PCD). That's a genetic condition affecting the cilia, the tiny hairs that line the body's airways, ears, and sinuses and move much as sea grass does on the floor of the ocean. When a person coughs, which is the body's effort to clear the lungs, normally functioning cilia aid the body in removing foreign matter. However, the cilia of people afflicted with PCD are brittle and don't move, so the lungs cannot clear themselves normally.

There's no cure or standard treatment for PCD. The adolescent and early adulthood years of PCD patients are described as a Cinderella period; it's when PCD is manageable. This would have been during the years when Jorge was most active water-skiing, snorkeling, and spearfishing. However, the progressive disease catches up with its victims when they reach their forties, and by their fifties, the lungs are unable to exchange oxygen at a sufficient rate. Many require portable oxygen. Their ultimate survival requires a lung transplant.

Jorge had been treated at Mass General in Boston since childhood. His pulmonologist, Dr. Walter O'Donnell, had mentioned early on the possibility of a lung transplant. Jorge was unable to expel the mucus collecting in his airways, and it became a real breeding ground for bacteria; Jorge suffered from recurring infections. But in the mid-1990s, lung transplant was still in its infancy; the mortality rate exceeded 50 percent.

At first, Jorge dismissed the idea of a lung transplant, but his condition continued to deteriorate through the 1990s and into the mid-2000s. Imagine having to breathe through a straw; that was life for Jorge as he entered his fifties and sixties. He no longer went for long walks with Leslie, no longer waterskied, no longer snorkeled for lobsters. Instead of walking, he traveled on a Segway and toted an oxygen bottle. Jorge was concerned that he would be too old, too sick, or too weak to be considered for a lung transplant, and he would need a double lung transplant. That meant a deceased donor and moral considerations beyond many people's ability to accept.

The deliberative process he underwent on his way to accepting a place on the transplant list was a long and complicated consideration of a number of factors including his age and physical state. He was plagued by self-doubt. To be considered for a transplant, a candidate had to be sick enough to require one but also strong enough to survive the operation, a paradox. Due to the lack of sufficient donor organs, potential recipients work hard to keep themselves healthy until a match can be found. However, their efforts at maintaining their physical strength often keep them from reaching the top of the transplant list. Jorge knew he met the first requirement, but he wasn't sure about his ability to survive the operation considering he was approaching his midsixties. And he worried about taking the place of a younger, more-deserving candidate, someone like a college freshman with his whole life ahead of him.

Jorge had to accept that only a lung transplant would save his life, and that would be a gift impossible to repay. *Why me?* he thought. *What makes me more deserving than anyone else, particularly someone younger, in need of such a miraculous gift?* His hesitation was not due to fear of surgery, or pain, or failure, or the consequences. What troubled him was the doubt he deserved such a gift.

He found his answer in his wife and his nieces and nephews. Leslie told him, "How do they know you're not a good candidate if they've never met you? They don't know how strong you are."

His wife became his focal point. He would do it for her as well as for his nieces and nephews, who had become like their own children. He would do it for those kids whom he had taught to water ski and spear fish. He would do it for all the years and memories they had made together and for the years and memories he hoped were to come.

Yes, the gift of life would be impossible to repay, but he would accept it for Leslie and his family. He knew that accepting such a gift would carry with it an obligation to the donor, nothing he would take lightly. Such a gift would have to be cared for, cherished, honored, and protected. Too many others were out there waiting for such a second chance. Jorge told himself, *This is something you do, but you have to do everything in your power to respect that honor you're getting. And make sure you do everything possible to keep those lungs in good shape.* Accepting transplanted lungs would be a lifesaver but also a heavy responsibility. He overcame his doubts with the help of Leslie and his new physician, Dr. Cesar Keller.

Cesar Keller is the epitome of a self-made man who overcame so many obstacles in life. He was born in Brazil to a Guatemalan father and a Uruguayan mother. Cesar's parents met while his father was studying veterinary medicine in Brazil. His surname is misleading but speaks to all he has accomplished.

Cesar's father founded the first veterinary school in Guatemala and became the dean of the faculty. At the time, Guatemala had only one university, La Universidad de San Carlos de Guatemala. It was 1968, and the Cold War was being fought throughout Latin America. Central American guerilla movements were supported by the Cuban government, which was seeking to export its own revolution throughout the western hemisphere.

The core of the revolutionary movement in Guatemala was based at San Carlos University. This rankled the elder Dr. Keller, who felt the academy was a place of learning—a place for education and preparation for a career. Cesar's father was not at all bashful in expressing his opinions on the matter, and that put him on the wrong side of the campus radicals. In time, threats began to come. First against him and then against his family. Fearing for his family's safety, the elder Dr. Keller took his family into exile in Brazil when Cesar was only fifteen.

Prospects for Cesar's father were no better in Uruguay than they were in Guatemala. After two years, the Kellers returned to Central America. Young Cesar had attended Jesuit schools all through his primary and secondary education in Guatemala. Unfortunately, despite his hard work in Brazil, there was no reciprocation between the schools in Brazil and his Jesuit high school in Guatemala. So when his father returned the family to Guatemala, Cesar had to repeat his last two years of high school.

The setback did little to dim the enthusiasm Cesar had for school. After graduating from high school, he was accepted into medical school at San Carlos University. Under the mentorship of Dr. Leon Arango, Cesar took an interest in pulmonary medicine, the study of the human lungs. He did very well at San Carlos and graduated after seven years second in his class.

In 1977, he began training in internal medicine but quickly expressed an interest in pulmonary medicine. A professor at Brooklyn helped Cesar get a fellowship at the Jesuits' Saint Louis University in Missouri in 1980. Cesar had a career-affirming experience with a patient in Saint Louis. As his patient got sicker, Cesar asked repeatedly, "Is there nothing we can do?" The only possible solution was a lung transplant. And at that time, the 1980s, lung transplants were the domain of science fiction.

In 1984, his fellowship at Saint Louis University as well as his J-1 visa were expiring; he packed up his textbooks and family and returned to Guatemala. Those were the Reagan years in Central America; those were the years of death squads and the contras. Central America was a violent, dangerous place. Leftist guerillas were fighting the US-backed governments of Guatemala and El Salvador. US-backed contras were fighting the Sandinista government of Nicaragua. Cesar returned and went into practice with his friend and mentor, Dr. Arango. He was making a good living and supporting his children, Cesar Jr. and Lorraine. He also taught pulmonary and critical-care medicine at the university in San Carlos.

In 1987, Costa Rican president Oscar Arias brokered a peace agreement that earned him the Nobel Peace Prize. Fighters on both sides of the conflict were suddenly no longer needed. As the combatant forces and militias demobilized, thousands of young men with few skills beyond killing and destruction were without work. Political violence declined, but economically driven street violence became a daily occurrence. Kidnappings for ransom became commonplace. Successful people such as Dr. Cesar Keller were especially vulnerable; he took to carrying a bag containing an automatic pistol everywhere. Violence was never far away. After his brother-in-law was murdered in front of his home, Cesar resolved to return to the United States.

A classmate from medical school was working at Methodist Hospital, Baylor College of Medicine. Cesar called his old friend and classmate. "Juan, if you hear of anything ..." His timing was serendipitous. There was indeed a need for someone like Cesar. A week later, Cesar was in Houston, Texas, being offered a job.

Cesar was excited to be working in pulmonology and grateful for the safety of his family. He became fascinated with the possibilities that lung transplants presented. There was a steep learning curve, but doctors everywhere were on it. He was encouraged to see patients begin to survive longer. One patient out of ten surviving was an improvement over zero out of ten.

After three years at Baylor, Cesar returned to Saint Louis University Hospital. Before too long, he was appointed the chair of the transplant department and was named chief of pulmonary and critical care medicine.

In 2001, the Mayo Clinic in Jacksonville wanted to build a thoracic transplant team to complement the success of their abdominal transplant practice. Then-CEO Dr. John Cortese explained that Mayo didn't want to undergo a long learning and experience curve; they wanted an excellent program immediately and wanted to start with the best.

By April 2001, Cesar Keller, an immigrant, was overseeing the lung transplant practice, one of the most prestigious positions in the medical profession. Who says America isn't the land of opportunity?

In the early 1990s, Jorge began redirecting his care to the Mayo Clinic in Jacksonville, Florida. The subject of a transplant had come up periodically with Dr. O'Donnell, Jorge's treating doctor at Mass General, but it took years of declining health before Jorge was willing to consider a transplant. The survival statistics were improving, and Jorge learned that Mayo was starting a lung transplant program in Florida. The staff at Mayo was committed to its success. Mayo was closer to Nassau, and he learned that southern hospitality extended far beyond Sunday dinner; people in the south were more likely to register as organ donors than were their northern neighbors.

However, his first consultation with Dr. Keller was less than encouraging. The doctor pointed out all the potential barriers to a successful transplant for Jorge—his age, the scar tissue from past surgeries—"But don't think this is not a possibility," Dr. Keller told Jorge over the phone. He asked Jorge to come to Jacksonville for an in-person consultation, and he ended up pleased to learn that Jorge was in much better physical condition than he had originally thought; he realized Jorge had taken good care of himself. All those exercises and years in the water had given Jorge the strength to make it that far, and Dr. Keller was impressed.

The rigorous and extensive evaluation took two weeks. Jorge remembers the ordeal as significantly worse than the transplant itself. Many of the tests were physically uncomfortable if not painful. And as is the case with all potential transplant patients, Jorge had to undergo a thorough psychological evaluation. Transplant patients needed the emotional and mental capacity not only to survive the operation but then also commit to permanent lifestyle changes. He came through with flying colors and was declared a candidate for a double-lung transplant.

But the moral gravity still haunted Jorge, and Dr. Keller could see that his patient remained conflicted. "Why should I take the place of someone younger?" Jorge kept asking. "Why *you*? Why *not* you?" was the doctor's reply. Dr. Keller explained that if he were in Jorge's shoes, he wouldn't hesitate. He'd jump at the chance to see his daughter's next accomplishment or witness his grandkids growing up.

Leslie also had to be vetted; she underwent her own battery of psychological evaluations. She had to be screened by the Mayo Clinic's social workers. Would she be a suitable caregiver? Despite having spent her adult life caring for her husband, the gift of a new set of lungs would bring additional scrutiny. Mayo leaves nothing to chance. Leslie is committed to Jorge, so it was no surprise that she passed with flying colors as well.

So Jorge was placed on the list. He was told the wait could be as short as a matter of weeks or as long as several years. Every three months, he would return to Mayo for an evaluation. Depending on the results of that exam, he would be given a lung allocation score from zero to one hundred. The Lung Allocation Score is a system to allocate lungs that combines the predicted risk of death during the year following listing (wait list urgency) with the predicted likelihood of survival during the year following transplantation. It prioritizes candidates most urgently needing transplant while receiving the greatest post-transplant benefit. Lung allocation scores take various factors into consideration—age, body mass index, and recent illnesses among them. Tests are run measuring pulmonary artery pressure, oxygen needed at rest, PCO_2 (partial carbon dioxide) levels. The higher the lung allocation score, the more the need for a transplant and thus the higher that patient's place on the waiting list.

For ten months, Jorge tried very hard to impress his doctors in those examinations. By March 2008, however, he was declining. Rapidly.

Reidulf Maalen is among the many who count the Bacardis as friends. Reidulf and Jorge had met during Reidulf's years as a captain aboard the Royal Viking and Crystal Cruise lines. They had been good friends since the late 1980s. Reidulf kept himself abreast of his friend's condition and knew Jorge's health was declining. He called the Bacardi residence one day in 2008 and spoke to Leslie alone. Jorge was not well, Leslie informed him. Would it be possible, she asked, for Reidulf to come to Nassau for a visit? She thought it might cheer Jorge up.

Under a beautiful March sky, the Bacardi's yacht, *Contigo*, lay anchored in the Exumas, a beautiful spot. The intensity of the vibrant blue water was matched only by that of the sky. A gentle breeze blew outside as the two old friends were chatting on the aft deck. Jorge, as he had been for some time at that point, was sitting in a chair. An IV was attached to the port in his chest. Reidulf was happy to see his old friend but not to see him in that condition. He felt more than a little guilty that they were out on the boat and not at the Bacardi's house in Nassau.

"You know, my friend. It's really good to see you," said the old sea captain.

"I'm glad you came," replied Jorge. His breathing was heavy and difficult.

"Listen. I realize you aren't in the best of health," said Reidulf. "I want you to know that I would be just as happy to be spending time with you at home."

"I am at home." Jorge managed a smile.

"I know. But what I mean is we didn't have to come out on the water. You might be more comfortable at your house."

But even Reidulf had to admit that Jorge's love of the sea was as strong as his own. On the water, Jorge was in his element. To be on his boat surrounded by friends and his wife made him complete.

Jorge looked wistfully out over the water. It was late afternoon, and the evening promised another magnificent sunset in a few hours. The water was a radiant aqua blue. The sky held dazzling white clouds. Off in the distance, a sailboat was being pushed along by the soft breeze. How many more times would he be permitted such a stunning view? How many more trips would he be able to take out on the water? At least one more. Of that he was certain.

The plan was to await the arrival of Joaquincito, Sonia, and their children after Easter. And then back to the Exumas. The kids would jump off the sundeck into the water while Leslie and Sonia admired them. He was looking forward to spending time with his nephew. Joaquincito was the son Jorge had never had. And soon they would all be together again, Joaquin and Sonia and their three children. No matter how bad he felt, that was all that mattered to Jorge.

"You know something?" Jorge asked, "this boat is probably going to be my coffin."

Reidulf knew that was probably true. Jorge's lung capacity had decreased to just about 20 percent according to his evaluation at Mayo earlier that week. To climb the eleven steps from his stateroom to the salon, he had to stop twice to catch his breath. Even before they returned to Nassau, Reidulf knew this would likely be the last time he would ever see his friend alive.

After a few days of fishing, the Bacardis and Reidulf returned to Nassau. Joaquincito was waiting for them. He was in Nassau on business and wanted to have lunch with his tio and tia before returning to Florida. Lunch that day was a difficult experience. Jorge was clearly not well. His breathing was heavy and labored. Conversation was difficult. His body was failing him.

The flight from Nassau took little more than an hour. The two men said very little to one another. Joaquincito and Reidulf were each lost in thought. Mostly, they reminisced about Jorge. The uncle who was more like a father, the friend who was more like a brother. They had shared adventures and laughs and stories and more than a few lies with Jorge. His condition left little doubt in either man's mind that his time was short. Barring a miracle, there would be no more fishing trips, or cruises, or games of *coroto*, a Cuban dice game that generated so much laughter after dinner.

The plane landed in Miami. They collected their bags, exited the plane, and walked through the terminal to the parking shuttle. Joaquin had offered Reidulf a ride up to Fort Lauderdale. They stood next to their respective cars looking at one another. It was a moment of clarity for them both; their worst fears could no longer be denied. They looked at one another and said in unison, "He's not going to make it."

play ball!

⋈

It's a perfect day for baseball. Perfect. The sun's shining. Puffy white clouds fill the sky. A soft breeze is blowing the deep-green leaves on the oaks that make up half the backyards in the neighborhood. A perfect day for baseball.

Chris pulls up to the Abdos' house as Brian is shooting baskets in the driveway. "Dude!" he calls out.

"What up?" replies Brian.

"We need to get up a ball game," says Chris.

"A what?"

"Ball game, dude. We need to get a game up. Right now."

He opens up the trunk of his car and retrieves a bat and his baseball glove. In his part of the world, they're gloves. Never mitts.

"Now?" asks Brian.

"Right now. C'mon, let's round up some guys and get a game up. Let's go."

It's classic Chris. It doesn't matter what else is going on, he had a great idea. He considers his such a great idea that the *sooner everyone gets onboard, the sooner everyone will realize just how awesome his idea is.*

Before long, Chris has Brian, Kevin, Matt Nolan, Matt's little brother Kevin, and a couple of Douville kids from across the street. There's not enough for a real game of nine on nine, so left field is closed—anything hit over short or third is an automatic out. Some guys have bats, some have balls, nearly all have gloves. Those who don't will share once the teams are picked.

"Where's Stack?" asks Chris to no one in particular. There are three Stack brothers, all of legal ball-playing age, and their services are needed at this moment. In Chris's mind, whatever else is going on right now will have to wait. They have a game to play, and the Stack household is right around the corner.

"Let's go get 'em."

Chris leads the small troop around the corner to the Stack residence. Like the Pied Piper at the head of a parade, Chris has his bat on his shoulder. His glove is hanging from the barrel. They approach the door. Chris rings the bell. Kenny's mom answers.

"Hi guys!"

"Hi Mrs. Stack. Is Kenny home?" It's a rhetorical question. They all know Kenny's inside. And so are his brothers, Jimmy and Tommy. The problem is that Kenny usually doesn't feel like playing ball.

"I don't know, Chris. Let me see."

"Thanks, Mrs. Stack," Chris replies. But it comes out as Miss Stack. The second syllable in Mrs. just falls off the sentence. Before she can close the door, Chris steps inside followed by his entourage. "We'll wait."

Surprised, Kenny comes downstairs from his bedroom. "What's up guys?" he asks.

"We're gettin' a game up, dude. C'mon."

"Uh. I, uh ... I'm right in the middle of something right now."

"Yeah. That's cool. Go ahead and wrap that up. We'll wait."
Chris just stands and looks at him. His bat is still on his shoulder.

"You'll wait?"

"Yeah, man, we'll wait."

Following his lead, the other kids nod approval.

Reluctantly, Kenny gathers up a glove and a cap and a younger brother, and they head to the ball field behind the Abdo house. The younger kids are thrilled. What better way to spend an afternoon could there be? Getting to play baseball with the big kids. Chris even drives! It's gonna be awesome. Chris has managed to incite an event the kids will remember for years.

The youths troop to the field where the art of picking teams is dictated by rules long ago laid down by the baseball gods. The older kids pick. Period. No debate. Chris has somehow managed to load the teams where it's him, Brian, and Matt against almost all the little kids. Somehow though, the baseball gods aren't pleased. If there's a universal arbiter of all karma, of justice, of what goes around comes around, it's the baseball gods. And somehow on this day, the gods are not pleased with the way the teams have been picked. And so after two at bats, Chris remains hitless.

Finally, with two men on base, redemption is at hand. Chris steps up to the plate. The pitch is grooved right down the middle. His eyes grow wide as his tall, lanky body begins to uncoil. With all the strength he can muster, he lets go a mighty swing. Pow! Skyward soars the ball.

"Dammit!" screams Chris. He slams the bat head into the dirt. Up in the air goes the ball. Chris looks into the field and sees one of the younger kids moving under the ball. It seems the baseball gods might smile after all. The younger boy circles unsure of himself. Chris breaks into a sprint. The ball falls innocently to the ground with a thud. Chris reaches first before the unfortunate younger boy can gather his wits, recover, and make a play.

"Yes!" Chris cries triumphantly. Finally, the game has attained the appropriate level of satisfaction. So elated is Chris that he unilaterally decides that nothing further is to be gained this day. As far as he is concerned, the game's over.

"Okay, guys. We're done."

And with that, he marches off the field the same way he came leaving the others to shake their heads in disbelief.

the call

TUESDAY, MARCH 25, 2008

LAUREL, MARYLAND

The telephone rang shortly before 5:00 a.m. No sound fills a parent with dread like that of a phone ringing at that hour. Ask any parent who's ever experienced it. Nothing good is ever at the other end of that line.

"Colin, honey, calm down. What happened?" Grace asked our middle son. I was instantly wide awake. I couldn't hear what he was saying, but like every mother, Grace just knew by the tone of Colin's first words that something was wrong.

"Where is he?"

Oh Jesus. It was Chris. Is he in trouble? In jail? Is he hurt?

No. Chris had collapsed at a friend's house. Grace heard Colin's voice catch, and she knew he was trying not to cry. She wanted to be as gentle and as strong as she could with Colin, but she wanted to know everything.

Chris had been taken to Tulane University Medical Center in downtown New Orleans. A fraternity brother was on his way to take Colin to the hospital. Colin had been roused by his friend, Jon Villien, the president of their fraternity; Colin was the vice president. Chris had been hanging out with friends when he said he didn't feel well, and then he had passed out.

Soon after, Colin had received a text from their friend, Colby, an EMT who had taken Chris to the hospital. It seemed Chris was actually snoring in the ER. Okay, confusing, but not as bad as what we'd been imagining. Then Colin got the call that sent him into a panic. Colby was on his way to get Colin, and Jon suggested he call us.

"Okay, Colin, you're doing the right thing."

Grace was calm. Years of mothering were in her voice. Colin said he'd call us once he got to the hospital.

Grace called the hospital, got the ER on the phone, and in a matter of minutes got through to the treating physician there. "Hi. My name is Grace Gregory. My son, Christopher, is in the ER."

"Yes ma'am. Your son was brought to the ER a short while ago. We've put in a vent to protect his airway since he's not responsive. There's no sign of trauma, so we don't know why he's not responding."

They had scheduled a CT scan. The ER physician was waiting for an MRI, and then Chris would be moved to the SICU, the special intensive care unit. Grace's heart was racing as she fought off panic. The words *intubated* and *nonresponsive* echoed in her head like an alarm.

"Okay, Chris's brother is on his way to the hospital now. He's in New Orleans. We're in Maryland," she said.

"Very well," said the doctor. "We'll be certain that his brother is permitted to be with him. I wish there were more

I could tell you, ma'am. We'll know more after the CT scan. Please feel free to call back."

Though Grace was a thousand miles from her son lying in a hospital, she knew as a mother she had to do something. Her next move was to contact the campus ministry office hoping to have someone go to the hospital to anoint Chris. She got the security office instead. She explained she was a parent of a student who was in the hospital and wanted to reach campus ministry. A short time later, the security office called back to tell us that Chris hadn't collapsed on campus—we knew that—but that someone from campus ministry would be in contact soon.

NEW ORLEANS

Colin waited outside in the early morning for Colby to arrive. He was nearly hysterical. Jon's words ricocheted around in his head like a super ball in a trash can. "Apparently, Chris isn't doing so well. You need to go down there and you should probably call your parents."

No sooner had he extinguished one cigarette than he lit another. Colby's car turned the corner, and Colin climbed in. Colby was stone silent. The fact that he immediately didn't tell Colin to put out his cigarette was another indication that things weren't good.

"Dude, what happened?" Colin asked.

"I don't know," Colby replied looking straight ahead.

They arrived at Tulane University Medical Center. Colby dropped Colin off at the ER entrance. An ambulance crew was reloading a stretcher and cleaning up some bandage wrappers when Colin ran past them. He told the staff at the front desk who he was, and he was asked to sign in. Despite his matter-of-fact demeanor, his trembling hands wouldn't permit him to sign his name legibly. A nurse in scrubs took him to Chris.

The lights were dimmed in the room where Chris was lying alone. A tube in his mouth connected to a medium-sized box was making a rhythmic, mechanical noise. The machine was breathing for Chris. Despite that, Colin thought his brother didn't look very much like a hospital patient. He still looked as if he were asleep and perfectly healthy but with an incredibly out-of-place tube as if med students were pulling a prank on a friend who had passed out at a party.

A nurse asked Colin some general questions about his brother. His age, general health, and previous injuries. She seemed unfazed as if he would wake up any second and that was just a precaution. She told Colin to talk to him, that maybe he could hear him and could use some positive encouragement.

As long as he could remember, Colin has had a fear of hospital beds. It was very uncomfortable for him to be in that room with his little brother actually in one. It's wasn't any med school prank. It was real. And Colin was very uncomfortable. He couldn't sit on the bed or even hold Christopher's hand. He sat on a chair next to him as he talked to his little brother through his tears. "C'mon, kid. You gotta wake up. I need you to wake up."

LAUREL, MARYLAND

I showered and got dressed for work knowing I wouldn't be there long. I left a voicemail for my boss in Atlanta asking for her to call me immediately. I booked a hotel in New Orleans and bought two one-way plane tickets. Still not knowing the seriousness of Chris's condition, I was figuring we might be in Louisiana a couple of days. Just long enough to find out what happened, get Chris healthy and discharged, and back to school or home.

Sometime around 9:00 a.m., the phone rang. It was Kurt Bindewald, the director of university ministry. Grace explained who she was and what had transpired with Chris, and that she wanted someone to go to the hospital. Kurt said he would make arrangements immediately. He gave Grace his phone number and offered to pick us up at the airport or do whatever else we needed. I'm certain that a freshman in the hospital is the worst possible thing for any university administration. My cynical side told me to expect Loyola to circle the wagons. Just the opposite happened. The entire university community opened up and started bending over backward for Chris and our family.

Colin called a short time later and put the ER doctor on the phone.

"There appears to be some bleeding in your son's brain," the doctor said very slowly. "As I told you before, there doesn't seem to be any trauma, so we need to figure out what's causing the bleeding. He's in line for a brain MRI."

Despite being a full-time nursing student, at that moment, Grace couldn't think of a single intelligent question to ask.

"He could have had some type of an aneurysm or a leaking vessel in the brain," the doctor said. After the MRI, Chris would be admitted upstairs, most likely in the SICU. He put Colin back on the phone. He sounded much more relaxed.

"He looks like he's asleep right now," Colin said.

"Okay, honey. We're flying down in a little while. Call me back when you know his room number or if you just need to talk. Are you okay?"

"Yeah, I'm fine. Matt's here, and Swantek and some of Chris's friends are here."

"Okay, sweetheart. We'll be there in a little while. I love you, Colin."

"Love you too."

Grace had two exams and three clinical rotations scheduled for the week. So before throwing some clothes in a suitcase, she called her boss and fired off a series of e-mails to her professors with the same ominous message: "I'm sorry. My son is sick. I am going to New Orleans, and I will call them and let them know when I will be back."

Gerry Nolan was sitting at his desk when his son, Matt, called. Matt and Chris had grown up together. They'd played sports and had attended the same schools until high school. Despite attending different high schools, they remained close since the Nolans lived next door to the Abdos. So Chris was always around one house or the other. Matt and Chris had reunited at Loyola New Orleans. It was only a little after nine in the morning, and Gerry could tell immediately something wasn't right.

"Dad, Chris collapsed," Matt told his father.

"What happened?" Gerry asked. He feared the boys, who had been rushing a fraternity, had drunk too much and something bad had happened. He was relieved to learn that wasn't the case. Chris had been just hanging out at a friend's apartment when he simply collapsed. His friends hadn't waited for an ambulance. They'd carried him to their car and made a beeline for the hospital.

"Dad, it doesn't look good."

"I should come down," Gerry said.

"I don't know, Dad. Colin said his parents were already coming."

Gerry hung up. He took a deep breath. The news made the blood drain from his face. As bad as it was, it was made worse by the sound of Matt's voice. Clearly, his son was shook up. Really, really shook up. *I should go*, he thought as he stared blankly at his computer screen. *It's bad. It's really bad.*

Gerry called his wife, Cathy, to break the news.

"Where is he?" Cathy asked.

"They're all at the hospital," Gerry replied. "Apparently, Eric and Grace are on their way down."

"What happened?"

"They don't know. Matt just got there. He'll call back when he knows something."

They hung up, and Gerry returned to his thoughts. He'd known us for years. He'd watched our boys grow up just as we'd watched theirs. Surely, there must be something he could do to help. He knew he could get away. He owned the company where he worked. He didn't need to ask anyone for time off. *If not for the Gregorys, then for the kids. For Colin and Matt.*

He thought of Matt just then. *Thank God it isn't my son.* As soon as that thought flashed through his mind, he regretted it though it was a natural thought for any parent. It was the realization that somebody else's son lying in a hospital room, not his own. For that, he was thankful and glad, but at the same time it seemed callous. It bothered him immediately and left him unsettled.

NEW ORLEANS

Colin lost track of time. It could have been thirty minutes or maybe two hours, but the nurse finally came into Chris's room in the ER.

"We're going to move your brother upstairs," she said.

"Where's he going?" Colin asked.

"The special ICU on the third floor. There's a waiting room right by the elevator. Y'all can wait there."

Together, Colin, Jenn, who was Chris's girlfriend, Colby, and Nick took the elevator to the third floor and went to the SICU waiting room. The sun was starting to rise over New Orleans. The tourists would be shaking off hangovers and the locals would be starting their workdays.

Dr. John Posey, the chief neurosurgeon, walked in and asked for Colin, who was impressed with his demeanor and poise. He thought, *You don't get to be the chief of anything without the ability to deliver good news, or bad news, in a calm, soothing tone.* The guy was good. He told Colin that there was no evidence of blunt trauma in the scans but that it was likely an aneurysm. More tests would be taken. The prognosis was wait and see. Aneurysms were serious but not necessarily death sentences or something that always caused lasting damage.

Somewhat relieved that at least they were getting answers, Colin sat down to wait and see.

LAUREL, MARYLAND

Mary Abdo was a second mother to Chris. Her sons, Kevin and Brian, had grown up with Chris. They had gone to grade school together and had played CYO basketball together, and when they grew older, all attended Mount Saint Joseph High School in Baltimore. The Gregorys and Abdos took turns carpooling the boys to school.

Mary and her husband, Brian, welcomed so many kids into their home, but Chris was different. He had a way of making himself at home no matter where he went. He had established what I call "refrigerator" rights among just a select few families whose love and acceptance knew no conditions or bounds. Besides their two sons, the Abdos had two daughters, Meghan and Kathleen. The younger of the two adored Christopher. Since age nine, Meghan was determined to become Mrs. Christopher Gregory. Whenever Chris appeared some Friday night at midnight after playing basketball with her brothers and announced, "Meghan, fix me a sandwich," a sandwich would be fixed.

At 11:00 a.m., Mary was reading her e-mails when the phone rang. She was unable to answer in time, so the call went to voicemail. Mary waited a few minutes and then checked the message. It was from Grace.

"Hi, Mary. It's Grace Gregory. We may or may not make your party."

Mary thought, *Now that's strange. Why on earth is she calling me about the party?* The annual Abdo Saint Patrick's party was an event not to be missed. It was scheduled for that coming Saturday night, March 29, but it was only Tuesday. Mary felt it odd that Grace would call so early in the week to say she may not make it, but there was also something odd in her friend's voice. Grace's next words made Mary's heart skip a beat.

"Christopher collapsed and is in the hospital. We're headed to New Orleans, so we may or may not make it." Instinctively placing her hand over her mouth, the devout mother of four said a quick prayer. "Oh my God," she uttered. *Christopher collapsed? It's serious enough that they're going down there.*

"What's wrong, Mom?" Kevin asked. He had just woken up and was standing in the doorway. Kevin and Chris had been in the same class at St. Joe.

"Chris is in the hospital. He collapsed. They don't know what's wrong. The Gregorys are on their way to New Orleans."

A dark sense of foreboding descended on the house. As kids of his age were in the habit of doing, he reached for his cell phone and typed a text message to Chris: "Hey man, just wanted 2 let u know how much I love you. Can't wait 2 see you when you get out of the hospital." He called Matt Nolan in New Orleans. Matt of course was already at the hospital waiting room. Kevin had to pack to go back to college in Emmitsburg, Maryland, the next day. His mind would be preoccupied to say the least.

TULANE UNIVERSITY MEDICAL CENTER

Matt surveyed the waiting area beginning to fill up with Colin's and Christopher's friends. Loyola was a small college, and the fact that there were two Gregory boys two years apart on campus meant news traveled quickly. It seemed that the semester would commence right there in the waiting room There seemed to be enough students to do so.

Fr. Jim Caime, SJ, and Kurt Bindewald were there when he arrived. And soon afterward, Fr. Ted Dziak, SJ, showed up. Matt was initially skeptical of their presence. *Great*, he thought. *I've seen these people around campus, but now we have to babysit them too.* He wasn't in the mood to meet new people. Matt asked Colin if there was anything he could do.

"Hey man, it's getting kind of full around here," Colin said. "And my parents are coming down. We're not going to know anything more until later this evening. I'd prefer this place not become a madhouse."

"Got it," Matt replied.

They decided they needed to stop the better part of the Loyola student body from showing up there. Since their phones were ringing nonstop, it was just a matter of telling people not to come. They would let them know if there was any news to share.

Matt let his mind clear. The rush of news and emotions had created a fog, and he needed to take a moment to just let it clear. He thought, *I'm definitely not going to class today. Or tomorrow. This is the most important thing I have to do this week.*

LOYOLA UNIVERSITY NEW ORLEANS

Ellie Trant and Christopher had met at the beginning of their freshman year. Ellie was from Grand Coteau, Louisiana, a quiet town off I-49 just north of Lafayette. Like many other students that week, Ellie was just returning from Easter break and was looking forward to catching up with friends at school. She sent Chris a message on Facebook but got no response.

Her phone rang. She saw Matt's number. "Hi, Matt. What's up?"

"Ellie, Chris is in the hospital."

She thought Matt was joking. That wouldn't have been unusual considering that Matt, Chris, and their friends were always joking with her. "Stop screwing around, Matt. That's not true."

"Ellie, I'm serious. He's in the hospital, he's unconscious, and we need you to please pray for him."

"Oh no," Ellie said. She felt ice developing in the pit of her stomach. Her new friend was in the hospital, and it was obviously very serious. Ellie knew Chris and Matt were rushing the Beggars fraternity. She feared that something stupid had happened and that there may have been horseplay or worse involved. Of all the friends she had made since starting at Loyola, Chris was her best. Besties they called themselves. An almost immature expression but one appropriate for their relationship. It described a closeness yet informality to the friendship that Ellie and Chris had developed. Besties.

TULANE UNIVERSITY MEDICAL CENTER

Fr. Ted and Colin decided to visit with Chris. Colin had had Fr. Ted in a class the previous semester. Chris looked a lot worse than he did earlier. It seemed that even more tubes had been connected to his little brother. It rattled Colin. Chris didn't appear ready to wake up at any minute. He looked like a hospital patient. In an ICU.

Colin started sobbing. Fr. Ted wrapped his arm around him. Colin walked out into the hallway and continued crying. The older man followed. Colin rubbed the tears from his eyes.

"I don't want Chris to see me crying like a little bitch," Colin said in between sobs.

"I think he'd understand," said Fr. Ted.

Colin walked out to the waiting room and felt he would lose his composure again. Fr. Jim took notice.

"You okay, Colin?"

"Yeah, I'm all right."

But Colin was anything but all right.

"I think I'm going to go get some fresh air."

"I'll join you," said Fr. Jim.

The two walked out of the waiting room leaving Jenn, Matt, and the others. Once out on the terrace, Fr. Jim pulled out a pack of Parliaments. He lit one and offered one to Colin. Leave it to a Jesuit to know just what to do at a moment like that. For all their academic rigor and reputation, Jesuits are great at knowing how to react to a crisis at a very human level. Colin didn't need any lectures on scripture or lessons on grace or the sacraments just then. He needed a cigarette. More than that, he needed someone to share that cigarette with. Not necessarily to talk with, just someone to be there and let him know he wasn't alone.

Over the next few days, the words "fresh air" became the signal between Colin and Fr. Jim it was time for a smoke.

CAROLYN HARRELL

In Shreveport, Louisiana, Carolyn Harrell and her husband, Horace, sat nervously at a desk at the admitting department at Willis-Knighton Medical Center. The sixty-four-year-old grandmother was in great discomfort. Carolyn was afflicted with liver disease and had been on the waiting list for a liver transplant for more than three years. As the admitting officer typed on her keyboard, a nervous Carolyn held the hand of her husband of twenty-seven years.

Carolyn Harrell had met Horace in November 1980. Mutual friends thought it was a good idea. They thought the two would get along. Maybe hit it off. Carolyn and Horace were both divorced. Each had children. But their friends thought an evening of dancing would be fun. The two divorcees reluctantly agreed. Immediately after being introduced, Horace exclaimed, "Look, I'm not interested in any kind of relationship here."

"Fine," responded the thirty-seven-year-old Carolyn. "Neither am I."

They married a month later at Christmastime.

The Harrells found that they shared a love of music and travel. Their love of travel sometimes took them on spur-of-the-moment trips to Colorado. More than once while sharing a meal at their favorite lunch spot, one would ask the other, "Where do you feel like going?" Almost as soon as the question was answered, they'd be heading off somewhere in their car.

Life was good for Carolyn and Horace. That was until she was diagnosed with liver disease. I'd always associated liver disease with heavy alcohol consumption. A common misunderstanding and definitely not the cause in Carolyn's case. Carolyn never drank alcohol.

The human liver is about the size of a football and sits very nicely under the right ribcage. A healthy liver cleans the body's blood supply, aids in digestion, and fights off infections. It's the only internal organ capable of regenerating. There are a number of causes of liver disease. It can be inherited. It can be caused by parasites or infections such as hepatitis. Autoimmune abnormalities can cause liver disease. The cause of Carolyn's liver disease was never clearly identified. Horace suspected that when they were living near Houston, chemicals that had leached into the water supply were the culprit. Enough folks had succumbed to cancers in the area that a class-action suit was launched.

Whatever the cause, Carolyn developed spots on her liver. And the condition grew worse. When the couple relocated to northern Louisiana, Carolyn came under the care of Dr. Robert McMillan at Willis-Knighton Medical Center.

As her disease grew worse, it became more painful. At first, a diseased liver becomes swollen and tender as it tries to fight off whatever is attacking it. If left untreated, it begins to scar. This scarring is called fibrosis. As scar tissue builds up, the liver doesn't function as well. Cirrhosis occurs when the scarring is so severe that it's irreversible. It may be possible to slow or stop cirrhosis but not reverse it.

The final stage of liver disease is liver failure that can take place over months or years. That was Carolyn's case. In December 2004, she was placed on the transplant list.

Patients waiting for liver transplants are assigned a ranking called a Model for End-Stage Liver Disease (MELD) score. MELD scores range from six to forty. People with the highest scores are generally the sickest, so they get first chance at donor organs as they become available. It's one of the cruel realities among everyone waiting for transplants. Patients do everything they can to stay healthy while waiting for a transplant, but their efforts sometimes prevent them from getting that life-changing call for months. The problem is the chronic shortage of donor organs in the United States, not the transplant community.

So Carolyn was listed. She went home to wait for *the* call that could come at any hour or maybe never. The call could bring jubilation and dread in equal doses. It could mean life for her but most likely tragedy for someone else.

For the longest while, it seemed that the call would never come. With each battery of tests, her MELD score went up. Slowly but surely, she began climbing to the top of the transplant list. If only a donor could be found.

In March 2008, Carolyn felt terrible. She became so sick and racked with pain that she called Dr. McMillan. He told her to come to the hospital.

NEW ORLEANS

Our flight from Baltimore was scheduled to leave around 1:00 p.m. Grace and I sat in the departure area not saying much. When you raise children, there seems to be a first time for everything. First words, first steps, first birthday, first day of school. Like new chapters in a book. The milestones in the life of a family. Chris was our youngest, and with the youngest, there's also a last time for everything. With each last time, a chapter closes. The last time you give any of them a bath, the last time you change any of their diapers. The last one you teach to drive. The last day of high school. I remembered picking Chris up when he was still a little boy and holding him in my arms with his head on my shoulders. I thought, *When I put him down, he won't be a baby anymore.* So I held him in my arms for the longest while wishing that moment would last forever.

I was clinging to the hope that Chris's hospitalization would be a temporary bump along the road of continuing first events for him. He was nineteen. Big and strong. His whole life ahead of him. We'd go down to New Orleans, get him out of the hospital, and maybe bring him home.

During the flight, Grace sat in silence and prayed the rosary. As she rolled the beads through her fingers, she offered another prayer. Her eyes were closed. Only her lips and fingers moved. The daughter of some friends of ours had recently suffered an episode similar to Chris's but had recovered. Grace was training to be a nurse. She knew what science and modern medicine were capable of. While she put her trust in science, she also put her faith in God. But as the Southwest Airlines 737 approached New Orleans, her sense of hope was being overshadowed by an ominous dread.

We took a cab to Tulane University Medical Center. The first time we had visited New Orleans was the weekend before Hurricane Katrina. We left Colin on a Friday at the conclusion of his freshman orientation in 2005. Two days later, he was back home watching New Orleans flood on TV. Like many kids of that freshman year, he couldn't wait to return to New Orleans. They genuinely wanted to be a part of the city's rebirth. So we had always marked the city's recovery during subsequent trips.

What we saw on the cab ride downtown was still disturbing some three and a half years later. Vacant buildings were everywhere. Signs of urban decay and stark reminders of the disaster from 2005 remained. The city was recovering but slowly. When we stepped inside the hospital, however, it was like entering an urban oasis. We found a clean, safe environment. In a city with entire neighborhoods destroyed, Tulane was a place where everything seemed to function. The floors were spotless. The staff was friendly and professional. We saw equipment, medicine—everything a patient and family wanted to see. We were hopeful.

We walked to the front desk shortly after 4:00 p.m. with our luggage in hand. The elevator doors opened, and an average-looking, forty-something man emerged dressed in black and wearing a roman collar. He introduced himself as Fr. Ted Dziak and asked, "Are you the Gregorys?" He offered to show us the way upstairs to the SICU. There, we found the waiting room filled with students and staff from Loyola. They had coolers of soft drinks and water and snacks. They had settled in for a long wait if necessary. They seemed nervous but hopeful. It was easy to see right away that they genuinely cared for one another. Colin stood to greet us, and when I hugged him, the emotion that was building finally flowed out of me and I began to cry. They were only the first of the many tears I'd shed.

Fr. Ted didn't know Chris. He didn't recognize him from Mass or from being involved in service projects. As a resident chaplain, Fr. Ted actually lived in Biever Hall, the same dorm as Chris. While he didn't know him personally, he did know of him. He had seen him around and recognized him as Colin's younger brother. Chris was not the kind of kid who would knock on Fr. Ted's door to seek confession or to discuss some urgent spiritual matter. The priest knew Colin, who had once been one of his students. He knew him also from working around campus and Colin's involvement in the Beggars. Fr. Ted was very familiar with the Greek system at Loyola.

Kurt Bindewald introduced himself and introduced us to Fr. Jim Caime. They're fine gentlemen, and they stayed with us for the next three days offering assistance spiritual and practical. No favor was too great. Jim would tell us the next day that they were happy to stay if we wanted or would leave if we wished. We asked them to stay.

Kurt and Fr. Jim had been the first to respond to the hospital after Grace's call to Loyola Tuesday morning. As with many colleges, there's a decision tree for emergencies involving students. The campus ministry office was often notified whenever a student had some kind of crisis. Sometimes, it was nothing more than a breakup with a girlfriend or boyfriend. Other times, as with Chris, the matter was much more serious. Despite Loyola's nature as a Catholic and Jesuit institution, the families of some students may not want a religious presence during a crisis. Hospitals are aware of this. Some hospitals are reluctant to work with clergy until they're assured that such a presence is in line with the family's wishes. Kurt and Fr. Jim were the first to go to the hospital, and finding the situation as serious as it was, they notified Fr. Ted and Loyola's president, Fr. Kevin Wildes, SJ.

Fr. Ted's first impression was that the students assembled in the waiting room were scared. There was a lot of hope and even optimism. But there was also fear. They had pillows and blankets, and it appeared that many had been there for hours. They all had the same nervous look on their faces. Ted had recognized Colin at once, and Colin had been genuinely relieved to see him.

TULANE UNIVERSITY MEDICAL CENTER

Matt Nolan was there as were Nick, Woody, and Colby, more of Chris's friends. Several girls were in the waiting room also. Mary Pendarvis was there, and Rebecca Reese. And of course we finally got to meet Christopher's girlfriend, Jenn. She had been driving home from work around midnight when she'd gotten a call from Nick Mangiello, a friend of hers and Chris's. "Something happened to Chris. You need to get here," was all he had said. Jenn had stopped by her house, changed clothes, and hurried to the hospital. She had been there since shortly after midnight.

Jenn and Chris had been dating since October. Our first hint of their relationship had come with that November phone bill monstrous enough to require delivery in one of those big, bulk-mail envelopes. I told people it had arrived in a box. It might as well have as big as it was. I jokingly asked if I got a discount from the phone carrier for billing by the inch. I thumbed through the billing statement—page after page after page of calls and texts to the same number. That was when he told us about Jenn. I had hoped she'd be in Arizona visiting her parents when we were there so we could meet her, but she was staying in New Orleans.

As I've written, though Christopher's first college semester wasn't the best, we decided to let him go back, and I'm glad we did. I still have his e-mails in which he expressed his gratitude for getting a second chance. Sending him back to Loyola was my way of saying, "I love you, and I trust you. Now get your act together." He did.

Chris's friends were introducing themselves when Jenn extended her hand. "I'm Jenn."

"So you're the reason my phone bill is so high," I responded awkwardly. Maybe not the best introduction, but we were as nervous as everyone there was, and I couldn't think of anything else to break the tension. I had a big smile on my face. I was genuinely happy to meet her. Jenn laughed and felt a little better. To meet your boyfriend's parents in a hospital waiting room is not something any young woman should have to endure, but Jenn is a special person, and she handled herself with tremendous class and poise.

Jenn had called her mother in Arizona at 4:00 a.m. that morning. She told her that Chris was in the hospital and what little they knew.

"Mom, I think they said he's bleeding in the brain," Jenn had told her.

"Jenn, that's not a good thing. Honey, people sometimes don't come back from that." And suddenly the nervous laughter wasn't so funny anymore. Jenn's call home had left her with a serious dose of reality.

We met the resident who was attending Chris in the SICU. His name was Dr. Jorge Alvernia. He told us they suspected Chris may have suffered a bleeding arteriovenous malformation (AVM) or possibly a ruptured brain aneurysm. An AVM is a congenital condition resulting in a tangle of blood vessels in the brain. AVMs occur in less than 1 percent of the population. The chances of an AVM leaking are 1 percent to 3 percent annually. And when they do leak, they are fatal only 10 to 15 percent of the time.

Approximately 2 percent of the population has unruptured brain aneurysms. If the vessel ruptures, it bleeds into the cerebral cavity and increases the pressure in the brain. Forty percent of ruptured brain aneurysms are fatal. And two thirds of those who survive them suffer from neurological deficits for the rest of their lives. The news was difficult to comprehend. What kind of life would Chris lead? What kind of care would he require? Brain aneurysms are more common in women than in men. And they're usually more common in people between thirty-five and sixty. But Chris was just nineteen.

They were watching Chris very closely and considering options to relieve the swelling. They asked our permission to insert an intracranial pressure monitor (ICP) to measure the pressure in his head. Apparently, the MRI had revealed a large bleed in his frontal lobe.

They allowed us to see Chris, but we had to wear masks, gowns, and gloves because hospitals around the country were confronting the spread of the MRSA virus. And we were told not to talk to him as all stimulation was to be avoided. We suited up and went in to see him.

There he lay. At first, I was certain he was just asleep. In the few seconds we were permitted to be with him, Grace couldn't breathe. Her big, strong, beautiful boy was not breathing on his own. Only a week before, he had been laughing and running after us as we drove past him at the Tucson airport. Pure joy was on his face as he hollered and waved and ran after us in his untied tennis shoes and shorts. Grace and I laughed at the sight as I intentionally allowed the car to coast past him and Colin.

The look on his face, that joyful smile was forever etched in our minds. But there he was lying there motionless, a breathing tube in his mouth. His big, strapping chest covered only halfway by a hospital sheet. It was more than she could bear. Grace held Christopher's hand and whispered, "We're here, Chris. Mom and Dad are here. We love you." They made her wear latex gloves to hold his hand. At that moment our hearts broke.

An attractive young woman with blond hair and a big smile entered the room and pulled the curtain closed. She wore green scrubs. She was Christopher's nurse. She went about her duties in a manner that betrayed the fact that she was a mother herself. She was mature but not old. She clearly loved caring for her patients.

"Hi, I'm Amy," she said in a friendly, soothing voice. "Are y'all his parents? I thought so."

Amy Schulingkamp was starting a three-day stretch, 7:00 a.m. to 7:00 p.m. each day. Chris had been brought into the SICU only a short while before Amy had come on duty. The nurse she'd relieved had told her basically the same things we knew. Chris had been with a group of friends and had collapsed right in front of them. Fortunately, his friend Colby was an EMT, and resuscitation measures were started right away.

Amy had taken the report from the night-shift nurse, but she wanted to compare the report to her own findings. She wanted to find out if anything had changed. Either an okay change or something else that needed attention. When Chris came up to her unit, he was not breathing over the ventilator. That is, he wasn't breathing on his own at all.

In Amy's assessment, Chris hadn't responded to any neurological checks. She shined a flashlight in his eyes, scraped a tongue depressor against the bottom of his feet. She tried deep-tissue stimuli and light-tissue stimuli. All negative. Chris had arrived in her unit the medical equivalent of a who-done-it.

We introduced ourselves, and Amy told us what she knew. They were still conducting tests. They were still hopeful. There was still so much they could do.

"Y'all are lucky," she said. "Dr. Posey is the treating neurosurgeon. He's the best neurosurgeon in New Orleans. If anyone can help your boy, he can."

Amy told us that if we wanted anything or needed anything, all we had to do was ask. She was as good as her word. Over the next few days, she would take care of Chris, us, and even Christopher's friends.

Later that afternoon, we met Dr. Posey, the neurosurgeon. He was an older gentleman who reminded you of the typical, trusted family physician. His years of experience and easy manner were apparent in his gentle bedside demeanor. He introduced himself and asked if we had any questions. Of course we did.

"What happened?" I asked.

"There's a tremendous amount of bleeding in your son's brain." He explained in more detail what Dr. Alvernia had said. I was in a daze and couldn't comprehend what he was telling us.

"Was there any evidence of foul play?" I asked.

"No, none."

"Did you do a toxicology screen?"

"Yes. It was clean. Nothing that would have caused this."

I breathed a sigh of relief. At least he hadn't been assaulted, there was no blunt-force trauma, and there was no overdose involved.

"I suspect a brain aneurysm is behind all this," he said.

He told us of several options to be considered starting with medications that would work to reduce the pressure. They would attempt a procedure to drain the fluid from his ventricles. The most drastic step would involve surgery. By the time he finished, I was numb. He asked if we had any other questions.

"Just one I guess," I said. "What are our lives going to be like a year from now?"

I expected him to tell me about rehab hospitals, physical therapy, and speech therapy. Maybe Chris would have to start college all over. Maybe after he learned to walk again. My father had suffered a stroke in April 1990 and died five months later. Grace's dad suffered from a fatal brain tumor and had died nine months earlier. We were too familiar with the effects of brain injuries.

"We don't know yet. We'll keep a close eye on his condition through the night. I suspect I can give you a better answer in the morning," he replied.

Dr. Alvernia informed us that the ICP had let them know the pressure on Chris's brain was eighty-one on whatever scale they used when it should have been between eleven and fifteen. Grace saw the monitor and thought, *This is not good.* Worse yet, during the procedure, they were unable to drain any fluid from his ventricles. Another bad sign. Dr. Alvernia described Chris's condition as "Grim. Extremely grim."

We spent the next several hours going back and forth between Christopher's room and the waiting room with Colin, Matt, and Jenn. Our boys' fraternity brothers were filling up the waiting room along with Jenn's sorority sisters, Delta Gammas. Fr. Wildes came as well. I had met him when Colin was a freshman. He had eschewed the private residences of many university presidents for an apartment in the freshman dorm. He had come to Loyola New Orleans from Georgetown

University. He's a bioethicist by training with advanced degrees in theology and philosophy. And an accomplished boxer. When I attended Georgetown as an adult student, I'd had a class with a young man who claimed Fr. Wildes had broken his nose in a sparring match. I didn't doubt it.

At one point, I realized MG had arrived. Morgan MG Ernest is loosely related to Colin and Chris. By loosely related, I mean MG's mother was dating my brother Mark's brother-in-law. MG and our sons had become familiar with one another through family gatherings at Mark's house. Birthdays and graduations would bring together the extended families. During the Fourth of July in 2007, MG learned that Chris and Colin would be in New Orleans. MG was going to go to Tulane, literally next door to Loyola. MG was happy to learn that he would get to know Chris and Colin much better.

The boys first connected in New Orleans at a bar then known as TJ Quill's. During the day, they focused on their studies. But at night, especially on Wednesday nights, they would likely run into each other. Whenever they did, the boys took the opportunity to strengthen the family ties. Their meetings were always very friendly, lasting at least an hour, as they all caught up on family news from Maryland.

MG was shocked when his mother finally got hold of him. It was proving to be a very busy semester for him, and his phone had been turned off to avoid distractions. When he finally spoke to his mother, he could tell something was terribly wrong. MG's mother, Patty, had only the sketchiest of details she'd gotten from Mark's wife, Kathy.

The Tulane freshman had been an EMT for over two years. He practiced that craft in suburban Washington, DC, a place where an EMT can get plenty of experience in a short time. He'd learned enough to know that whatever happened to Chris was very serious. He knew also that Colin, Grace, and I would need support. Instantly, the clinical part of MG took over, and he called his own fraternity brothers to say that he wouldn't be at a scheduled pledge meeting that evening. After dropping off his books at his room, he departed for the hospital.

My mind was having difficulty processing everything. I couldn't concentrate, and I was very confused about anything besides Christopher's condition. Yet I felt I had to put on a good front for Grace and everyone else. Colin was introducing us to several girls who happened to be friends of his and Chris. Among them was Fiona, a girl he was dating. It was one of those confused moments when everyone was introducing himself or herself to Grace and me. I stepped in it big-time when I extended my hand to one of the girls and said, "Hi. I'm Chris's dad."

She looked at me strangely. "I'm Jenn." She didn't have to say, "Don't you remember? We just met."

I was embarrassed and ashamed. I'd never been good at remembering names and faces, but that gaffe was inexcusable. Chris meant the world to her. Meeting us under normal circumstances wouldn't have been easy, and with her boyfriend down the hall on life support, meeting us had to be a nerve-racking experience at best. One more thing to pile on the pile.

"I'm sorry, honey. I'm having a bad day," was all I could get out. I had to excuse myself.

LAUREL, MARYLAND

At some point on Tuesday, the entire Abdo family contemplated flying to New Orleans. Mary called Gerry and asked if they should come. To many people, such an idea might have seemed overboard. But that was the kind of person Chris was. People wanted to hang out with him. He was a really likeable guy. Ever since he was a boy, he was what I can only describe as naked. He was the most genuine, unpretentious boy you'd ever meet. And especially with the Abdos and with what Chris had been through with them, the whole family wanted to go as soon as they heard the bad news.

"Mary, I wouldn't do that if I were you," Gerry told her. "I think I'm going to go down. But let's see what happens overnight."

"Are you sure, Gerry?"

"Mary, I'm positive. The last thing Grace and Eric need is to worry about how everybody else is doing."

And that was that.

Kevin Abdo especially wanted to go. He and Barry Fitzpatrick, Mr. Fitz, Chris's high school principal, were contemplating the idea. Matt told Kevin to wait. Matt and Kevin were two of Christopher's best friends. Matt could tell that Kevin desperately wanted to come down. They were all just waiting, Matt told him. There were already many people there, and whatever was going to happen was in the hands of the doctors.

Everyone was just sitting in the waiting room. There was little anyone could do. "Stay home," Matt told Kevin. "Just keep praying."

TULANE UNIVERSITY MEDICAL CENTER

MG could tell his mom hadn't had the full picture when she'd called. When he had first heard the news, the EMT in him took over. But Chris was in bed, not breathing on his own. The scene was surreal. He had seen his share of motor-cycle accidents on the Capital Beltway. He'd picked up enough broken bodies to learn how to protect himself emotionally. But this was difficult.

Part of it was his familiarity with Chris, whose personality was sometimes bigger than life. He was real. Always with a big smile on his face. Always happy. To know Chris like that and see him like this was more than disconcerting.

MG had overheard all the conversations about tests, possible diagnoses, and potential outcomes. In his heart, he shared the hope that the rest of Chris's friends in the waiting room were feeling. *There are still tests to be done*, he thought. *There's still hope.* But the EMT in him also said that loss of neurofunction was a one-way street. As soon as he saw Chris was intubated, he knew it was bad. MG's heart wanted to tell him there was hope, but his head told him Chris was never going to sit up in that bed.

Brant Langlinais was sixteen months on the job in the SICU. He had graduated from the nursing program at Louisiana State in December 2005. He was a member of the Katrina class. He'd had to finish his studies in Austin, Texas. He had been working as a registered nurse in the SICU at Tulane for sixteen months and had already witnessed more than his share of tragedy.

Brant was engaged to Michelle, a real heroine. She had worked at Baptist Hospital in New Orleans during Hurricane Katrina. She elected to stay on duty at the hospital during the worst of the storm caring for the patients trapped there. She was among the last living souls to be evacuated. She was rescued by a Cajun fisherman and his son who managed to get her out a window and into their boat. Brant and Michelle were to be married in May.

Brant wasn't quite numb, but the intensity and pace of the SICU had started to make him perhaps a little hardened to tragedy. The emotional strain of caring for severely injured or ill patients eventually builds on all nurses. It's a natural byproduct of the daily life-and-death drama that unfolds before their eyes. He was receiving "report" from Amy, the day nurse. Nurses everywhere do it. As they hand off a patient to another nurse, they report on the patient's condition. Their vital signs. Medications. Diagnoses and prognoses. As well deserved as is the credit that goes to physicians, the nurses manage the care of the patient. They are in the room hours at a time day and night caring, cleaning, monitoring, feeding. And as would be the case with Chris, caring not just for the patient but for the families as well. It's a noble calling. Those who perform the job well can have a lasting impact on the lives they come in contact with. And they're often not soon forgotten.

Amy hadn't been on duty when Chris was admitted to the SICU from the ER, but she'd taken over his care at the beginning of her shift earlier that day. Brant looked the young man over as he listened to Amy. A nineteen-year-old had been brought to the ER by his friends, not in an ambulance. Really? He kept waiting for the part about drugs, alcohol, or foul play. That was the case more often than not with guys Chris's age. A college student away from home in the Big Easy. Big Trouble.

The ER wanted to stabilize Chris and get him up to the SICU for closer observation and monitoring. So they had pumped him full of vasopressors to keep his blood pressure up. Levophed in particular. A patient's blood pressure is like an airplane engine in flight. The most critical gauge on the control panel is the tachometer that measures RPMs. Just keep the RPMs up and the engine keeps running. The props keep turning. The plane keeps flying. Same idea with the human body especially when it's in trouble. The bad news with vasopressors is that in addition to keeping a patient's vital signs up, they can have deleterious effects. Brant thought about that for a moment.

"So what happened?" he asked Amy.

"Visiting a friend's apartment. Said he felt like he was gonna pass out, and he did just that."

"Really. Toxicology screen?" asked Brant.

"Negative."

"You serious?"

"Yep. No trauma either. Might be an AVM. His family's from Maryland. His brother and all their friends from school have been here all night."

Amy explained the steps she'd gone through all day long with Chris. She explained the neuro tests she had performed all without response. She explained the ranges of his vital signs. She explained every detail of every test so Brant would have something, a base line, to compare his own assessment to.

Brant noticed Chris's heart was racing and his blood pressure was high. The result of the vasopressors.

Amy said goodnight. She would return at 7:00 the next morning. Brant began to survey the room and Christopher's belongings. He picked up the bag containing Chris's clothes and noticed grass on the boy's shoes and shirt.

"All right, no foul play, but maybe some horseplay?" he asked the unconscious boy. Brant looked at the feet protruding from the sheet. "Damn, you got some big-ass feet, boy." Christopher's temperature was still quite high. Over 104 Fahrenheit. Brant decided on an ice bath to cool his patient's body. He decided to start backing down the meds. Perhaps his body could regulate its own body temperature. After turning down the meds, he placed ice packs in Chris's armpits and on his groin. Before long, his body's temperature was down to 101.

Brant looked over his young charge. *Why are you here, man?* Chris was motionless. It wasn't adding up. Brant pulled the sheet down over the boy's muscular chest and shoulders. The boy was intubated. A machine was breathing for him. He had an IV, and he was catheterized. Electrocardiogram leads were placed on his chest. Beyond that, this was a healthy young man. *No drugs, no booze, no violence?* Some patients make their own beds as the saying went. But Brant sensed this was not the typical New Orleans gangster with a gunshot wound. Nor was he some irresponsible young man convinced he was bulletproof. That could just as easily have been himself a few years earlier. Satisfied with his patient's condition, Brant decided he needed a soda.

Fr. Ted asked if we'd had anything to eat. We hadn't. He offered to take us to get something. We decided to go to a McDonald's where I could also pick up rations for Colin, Matt, Jenn, Fiona, and the rest of the folks. I asked Fr. Ted how he had happened to come to Loyola. He was originally from Chicago. He was working in Korea when he suffered a serious leg injury in a motorcycle accident. It was during his convalescence that he decided to become a priest. He joined the Jesuits in the order's New England Province and studied education and theology. He has extensive experience working in the Caribbean and Latin America. He had spent time at Boston College working in and studying university administration. After Hurricane Katrina, his superiors in the order told him there was a pressing need in New Orleans. He'd been there ever since.

My cell phone rang.
"Hello?"
"Hey Mr. Gregory, it's Brian Abdo."

"Hey man."

"What can you tell us? How's Chris?"

"He's in a coma. They're doing some tests. They're keeping an eye on him. Maybe tomorrow they'll know more."

"What's wrong with him?"

"They don't know."

Brian's voice thundered through the phone. "Well somebody down there better figure out what's wrong!"

That's when I realized I wasn't speaking to the elder Brian but to his son, Little Brian, who was two years younger than Chris. I told him what I knew, which was little. I promised to call his parents as soon as I had something substantive to share.

We purchased burgers, fries, enough for the kids in the waiting room, and headed back to the hospital. When we got there, we left the food with the kids in the waiting room. Most of them didn't seem interested in eating. I found Jenn sitting by herself on the terrace outside. She had been in Chris's room for a while, and when she returned to the waiting room, she found it full of fraternity brothers. Overwhelmed with emotion, she'd sought a little peace and quiet on the terrace outside. I apologized for my earlier gaffe, and we just sat there chatting for few minutes about nothing in particular. I stood and said, "Jenn, come here." I wrapped her in a bear hug. "It's gonna be okay." We walked around the corner to a soda machine.

Around 9:00 that evening, a young man in hospital scrubs walked out to the waiting room and asked who we were there to see. It was Brant, Christopher's nurse that night. We instantly felt comfortable with the guy. Maybe it was because after having raised three sons, we were just plain used to having men around. Brant gave us the immediate impression that he knew what he was doing. He told us Chris was cleaned up and ready for visitors. We gowned and masked up.

Chris was pretty much as we had left him. It was a sight that remains seared into my memory. He looked so peaceful. But for the IV, the ventilator, and the ICP, he looked as he always had. It was so hard to comprehend how much danger he was in. The mechanical, rhythmic sound of the ventilator was joined periodically by the beeping alarm of the IV when it required attention.

"Go ahead and talk to him," Brant told us. "I think he knows you're here."

We didn't know if he did or didn't. "Hi pal," was all I could think to say. "We're here. We love you." I was otherwise speechless. We sat there for the longest time holding each other's hands including Chris's. He didn't squeeze back. He seemed so fragile. I desperately wanted to hug him. Pick him up and cradle him in my arms just as I had when he was little. I wanted to tell him I was there, everything would be okay, I'd take care of everything. But I was afraid I might disconnect him from what was keeping him alive. All we could do was look at our son and cry. We were helpless. We were numb.

We left the room and told Jenn, Matt, and Colin they could go in and see Chris for a while. We had to remind them about the rules about gowns and gloves. We warned them about all the tubes and machines they'd see.

LAUREL, MARYLAND

Kevin Abdo stayed at home that night. He had to get up early Wednesday to be back at school for a 10:00 a.m. class. He made sure his bags were packed, his books and computer were ready, cell phone nearby—all the college freshman essentials. Before getting into bed, he dropped to his knees. He prayed for ten minutes. He prayed hard. He prayed God would spare his best friend. He reflected on all the years he and Chris had been together. How they had drifted apart and fallen out with each other in their senior year. How Chris had become a big brother to Brian, Kevin's brother. How Chris had been there when the family learned of Kevin's uncle's death, and how he had comforted Kevin's dad.

Kevin thought about their reconciliation during their senior retreat. It had taken not one but two cigars before the two successfully put to rest the issues that had caused them so much heartache. Kevin swore then never to take their friend-ship for granted.

Kevin thought he should go to New Orleans to be with his friend. He climbed into bed and turned off the light wondering what the next day would bring.

Amy was mentally exhausted. It was only day one of a three-day stretch, but Chris had her racking her brain for a reason why he was in the SICU. If only Chris could have been able to communicate, she might have understood his situation more. But that wasn't the case.

Before heading to bed, Amy texted Brant, "Any change?"

"None," came the reply in seconds.

Amy had had some patients come into her care in whom after some hours she'd seen a change for the better. That's all she wanted for the nineteen-year-old in her SICU. An improve-ment in his condition. Any improvement.

She called it a night. Perhaps the next day would bring some answers. Maybe even a plan. Hopefully a change for the better.

NEW ORLEANS

Ellie Trant was completely distracted during dinner with her friends. Roslyn, Amy, Alicia, and Ellie had been friends since high school in Grand Coteau. The four hadn't been together for some time, and Ellie was looking forward to catching up with the others. That was until Matt's call earlier that day. Ellie kept worrying about Chris and what circumstances had led to his ending up in an ICU.

Her friends sensed her uneasiness as Ellie shared the news and her fears for Christopher's condition. Her friends tried to ease her concern. "He's strong," they kept telling her. "He'll be fine."

At the end of their evening, Ellie bade her friends farewell and called Matt again.

"How is he?" she asked.

"He's the same. Unconscious," Matt said. "They don't know what caused it. He just collapsed."

"Who all's there?"

"Who isn't? Jenn's here, and Nick, and all the Beggars, and Rebecca and Kurt and Father Ted. Everybody."

"Maybe I ought to—"

"No, don't. You don't want to see him like this."

TULANE UNIVERSITY MEDICAL CENTER

Kevin Drohan, Nick, Woody, Steve, Dan Whalen, Dan G, Nick Payne, John Villien—all fraternity brothers of Colin's—had just showed up. The boys arrived just after visiting hours. They were initially turned away at the ER entrance, but they refused to take no for an answer.

The mood in the waiting room was one of nervousness. Nick Mangiello was trying to break the tension with some comic relief. Once or twice, he even picked up the phone to the nurse's station in the SICU.

Sometime after nine, two hospital security guards arrived and told everyone that visiting hours were over, that everyone but immediate family had to leave. These were not your average security guards. They were the night shift. They were two big guys, early thirties, muscular, tall, armed. And they weren't going away.

"Okay, man, we'll be out in a minute," one of Chris's friends said. He was betting on the hospital cops issuing a warning and finding something else to do. But the cops didn't budge.

"Folks, if you're not immediate family members, you're leaving. Now." A command, not a request.

"Okay, guys," I said. "You all look like you can use some sleep."

Coolers started closing. Trash made its way to the trash can. Shoes went back on feet. The migration started slowly, but it started.

"Seriously, folks. Y'all gotta go home," said the bigger cop.

John Villien spoke up. "C'mon, y'all. Let's let everyone get some rest."

Grace and I walked with the kids and with Fr. Ted toward the elevators. Colin pulled us aside.

"Dad, Jenn wants to stay," he said. I looked at her and at Matt. It was obvious they were physically and emotionally exhausted.

"Look," I said. "Why don't you guys go get some sleep. Chris isn't going anywhere tonight. We can all come back in the morning." Then I heard MG's voice.

"I'm staying too. Tell them I'm his cousin. Seriously. I am."

I guess he was. And the big freshman looked like he wasn't planning to take no for an answer.

At every turn, the crowd kept expecting the two security guys to convince themselves that the students were actually on their way out and then go look for something else to do. They didn't. The two big cops walked the crowd every step all the way out the door and didn't go back inside until they saw the kids actually enter the parking garage.

"That was sweet of them," I said to Grace and Colin. "Even if they were all half in the bag."

The cops were actually pretty cool. They said goodnight, and we went back to Chris's room. As before, we put on gowns, caps, and latex gloves. As we sat there in silence, the day's events replayed in my head. The call from Colin. The flight to New Orleans. Matt, Colin, and Jenn. Frs. Wildes, Jim, and Ted. Seeing Chris in the SICU. Realizing we'd been together only a few short days ago and now look at him. Look at my boy. Dr. Alvernia's assessment that things were grim. Extremely grim. So many thoughts swirled around in my head. Still, I had hope. I figured that the next day, we'd come back and Chris would be sitting up eating cereal. These people knew what they were doing. We'd get to take him home. At worst, they may have to operate. He may have a long road ahead, but he'd be okay. He'd make it.

"Where y'all staying?" asked Brant.

"Holiday Inn across the street," I replied.

"Do you want to give me your cell number? If anything happens, I can call you."

We exchanged numbers, and Brant left us alone in the room. We said goodnight to Chris. I leaned over and whispered, "Chris, this is Dad. I want you to know I love you. Okay? I love you very much. Listen to me, son. Put your hand in God's hand, okay? Put your hand in God's hand."

freshmen

⨯⨯⨯

Chris had come a long way in the four years Mary and Brian had come to know him. They had known him for years of course but never really as part of the family. The boys had gone to grade school together and played basketball on the same CYO team. But Chris was very much a child then, and it wasn't until high school that Chris's sense of humor developed.

On their first day of high school, it was Mary's turn to drive to Mount Saint Joe. She had test driven the route before and was confident about how long it would take. Except she hadn't counted on rush hour. So on their first day as high school freshmen, Kevin and Chris were late. Mary was frantic. Kevin was having a nervous breakdown right in front of her. Chris was in the backseat with a look on his face that said, "Whatever. What's the big deal?"

As Mary pulled up to the school, there was the formidable Mr. Norton standing out front. As though she were trying to talk a state trooper out of writing a ticket, Mary jumped from the car and began to plead for mercy from Mr. Norton. Norton was having none of it. His attitude was, "Ma'am, get back in the car. I got this." And that's how their high school careers got started.

Chris said very little those first few weeks of school. Just the normal coming and going of high school students. As homecoming approached, Kevin agonized over who he should ask to the dance. It was as big a deal at Saint Joe's as it is at most high schools across the country. As Kevin began verbalizing his possible choices, Chris started to weigh in. Usually, his commentary was limited to a response to Kevin's candidates. "I don't know, Kev," or "Maybe not." For two days, the conversation in the carpool focused on nothing but Kevin's date for homecoming. Chris was up front next to Mary. Kevin finally announced that perhaps he didn't think he'd ask anyone. Chris turned to his friend in the backseat, extended his arms, and in a complete deadpan voice said, "If you can't find anyone else, Kev, I'm here for you."

Oh my God, Mary thought. He's really funny.

And as the months progressed, Christopher began to feel comfortable enough to share his sense of humor. In the mornings especially, the radio became an immediate topic of discussion. Especially if Kevin put on a rock 'n' roll station.

"I'm so sorry about your son, Miss Abdo," Chris would say instinctively dropping the second syllable. "I'm sorry he listens to that devil music." And then purely tongue in cheek, he'd ask, "Why don't you put on that Christian rock station we like?" After no response from Kevin, "Would you please put the radio on the Christian rock station? It's the only station I listen to. Right, Miss Abdo?"

Chris gave the impression that he was merely tolerating Kevin and that the sainted Mrs. Abdo deserved so much more from her son. "Kevin, do you kiss your mother with that mouth?" he'd ask sometimes. "I'm sorry about the way Kevin turned out. You deserve so much better. I mean, you seem like a nice mother."

nic whitacre:

THE ACTIVIST

Nic Whitacre was twenty-seven when he kissed Michelle Hebert for the first time. They were guests at a party, and Nic had just been dumped by his girlfriend. It was 1989. They've been together ever since.

Nic was originally from Texas, but he'd grown up traveling the world with his father, a Church of Christ missionary. Nic's dad typically ministered at army bases in Europe; that meant Nic had attended kindergarten in Germany and had grown up exploring sites like the Louvre and Notre Dame. But by the time his high school years arrived, the Whitacre family had settled in Shreveport, Louisiana.

Type 1 diabetes (T1D) used to be called juvenile-onset diabetes. It afflicts one of every five hundred people. It's much less common than type 2 diabetes. T1D accounts for from 5 to 10 percent of all diabetes patients. People with Type 1 don't produce insulin. Rather, their pancreases don't produce enough insulin. The body's immune system attacks the cells in the pancreas that are supposed to produce insulin. Nic Whitacre had been diagnosed with T1D, and at age thirteen, he became insulin dependent. Little was known about the disease in the 1970s, and Nic lived life as best he could.

He attended Louisiana State University-Shreveport, but like many successful people had not graduated. A born entrepreneur, he found himself in pharmaceutical sales and then opening a chain of movie theaters. Nic was in the business of opening theaters in 1990 when he and his bride moved to Southern California. Shortly thereafter, he went into the insurance business. It turned out to be a fortuitous career move for someone with a medical future like his. Nic was a very successful insurance salesman.

He and Michelle moved from Mission Viejo to Escondido, and he moved from sales into management. At the peak of his career, he was a regional sales development manager responsible for developing and training a sales force in Southern California. The Whitacres' ship had come in, or so it seemed. And then he started throwing up and couldn't stop it.

From nearly the beginning of his battle with diabetes, Nic developed neuropathy, a condition resulting in nerve damage that produces tingling in the hands and feet. It's similar to the sensation you get when you hit your funny bone, except in Nic's case, it never went away. He also developed gastroparesis, a condition among diabetics that causes damage to the vagus nerves. As a result of gastroparesis, the muscles of the stomach and intestines don't function properly and food does not travel through the digestive system in a normal manner. Nausea, vomiting, and heartburn became part of Nic's daily life.

In his thirties, Nic began to suffer from diabetes-related vision problems. For several years, he was unable to see out of one or both eyes. He relied on others to perform the routine tasks of daily life: picking out his clothes, preparing his meals, putting a knife or fork in his hands. He even relied on others to help manage his medical care including injecting insulin and taking medications.

For six years, Nic attempted to manage the symptoms. In 1994, he was hospitalized five times. By 1999, the situation was out of control. Doctors were simply throwing drugs at the problem like firefighters pumping water at smoke but not attacking the deep-seated fire. They prescribed Ativan, Xanax, Zofran. At best, the drugs merely masked the symptoms. Nic grew sicker by the day, and his illness affected his ability to perform his job. In 1999, he was hospitalized two dozen times. Eventually, his employer told him to report for work or go on disability. Nic went on disability. To facilitate the medications he was receiving, he had to have a port implanted in his chest.

In 2000, unable to work, Nic and Michelle moved to a condo in Houston, where they would be close to the support of Nic's family and friends. They'd been to specialists all over the country. Due to the frequency with which Nic was hospitalized, a standing protocol was developed at area hospitals. When he became violently ill, doctors would administer a cocktail of Thorazine, Benadryl, and Ativan. He would usually recover within a matter of hours or at most a couple of days.

In between the bouts of distress, Nic came to appreciate life's little moments of peace that become so dear when all else was chaos. *Every moment is a precious moment,* he said to himself. Every moment to love his wife, share a laugh with a friend, or enjoy a favorite song. Those moments most of us take for granted. Those of us who wake up and go about our days and grouse about catching one traffic light too many. Those of us who never suffer anything worse than inconvenience. We don't appreciate the little moments, the precious moments, but Nic sure did. He got along by remembering something his grandmother had told him: "Nic, you can do anything for five seconds."

By 2007, Nic had come to appreciate the precious moments in between the seemingly endless trips to hospitals. All thirty-nine of them in that year alone.

Nic looks back on those years and simply says, "It's a hard way to live."

In 2004, Michelle's brother, Mike, and Mike's wife, Stephanie, purchased property in Slidell, Louisiana. The Whitacres moved into the house shortly thereafter. Slidell is a small community across Lake Ponchartrain about twelve miles from New Orleans. It's a simple suburban community whose inhabitants aren't unlike their neighbors in the Crescent City, decent folks quick to help neighbors when needed. It was a small but comfortable townhouse suitable for Nic and Michelle. Unfortunately, their stay didn't last long.

August 23, 2005, was a Tuesday. Nic was watching TV in his living room. What he saw on the weather report terrified him. A category-5 hurricane was building in the Gulf of Mexico. Living in Louisiana and Houston had given him an appreciation and a sober respect for tropical storms. But this was a monster the likes of which he'd never seen. The satellite imagery showed a system stretching nearly from Florida to Texas and covering the entire Gulf of Mexico. It was a storm packing significant winds, and it was picking up strength as it traveled across the gulf's warm waters. Worst of all, it was on a path where the eye would travel right over New Orleans. Nic and Michelle immediately understood their predicament. It was no time for a hurricane party. They determined what material possessions they could afford to lose, loaded the rest into their car, and headed for Houston. Among the items they snatched up were two milk crates filled with Nic's medical records. They left behind their wedding pictures.

By the time Hurricane Katrina slammed into New Orleans, the Whitacres were in Houston. They planned to continue on to San Diego, to Michelle's family. But in El Paso, Nic fell violently ill. He suffered from fits of cyclic vomiting. They pulled into a hospital ER. Michelle desperately tried to explain to the El Paso doctors the standing protocol that had been used somewhat successfully in the past. Michelle pleaded with the doctors and showed them the milk crates with all of Nic's medical records but to no avail. Finally, Michelle was able to convince an older, experienced nurse to convince a young doctor to prescribe Ativan for Nic. His symptoms subsided enough for Nic to check himself out of the hospital AMA, that is, against medical advice. Nic and Michelle continued on to California.

For the next four months, Nic slept on an air mattress in his brother-in-law's office. His physical discomfort was compounded by the absence of his wife. Michelle had to return to Louisiana. Someone had to clean up their house after the storm. And to maintain their health coverage, she had to continue working. When she could, she'd fly to San Diego to be with Nic. The presence of his wife eased his loneliness but did little for the burning discomfort that came with the uncontrolled vomiting. Those were a difficult four months for the Whitacres.

With the new year came an opportunity to return to Louisiana. Nic and Michelle qualified for a FEMA trailer. They returned to Slidell. However, within days of their return, Nic's vomiting became worse than ever. His days became unending periods of misery. Nic did all he could simply to make it through the day.

Alone in a tiny trailer, Nic simply existed while his wife earned their living. It was later discovered that the trailer in which they were living, like thousands of similar trailers, emitted toxic levels of formaldehyde, a carcinogen. Nic had spent eight months in a trailer inhaling the chemical in the same concentration as would a professional embalmer. Government tests determined the levels to be five times higher than those found in most modern homes.

After eight long months, the Whitacre's home was repaired and habitable. Nic was grateful to be back in his own home. His vomiting had subsided, but he began to notice swelling in his legs. His doctor prescribed Lasix, a diuretic. His gastroparesis, high blood pressure, and his long-term diabetes were all catching up with him. Nic was in serious trouble.

On September 9, 2006, Nic felt he was catching the flu. So around 8:00 that evening, he went to bed. At 3:00 in the morning, Michelle, who was in the living room, was startled by the urgent barking of their dog, Lucas. Lucas was running back and forth between their closed bedroom door upstairs and the downstairs living room where Michelle had fallen asleep. Michelle went upstairs to check on Nic. The scene she found terrified her. Nic was purple. Gurgling sounds emitted from his mouth. His lungs were filling with fluid, and he was desperately trying to breathe. There was blood on the walls of the bedroom, and it seemed that in a panic to breathe, Nic somehow had thrown himself out of bed and up against the wall. That must have been what startled Lucas. Michelle called 911, and Nic was rushed to the hospital and admitted to an ICU. His kidneys had failed.

The next two weeks are a haze for Nic. He recalls seeing Michelle in the ICU along with his sister-in-law, Stephanie. Two weeks after being admitted to the ICU, he awoke to a sticking sensation in his neck. A dialysis nurse was inserting an IV.

Nic had developed end- stage renal failure. His kidneys were no longer able to function at a level necessary for day-to-day life.

Those suffering from end-stage renal failure have two options—dialysis or a kidney transplant. Kidney failure can result in many complications including anemia, dementia, and seizures. Also possible with diabetes sufferers is the loss of the big three: eyes, toes, and kidneys. During his time in California, Nic had been blind in one or both eyes for two years. He credits his ability to see to some brilliant California eye surgeons.

When he awoke in the ICU, he was told his kidneys had failed completely. He was prescribed maximum doses of Demerol for his back pain. He was seen by orthopedists and infectious disease specialists. His initial dialysis experience, however, was far from perfect. Nic received absolutely no training in living with dialysis. "Watch your fluid intake" was all the instruction he was given. Of the first sixteen, yes, sixteen temporary access points, none worked successfully. However, Nic had been set up for dialysis that would last at least five hours a day three times a week.

In October 2007, Nic received a call from his sister in Houston. The Whitacre clan are big football fans. Nic's sister wanted him to come to Houston for a Texans game. The plan was that Nic could get dialysis in New Orleans on Friday, drive the five hours to Houston on Saturday, take his nephew to the game on Sunday, and get dialysis on Houston on Monday.

Nic had always been a sports junkie. And he was renowned among his family and friends for his knowledge of sports trivia. But Nic was having trouble remembering sports statistics, and Michelle was concerned. So they arranged for him to be seen by his mother-in-law's boss, a neurologist, while in Houston.

When Nic walked into the neurologist's office that Monday, the doctor took one look at him and called 911. Nic's face was swollen and jaundiced. His eyes were nearly closed. Due to the lack of good advice he had received from his original dialysis center, Nic's kidneys were not being completely cleaned and the toxins in his bloodstream were accumulating throughout his body including his frontal lobe. That was why he could no longer remember sports trivia.

For the next three months, Nic was on dialysis daily. An MRI revealed cracks in his spine from T1 to T5, most likely from throwing himself out of bed the previous September. He was fitted for a custom back brace that he wore for the next six months.

In early January 2008, Nic returned to New Orleans. He had decided to get on the transplant list. Organ transplants are neither cheap nor simple. They require a lot of money and extensive research. Nic looked at the transplant programs at Baylor University Medical Center in Houston and Ochsner Medical Center in New Orleans. Ochsner took Medicare. Nic always knew that he would require a pancreas transplant as well as a new kidney. A new pancreas would eliminate the diabetes that was causing his kidney failure. The pancreas would be the tricky part because the organ is so fragile. Nic had friends and family willing to be live donors. But the pancreas is transplanted only in conjunction with a kidney transplant. He also took the opportunity to cut ties with his old dialysis center and found a facility where he felt in better hands.

The kidney-pancreas transplant program at Ochsner is tied with that of Ohio State University's for the distinction of being busiest in the country; it performs over twenty such procedures every year. Kidney-only transplants and liver transplants are more common. Kidney-pancreas transplants (K-Ps) are rare and complicated. The procedure itself usually takes between three to five hours from the first incision to the final staple

depending on how many people assist. Usually, the team con-
sists of two surgeons, a resident, an anesthesiologist, a scrub
tech, a circulating nurse, and a surgical first assist. It can be a
crowded operating room.

Kidney-pancreas transplants are heterotopic in nature—
the implanted organs aren't placed in their normal anatomical
positions. Liver transplants, as is the case with heart and lung
transplants, are orthotopic in nature in that they go in the same
locations.

Standard teaching has it that the pancreas will be placed
on one side and the kidney on the other. The kidney usually
goes on the left. The implanted organs are often placed in the
groin or pelvis of the transplant recipient. The pancreas has
blood flowing through it, arterial inflow and venous outflow.
The urine that comes out of the kidney has to be channeled
to the bladder through the ureter. The sutures used to connect
these vessels and organs are finer than human hairs. The wall
of the bladder, the mucosa, to which the organ is sown during
a transplant is so thin that you can see through it. It's a complicated surgery, and those who perform it marvel that it actually
works. It's a testament to the healing power of the human body.

The prescreening process at Ochsner is similar to those at
other transplant centers; patients have to be sick enough to need
a transplant but strong enough to survive. Thorough psychological screening is also included to be certain the transplant
recipient will respect the donated organ and protect it. Anyone
who has ever met Nic knows that especially in those darkest
hours, he has always been desperate to live. Even if it was only
for five seconds at a time, Nic Whitacre's desire to live never
faltered. He would protect the donor organ as best he could.

In the months waiting for his transplant, Nic coded six
times. Coded as in cardiac arrest. Michelle would recognize

Nic's symptoms and call 911. Sometimes, he coded at home, sometimes in the hospital, sometimes on the way to the hospital.

As his health failed, continued dialysis became an increasing problem. The permanent access points for dialysis never worked properly, and the temporary catheters—sixteen—that had been installed had failed. So too had the two fistulas and the four Gore-Tex tubes that had been implanted.

In March 2008, Nic met a new vascular surgeon, Dr. Britt Tonnessen, a graduate of the Mayo Medical School in Rochester, Minnesota, the medical school program of the Mayo Clinic. Her goal, she explained to Nic, was to keep him alive until he could receive a kidney and pancreas transplant. "We're going to do something outside the box," she told Nic. They would find some place, any place, to install a port to allow dialysis to continue until a transplant could be done. She recommended an angiogram.

a close call

$\times\!\!\times$

High school boys can sleep at will. Whether on the way to school or right after school. But Chris liked to talk in the car, so he soon found himself in the front seat no matter who was driving. In the mornings, I would listen to C-Span, the public affairs broadcast from Washington, DC. Big Brian Abdo listened to NPR. Chris could take an interest in either and share a discussion on any topic on the radio. Big Brian enjoyed having Chris in the front seat. He would talk while everyone else would sleep. Chris would talk about Boy Scouts, sports, politics, family—anything.

One day as they were headed south on I-95 after school, Brian had just merged on to the highway when a huge tractor tire fell from the truck immediately in front of them. Big Brian jerked the wheel to the right and onto the shoulder just as the huge tire was about to land on the windshield. When a second tire fell from the truck, Brian swerved the other way. As he and Chris looked in their rearview mirrors and Kevin turned to look out the rear window, the tires started ricocheting off cars and causing chain-reaction collisions behind them. Brian could hardly breathe as he felt the blood rushing back to his face. He noticed his hands were trembling.

Big Brian was unable to speak. Almost as a matter of fact, Christopher broke the silence. "First of all, Mr. Abdo, that was a cool move."

arthur jackson—mac

><del>×</del><del>×</del>

"C'mon Mac, gimme two more minutes." Mac was getting light headed, faint. He had been on the treadmill for nine minutes, and the doctor had steadily increased the incline on the machine. He was sweating profusely, and his breathing was labored. "Two more minutes, Mac. C'mon, you can do it." Mac didn't have two minutes left in him. He lost consciousness and passed out.

When he came to, Mac was surrounded by doctors and nurses. He had been feeling poorly up to that point, and his doctor wanted him to undergo a stress test. The test itself nearly killed him. But the results were conclusive. It was October 2006. At age fifty-six, Arthur Jackson was diagnosed with congestive heart failure, CHF.

It happens when the heart weakens and is unable to pump strongly enough to maintain sufficient blood flow to the body. It's just like grade school science. The body's blood carries oxygen and nutrients from the lungs to the body through the cardiovascular system. When the heart isn't physically strong enough to perform this function, the body becomes congested with fluid. If the right side of the heart fails, blood backs up in the liver and legs. When the body retains fluid, the extremities may become swollen. People like Mac suffering from CHF experience a greatly diminished quality of life. They tire quickly, suffer bouts of dizziness, and experience weakness and shortness of breath.

As the body attempts to compensate for the decreased blood flow, enzymes may be released that result in increased salt and fluid retention in the kidneys. Muscle fibers may break down and lead to an inability to exercise. Generally, as the heart begins to fail, the entire body starts to fail with it. The person suffering from CHF slowly begins to break down physically.

The progression of congestive heart failure can be measured in four stages, A to D. Stage A (sometimes called Class I) is the mildest. At that point, there are no limits to physical activity and symptoms are usually not readily apparent. Mac's life would have been very normal at that point in the progression of his disease. He didn't even know he had it. But as patients decline through Stages B and C, they exhibit symptoms associated with heart failure. They experience greater limitations on physical activity and earlier and more-frequent fatigue.

Treatment for CHF ranges from dietary modification and exercise to medication and even heart transplant. People in Stage A heart failure will be prescribed medications such as angiotensin-converting enzyme (ACE) inhibitors and beta-blockers to exercise. ACE inhibitors widen the blood vessels and thus lower blood pressure. Beta-blockers slow the heart rate and lower the body's blood pressure.

In severe cases, those classified as Stage C, a cardioverter-defibrillator (ICD) may be surgically implanted. Mac would ultimately have this procedure done. This was a device implanted in Mac's chest and attached to his heart with small wires. Mac's ICD would monitor his heart rhythm and upon detecting a potentially dangerous rhythm would send a shock to Mac's heart. The result would be a correction to his heartbeat. And in the most dire cases (Stage D), the patient may be listed for a heart transplant.

Heart failure is a worldwide issue. Its causes can be genetic or due to a person's lifestyle. It's an equal-opportunity killer. The most common causes are high blood pressure and diabetes. Heart failure doesn't attack based on ethnicity or race though African Americans tend to have a greater incidence of high blood pressure and experience more heart failure related to hypertension.

Mac is a baby boomer. He was born at Dekel's Clinic in Jonesboro, Louisiana, in 1949. He's the oldest of twelve born to Marion and Sarah Jackson—eight boys, four girls. They grew up a close family. Mac's father, Marion Jackson, served in Italy with the Army Air Corps during World War II. Returning home after the war, he worked the family's small farm and at a sawmill. The forty-acre Jackson farm produced corn, peanuts, and watermelons.

Sarah Jackson was a stay-at-home mom. She and her husband insisted on taking the Jackson children to church, and disobedience wasn't tolerated. The kids went to school and did their chores without complaint. The eleven surviving children (one had died from crib death) shared everything growing up. If Marion and Sarah provided a bicycle for Christmas, the Jackson kids shared it; there were never any disputes about "This is mine!" Like the rest of his brothers, Mac was your average, normal youngster.

"We were just your normal 'bad' kids," said Carl, one of Mac's brothers. Mischievous but not malicious. They swung from vines hanging from Louisiana trees. They chased rabbits through the fields and would laugh while the rabbits would become quickly exhausted and disoriented and eventually turn right into the path of their pursuers.

Growing up, Mac was shy and introverted. He learned to play the trumpet and became good enough to be the lead trumpet in the high school band. Mac was an excellent student in high school. He was especially sharp in math and science. He was one of those rare individuals who always did well on tests seemingly without effort. In Louisiana during the fifties and sixties, all students were required to take standardized state tests. It was something of a competition. First at the local level and then at the regional level. The best students competed at the state level. One year, Mac showed up ten minutes after the test had begun. So sharp was he that he was finished for half an hour before the next student completed the test. Mac won the highest honors effortlessly.

After graduating from Shady Grove High School in Saline, Louisiana, Mac studied electrical engineering at Southern University. He originally wanted to be an architect and design buildings. A college advisor suggested he switch subjects, and so Mac earned a BS in electrical engineering in 1973.

While at Southern, Mac was enrolled in the school's Army ROTC program. After college, he entered the army, went through basic training, infantry school, and Ranger school. Growing up in rural Louisiana had made Mac a fit young man. But in 1973, the army was winding down the war in Southeast Asia, and there wasn't a significant need for new second lieutenants. Mac was mustered out of the army.

His electrical engineering degree landed him a job with Exxon. Mac's reputation for immediately responding to requests earned him the nickname Stat as in the medical term for "Now!" Mac's dad believed in hard work, and he passed that trait on to his children. He traveled a lot in the thirteen years he worked for Exxon. Much of his time was spent in Venezuela. He was on loan to the Venezuelan government and assisted in developing that country's oil industry. He also picked up Spanish, a language he can still speak after a little prompting. Mac and others doubled the size of Venezuela's oil refineries by installing and improving generating pumps and boilers. In his two years there, Venezuela's oil production doubled. In 1986, Mac left Exxon. Oil refineries, he explains, "are dangerous work."

His love of physical fitness led Mac and a friend to form a track club for young people. The Baton Rouge Striders were a group of youngsters composed mostly of sprinters and mid-dle-distance runners. Working out with the club kept Mac in great shape. The team traveled to events from Corpus Christi, Texas, to Jackson, Mississippi. They had a grand time and were quite competitive.

Mac is a shy, gentle, soft-spoken soul who is very easy to like. He's also very private. He had a daughter with his first wife in Baton Rouge. That marriage ended in divorce. Then in 1999, he married again, that time to a woman fifteen years his junior. His second wife brought a daughter to their marriage, and together, they had a son, Christopher. Mac loves being a father.

The fifteen-year difference in ages caused problems for Mac and his second wife. She had difficulty accepting the fact that Mac was more settled down than she would have liked. But a man of fifty is pretty much set in his ways. For five years, Mac was in and out of hospitals. Maybe his new wife was in denial. Maybe she thought that Mac's health problems were nothing more than his age. Before long, their relation soured, and Mac moved out of their house.

But Mac had always been an active person. That's why his heart problems were so difficult for him to understand. He had always been a vision of health; he didn't smoke or drink, and he stayed in shape. So when Mac began feeling poorly and couldn't recover from physical exertion, his doctor suggested that stress test. That's when his congestive heart failure was diagnosed.

Mac continued to work after the stress test. In the months following the test, he continued to feel bad but not as bad as what he'd experienced during the stress test. The symptoms were usually little more than just feeling weak. Sometimes, the weakness would be accompanied by shortness of breath. But usually, he just felt tired and wanted to rest. Climbing stairs became a chore. At one point, the personnel manager at his workplace took him aside. His health was affecting his job performance. He suggested Mac go on disability.

Then one February afternoon in 2007 as he was getting ready for work, he felt a severe shortness of breath. He bent over but couldn't straighten up. An ambulance was called, and he was rushed to Jackson Parish Hospital. The following week, he saw Dr. Billy Smith, a cardiologist at Willis-Knighton Medical Center in Shreveport.

In the months that followed, he was in and out of hospitals all over Louisiana. Jackson Parish Hospital in Jonesboro. Willis-Knighton in Shreveport. Glenwood Regional in Monroe. The physician at Glenwood saw Mac twice and refused to see him again. "It looks like you need a heart transplant," Mac was told.

In search of a second opinion, he ended up at Ochsner Medical Center in New Orleans. There, he came under the care of Dr. Hector Ventura, who like so many other physicians in this story is Latin American. Born and raised in Buenos Aires, Argentina, he was educated at the National University School of Medicine. He went to Ochsner in 1981 for an internship and residency in cardiology. He completed a fellowship in heart failure and transplantation at Loyola University in Chicago. He returned to Ochsner in 2000 and assumed the role of director of the cardiomyopathy and heart transplantation section. Despite his extensive knowledge of heart transplantation, Dr. Ventura isn't a surgeon; he's a treating physician who cares for patients before and after transplant.

On New Year's Day in 2008, Mac was sitting in the waiting room at Ochsner when he began to feel light headed, then nauseous. He started sweating profusely. Mac's brother asked the nurse for oxygen. When the nurse took one look at Mac, she hit the code button and the hospital sprang to life. Doctors and nurses seemed to come out of the woodwork. Mac had gone into v-fib, ventricular fibrillation, which happens when the heart's electrical activity becomes disordered and the lower chambers of the heart begin to flutter instead of beat. The heart cannot perform its normal job pumping blood when it goes into v-fib. Had the event not happened at the hospital, Mac likely would have died as v-fib usually results in cardiac arrest.

The responding medical personnel were able to resuscitate Mac by shocking his heart. He was admitted, stabilized, and discharged four days later. Mac had an internal defibrillator installed. And for a while, his health seemed to improve. But he was still plagued with weakness and shortness of breath. Time was running out. Mac was placed on the national organ transplant registry.

His first call came in February 2008. After yet another weeklong stay at Ochsner, Mac was at home when he received a call informing him that a heart had been found. When asked how soon he could be en route to New Orleans, Mac replied, "Well, I feel pretty good right now." Mac was elated and scared.

"Are you turning down this heart?"

"No ma'am," he replied.

"How long will it take you to get here?"

"Six hours."

Six hours to a new lease on life. But six hours is starting to push the limits of the ischemic time of a donor heart, that is, how long it or any other organ to be transplanted can survive without blood flow. Six to eight hours is the longest time a donor heart can remain unoxygenated and still be viable for transplant. Beyond eight hours, the odds of a favorable outcome begin to decline. Organ donors are usually found as the result of a sudden tragedy. And when their families choose to donate their organs, multiple organs may be transplanted. If a recipient in need of a lung or pancreas was closer to death than Mac, the recovery surgery might have to proceed with Mac not in place. It's a delicate ballet. Timing is everything.

Mac would have to make the trip, undergo the inevitable testing and preparation, and then undergo the surgery. Mac called two of his brothers and headed to New Orleans. The three-hundred-mile drive should have taken six hours. He accomplished it in four. Mac was prepped, shaved, and sedated when the recovery team concluded the donor heart was not a viable match. After another four-day stay, Mac went home to Jonesboro and an uncertain future.

Back at home, Mac did his best to make the most of life. But he was sick. Very sick. Too sick to work. He worried about providing for Chris, Ashley, and Stephanie. His son, Christopher, was just reaching maturity, that age when a young man needs the presence of an adult male in his life, and Mac worried that he might not be there for him. Ashley and Stephanie were off in college, but Chris was still at home just entering high school.

And so as February turned to March, Mac cherished his days with Chris and tried his best to live a normal life despite the constant weakness and shortness of breath. And he waited for the phone to ring.

wednesday, march 26, 2008:

THIS IS DEATH (PART I)

TULANE UNIVERSITY MEDICAL CENTER

We didn't sleep well. We got up early. We showered and dressed. I noticed what seemed to be a never-ending parade of military personnel in and out of our Holiday Inn. I figured they were in transit to and from the Middle East. We later learned that the Louisiana National Guard was working side by side with the New Orleans Police Department. With a large number of police officers still displaced from Hurricane Katrina, the city was depending on the guard to augment the police force. So in between patrols, the Holiday Inn served as a barracks and police station.

About quarter to seven, we left the Holiday Inn and walked up Loyola Avenue. As we approached Tulane Avenue, diagonally across the street was a vacant building. The smell of mold was overpowering, and we saw huge rats scurrying in and out. The contrast between the inside of Tulane Medical Center and the street outside couldn't have been starker. We signed in at the desk, got our visitor's badges, and made our way to the third floor.

We told the nurses at their station that we were there to see Chris. With the start of a new day came optimism that Chris's condition would improve. We knew Chris was in good hands. He was in the right place. I thought, *Let me go get my boy and take him home.*

Perhaps the medication they had given Chris had indeed lowered the pressure in his head. At the very least, they'd have a treatment plan and we'd be able to find out more about how long we could expect him to stay in the hospital. We saw Dr. Posey reviewing charts on a desk outside Christopher's room. He looked up and said good morning. He didn't smile.

"We should talk."

It was all he needed to say. I felt a knot in my stomach, the primal fear that we first experience as children when we are truly afraid. It was something in our DNA. A feeling that gripped the first cavemen when they faced the first sabre-tooth tiger. Warning bells started going off inside me. Dr. Alvernia was nearby, and Amy, the day shift nurse, was in Christopher's room. The three of them ushered us around the corner to a small conference room. I started thinking this would not be good news. I feared they would tell us that surgery was our only option. Dr. Posey spoke.

"Christopher's condition has deteriorated overnight. This is death."

Just like that. Point blank. Between the eyes. "This is death." I couldn't breathe. I became lightheaded. I can still hear the tone and volume of his voice as he delivered the news. I can still hear the inflection of his speech, and I can still see the look on his face. It was matter of fact but not without tremendous empathy.

"Oh no," was all I could get out.

"I'm sorry," said Dr. Posey.

I put my head down on the conference room table and began to sob almost immediately. Beyond the immediate shock and horror, I felt that my existence had somehow been suddenly, violently, and inalterably turned upside down. It wasn't right. It didn't make sense. Children aren't supposed to die before their parents. *This is wrong. This is all wrong. It's completely backward. I came to get my boy, and they're telling me I can't have him. Ever.*

"Isn't there anything you can do?" Grace asked.

"No. We're terribly sorry."

I began to cry uncontrollably. Grace was doing the same. Only after a few seconds was I able to turn to Grace, and we held each other in our arms unable to speak, just crying. The doctors and Amy sat there looking quite uncomfortable. They took no pleasure in having to do this. After what seemed the longest of pauses, Dr. Posey asked us to start thinking about donating Christopher's organs.

I knew very little about brain death. I'd heard the expression in the past and knew only that it was final, irreversible. There's a lot of misunderstanding about brain death. Here is what it is not. It's not a coma. It's not the same as a persistent vegetative state. It's not a semifinal state of death perhaps where the heart continues to beat. It is death. It is final. The heart is part of the autonomic nervous system and will continue to beat as long as the lungs provide oxygen. But the lungs will not function on their own after brain death. Chris's were functioning only because they were being supported by a ventilator.

In 1981, the Uniform Declaration of Death Act (UDDA) was drafted as a nonbinding model for the states to following in enacting their own criteria for declaring someone dead for legal reasons. The UDDA met the approval of the American Bar Association and the American Medical Association. The UDDA provides two definitions of death. First, it is the irreversible cessation of circulatory or respiratory functions. And second, it is the irreversible cessation of all functions of the entire brain, including the brain stem. The need to adequately define death for legal reasons was driven not just for the benefit of the organ donation community. Criminal cases require such a definition for homicides. Wrongful-death suits and life insurance claims also require a determinative description of death. And so the UDDA addressed those needs. But many people have a hard time wrapping their heads around the concept of brain death.

From the time we arrived on Tuesday until we left him early Friday morning, Christopher looked as if he were sleeping. He had a pulse. We felt warmth in his hands. His chest rose and fell with every breath. But those breaths were the result of air being forced into his lungs.

His brain no longer functioned, and it never would again. He would never again speak. He would never tell any more jokes. He would never laugh again. We would never hear him play the guitar again. He would never walk or talk or hear or see or hug his mother or call his grandmother or annoy his brothers. Never again. The brain stem controls the central nervous system. It makes the lungs function. The doctors would keep him on the ventilator until additional tests could be performed that would confirm brain death.

I think I called my brother, Mark, first. I told him that Chris was brain dead. Mark was at our mother's apartment. My brother Joe was there along with John.

"This is death. That's what they said," I told him. They'd perform an apnea test later to confirm their diagnosis. They could wait a little while to allow family to get to the hospital. But he was brain dead. As if somehow that was different from being dead dead. I still didn't understand the definition of brain death. Only its finality.

"I see," Mark replied. "Do you want to tell Mom, or do you want me to do it?"

"Would you do it please? I don't want her to hear it over the phone." I think she may have actually been there with him, but I needed to do this in little steps for myself as much as for anyone.

"I'll take care of it," he said.

"And I need someone to please get John to the airport."

Amy had known before we had even arrived that Dr. Posey would have to have the "talk" with us. Dr. Posey had gotten in early to check on Chris. He had asked Amy about Chris's vital signs, the ICP, and other diagnostic tests that had been ordered.

Having read the test results, the nurse had a gut feeling. She could read the scores as well as anyone, and she knew that the pressure inside Chris's head was the reason for the negative brain stem function. Amy was frustrated that nothing seemed to be the obvious cause of Chris's condition. If she knew what was wrong, she would know what had to be done. Chris was not the first young man who had died in her care. But usually, there was a known reason. A car accident. Even a suicide attempt. But there was nothing like that in Christopher's case. There was nothing—no clue, no reason—and it frustrated her. Chris remained a mystery. *Why is he bleeding in his brain? Why can't they stop it?* She knew that the next step that morning would be the talk. It seemed to her that Dr. Posey was taking this case especially hard.

Amy stood in the hallway with Dr. Posey and the charge nurse that morning.

"How do you have this conversation with people?" she asked.

Dr. Posey looked at Amy and took a deep breath. "The only thing harder than having to deal with it myself is having to tell another parent."

He related to Amy and the charge nurse the circumstances of his own son's death. His son was nearly the same age as Chris and had died under the same circumstances. It was obvious to Amy that the doctor was struggling with having to break the news to the parents of such a young and otherwise healthy boy. They didn't teach that in medical school.

NEW ORLEANS

Somehow, Matt had gotten word from Mary Pendarvis. They had spent the night at Rebecca's house on Jefferson Street in the Uptown section of New Orleans. Matt was planning to get Jenn and Colin and return to the hospital as soon as they got up. He wanted to get up extra early and try to get at least a little work done on a school project he'd been forced to neglect. He'd been given an extension already. And then the first call came that Chris was in the hospital.

Matt took his phone out onto the porch of Rebecca's house. He wanted to fill Mary in on what he knew from the previous night. It quickly became obvious that Mary knew more than

Matt did at that moment. Mary told Matt what Dr. Posey had told us. That during the night, Chris had lost brain function. He was gone.

Matt went inside and woke Kevin Drohan. The big, red-headed youth wiped the sleep from his eyes and lifted his head to look at Matt.

"Mary just called," said Matt.

"Yeah?" replied Kevin.

"Chris lost brain function overnight." Matt paused. "He's dead, man. He's gone."

"Oh shit." Kevin sat up and looked at Matt. Then he laid his head back on the air mattress as the news sunk in.

"Dude, we gotta tell Jenn," Matt said. His voice was already cracking.

"Oh shit."

Kevin got up and followed Matt outside onto the porch. The two were numb with disbelief. Before they could figure out what they would tell Jenn, who was still asleep in the back bedroom, they started crying. They knew it was not going to be easy and that the scene would not be pretty. They couldn't believe Chris wasn't coming back. His goofy laugh. His silly jokes. His random comments. Everything that made Chris the bigger than life personality that he was was gone.

TULANE UNIVERSITY MEDICAL CENTER

Colin walked into Christopher's room. He had been brought by Kurt Bindewald, who just couldn't do enough for anyone and everyone. Grace and I stood at the foot of Chris's bed. Tears were rolling down Grace's cheeks. She was sniffling nonstop. The look on Colin's face said that he was already expecting the worst. Grace gave him a tight squeeze and didn't let go. "Chris is brain dead," she said.

Colin started crying. Immediately. No dawning realization or slow-motion reaction. Like everyone else, once they heard the news, it was immediate and all-out bawling. In an instant, he realized it was over. Some people may have held out hope a while longer, but not Colin. He may not have been a physician, but he knew physicians used the term "brain dead" because they meant it. It carries all manner of terminal implications. Life as Colin had known it had ended that moment. The old world, the one in which he and Chris had explored woods and creeks together, and jumped on furniture to avoid the lava on the floor, and fought in the snow, and played sports, and gave their poor mother hell together, and eventually snuck beers and cigarettes late at night together, and went to New Orleans and chased girls together—that world was gone forever.

LAUREL, MARYLAND

Gerry Nolan had never heard his son so distressed.

"Dad, he's dead. They said Chris is dead!"

Matt was crying on the phone.

"I'm right here, son." It was all Gerry could think to say. He was thousand miles away, and he wanted desperately to be with Matt in New Orleans.

"They said that overnight he lost his brain function!" Matt said.

The boy was taking it very hard. Gerry thought for a second and suddenly remembered how he'd felt the previous day when he was grateful and happy it hadn't been his son in the ICU. Worse yet, it was the son of friends who was in trouble, people the Nolans were close to. *I need to be there*, he thought. *I need to be there for them.* He dialed his wife at work.

"Cathy, it's bad," Gerry told her. "It's a lot worse than we thought. I'm going to New Orleans."

Gerry raced home, threw some clothes in a suitcase, and headed to BWI Airport. His mind racing a thousand miles an hour, but at the same time, he laser focused on where he knew he was needed. If he could get to New Orleans, he could be of some help and feel useful. He could be there for Matt and for everyone else. But he had to get there first.

NEW ORLEANS

"Jenn, wake up." Matt gently shook Jenn by the shoulder. Jenn wasn't able to sleep alone at her own house, so she had spent the night at Rebecca's. "Jenn. Wake up. I have to tell you something."

The exhaustion had taken its toll on her. The sun was not fully up. She slept deeply enough that the trauma of the previous day had been mercifully forgotten. She opened her eyes and saw Rebecca leaning against the doorjamb, arms across her chest. As soon as she recognized Matt and the place where she slept, it all came rushing back. Dread washed over her. It was not a bad dream after all. It was real.

"Jenn," Matt said taking a seat on the side of the bed. Rebecca's eyes were red. "There's something I have to tell you. Chris is brain dead." He tried to be as gentle as he could, but there was no easy way to say what he had to. "He's not coming back. They're going to donate his organs."

The gravity of the situation landed with its full weight. It wasn't fair. Things like this don't happen to people like Chris.

Things like this aren't supposed to happen to her. Despite the past two days in the hospital, having heard the talk, seeing the tears, and being there as the mood turned from hope to something much darker, Jenn had held out hope. If nobody else would hope, she would. She would hold out hope for both of them. If she had to do it all by herself, she'd will her boyfriend back from the darkness. She wouldn't give up on Chris. Even if the doctors and the nurses and everyone else in the world had given up, she wouldn't give up on Chris.

But he was gone. She felt as though she were the last person to realize that fact. It was too much. She sat up and began crying hysterically. Her crying was loud, uncontrollable, continuous. *This can't be happening.*

After a few moments, she bolted from the bed, raced to the bathroom, and threw up.

BALTIMORE

Gabe Scasino had been Christopher's Spanish teacher during his sophomore year at Mount St. Joe. Gabe was a patient and compassionate soul, and he and Chris had hit it off. The two remained friends throughout Chris's time there and even after he went off to college. So Gabe was shocked when Little Brian called with the news Chris was in the hospital.

"What's wrong with him?" Gabe asked.

"They don't know. There seems to be a lot of bleeding in his brain. It's very serious."

"What are they doing for him?"

"I talked to Mr. Gregory last night, and he said that they weren't really sure what was wrong but that they might have to operate," Brian said.

Gabe was having a hard time comprehending the serious nature of Christopher's condition. But what Brian said next landed on him with a shock.

"Gabe," Little Brian said, "please pray for Chris."

"I will."

Little Brian said he'd started a Facebook group and would post whatever information he received. They could all keep one another informed of the events in New Orleans.

Gabe sat down for a moment staring out the window. He could see Christopher's face and hear his voice. He could remember not just the last time he saw him; a hundred other images of Chris in class, in the hallway, at basketball games emerged from his memory all at once. The memories were like a cloud engulfing Gabe. *This can't be happening.*

EMMITSBURG, MARYLAND

Kevin's cell phone vibrated in the middle of class. He had just arrived back at school that morning and was in his first class of the day. He checked it as soon as he was in the hall. The voicemail message sent a chill up his spine. He dialed his passcode and listened with butterflies in his stomach. It was from his father. Big Brian wanted to meet him in the Bradley Hall parking lot. Kevin slowed his pace. Slowly, very slowly, he walked across the campus. It was still winter in Emmitsburg. The trees were bare, and the air was cold. An even colder, icy sensation welled up in his chest. As he approached the parking lot, Kevin saw his father and his girlfriend, Allie, next to the car.

"Hey Kev," said Big Brian. His eyes were moist. He put a hand on his son's shoulder. "I'm just going to tell you. Chris is brain dead."

Kevin's knees gave out. Brian and Allie caught him as he fell into the car. Bad had just gone to worse. His best friend was dead. He started crying. As much as they tried, Allie and Brian could offer little solace.

TULANE UNIVERSITY MEDICAL CENTER

With what seemed to be a dramatic flourish, Amy threw open the curtain around Chris's bed. "Y'all don't need to put on gowns. And you don't need gloves either," she said. The rules of the SICU it seemed had just been tossed out the window.

We sat there in stunned disbelief. We were clearly somewhere we'd never been before and were having a difficult time adjusting. Amy seemed to sense that right away.

"Can I get y'all something?" she asked. "Would you like some coffee?"

"That would nice," I said. Her offer of coffee was more than a courtesy. It seemed she was throwing her arms around us.

"Did they tell y'all about the apnea test?"

"I think he mentioned it. What's an apnea test?" I asked.

"I'll let the doctor explain it. But basically, they're gonna have to perform a test to confirm Chris is really brain dead."

She explained they would have to disconnect Chris from the ventilator and see how he responded. That would determine if he was indeed brain dead.

"Any idea when that'll be?" I asked.

"Some time later on this afternoon or tonight. Y'all have family on the way?"

"Yes. Chris's brother, John."

"That's right. They're gonna wait for him to get here."

Amy shared with us that she had gone to Loyola as an undergrad to study nursing. She was currently working on a graduate degree at Loyola. She, Chris, and all those kids in the waiting room were classmates; they had at least that much in common. So Amy had a reason to connect with us. And a bond was already starting to form between her and them and us. A community of sorts was in its infancy, and the usual barriers that so often keep people apart began falling. Amy was not only part of the Loyola community; she was also a single mother and was very close to her brother. It didn't take her long to identify with Chris and us.

JACKSONVILLE, FLORIDA

Jorge and Leslie Bacardi were at conference table across from Dr. Keller at what was supposed to be a routine checkup at the Mayo Clinic. Dr. Keller was alarmed at Jorge's condition. His health was declining rapidly. All the tests indicated that a transplant was needed as soon as possible. The conversation had taken on a most urgent tone.

"Listen, Jorge," Dr. Keller said. "I want you to think about the possibility of waiting for a transplant here. In Jacksonville."

The Bacardis looked into the physician's eyes quizzically and with concern. Leslie spoke first. "Here? You want us to stay in Jacksonville?"

"Let's say that you're in Nassau. When we get the call that there's a donor, you may not get here fast enough," Keller explained.

"I see," Jorge responded. "I think I can make it here in three to four hours. Maybe four to five."

"That may not be fast enough. You may not have four hours. Sometimes, the OR time is only in one hour."

Dr. Keller explained the complexities of the timing. It would be the donor hospital that set the OR time, the time the donor would be taken to the operating room. All the recipients would have to be in place based on that time. If a candidate for transplant couldn't be in position in time, he or she might have to pass up the opportunity.

Jorge nodded. He felt terrible. Breathing, the one human function most of us take for granted, was a struggle for him.

"Why don't you think about bringing *Contigo* here to Jacksonville?" Keller asked. "At least there you'll be close, comfortable and in familiar surroundings."

"Let me think about it," Jorge said.

The Bacardis stood. Jorge and his doctor shook hands. Leslie gave Dr. Keller a hug, and they left. On the drive to the airport, Jorge was deep in thought. He would have to bring his yacht from Nassau and dock it at a marina in Jacksonville. But that was the least of his problems. It was Wednesday. They had planned to meet Joaquincito and Sonia on Friday for a week of fishing in the Exumas. If a donor became available while they were away, well, *So be it*, he thought. He looked at his wife. Leslie had cared for him for far too long to think about giving up just then.

NEW ORLEANS

Ellie woke up to the familiar sound of a text message on her phone. She was still drowsy, and she wanted to just lie in bed and relax. Her mind was blank. Not thinking, just resting. There was no noise outside. She knew she had a class to get to, but she was certain she still had time to just lie there for a bit. So she did. And then suddenly *Chris!* She was jolted awake not so much by her phone but at the recollection of the previous day's events. *Chris! How is he?*

She reached for her phone. The message was from Jenn. One heartbreaking sentence: "He's not going to make it." Ellie's heart raced. She couldn't believe it. She dialed Jenn, who sounded as if she were hyperventilating when she answered.

"He's not going to wake up," Jenn said crying. She could barely talk, and Ellie didn't know what else to say. They hung up, and Ellie called her mother in Grand Coteau. Mary Claire asked her if she wanted to come home. It was only a couple of hours away; she was willing to come and get her.

"No, Mama. I have to go to class."

Ellie hung up and called Cesca and Caroline. They had heard the news already. They were all crying. They were confused. They were scared. *Chris is dead? This can't be happening. Not Chris.* They hadn't had the chance to hang out after spring break to swap stories about vacations and what was happening back home. Everyone knew Chris and Colin had gone to Arizona, and everyone wanted to hear about what kind of mischief they'd managed to get into. *Chris is dead? This can't be happening.* If the previous day was bad, this was ten times worse.

After showering and dressing, Ellie walked to class looking for anyone she might know, any friendly face. She saw her history professor, Dr. Eagle, across the Peace Quad. Ellie walked over to him. Their eyes met, and Ellie burst into tears. Not an unusual occurrence for a college freshman, he thought, but somehow, Dr. Eagle sensed something serious had happened. Ellie told him about Chris.

"Don't go to class, Ellie. Go back to your room. Take it easy, okay? You don't need to come to class. We'll take care of it."

Grateful for his understanding response, Ellie returned to her dorm room, buried her face in her pillow, and cried herself back to sleep.

TULANE UNIVERSITY MEDICAL CENTER

Dr. Posey entered the hospital room. Grace was sitting in a chair holding Chris's hand. Fr. Ted stood in the door as I was looking out the window staring at cars on the street below. The tall, grandfatherly doctor asked if we could speak in the hall.

"Yesterday, you asked what your life would be like a year from now," he said.

"Right."

"It's going to take a while. It's going to take about a year at least. But you'll get better."

I just looked at him. I had no idea how to respond. At that moment, I didn't think I would ever want to get better. He didn't say we'd get over it. He said we'd get better.

"I know how you feel. I know exactly how you feel. I can tell you this from experience. You see, I lost my own son exactly the same way. He was exactly the same age as Christopher. He was in college, and he died exactly the same way. For a year, I carried a rock in my hand. He'd given it to me when he was a boy. And I never put it down for a whole year. It was always in my hand. Find something that belonged to your son and keep it with you at all times as a constant reminder of him."

I didn't know what to say. I didn't know that we were being initiated into a special community. At that moment, we were being welcomed into a club nobody wants to be a part of but whose members acknowledge they alone understand what each other is enduring. That never again would we experience joy. That the best we could ever again hope for was a day that just wasn't too bad. We didn't realize it at the time, but Dr. Posey was the first to welcome us into that fraternity. He was among the very few who would understand how important that connection is to other grieving parents.

Fr. Ted had been to hospitals dozens of times in his thirty years as a priest. He'd seen his share of tears and raw emotion as families coped with uncertainty and tragedy. He knew that medical professionals often kept their patients at arm's length careful not to become too emotionally attached. But he'd noticed something in Amy—a medical professional for Chris, a counselor to his parents, and a big sister to his friends. Ted thought, *What a caring, pastoral person.* And then Dr. Posey and what he had just shared about his own son. Something intensely private and personal. He didn't have to share that, but he did.

The medical staff at Tulane, especially those caring for Christopher, had a sense of warmth and empathy for everyone there. Ted thought it very rare indeed. In all his visits to hospitals, he'd never seen that level of emotional commitment to a young man and his family. Maybe it was the circumstances. Maybe it was the outpouring of love from his friends outside, but something genuine was happening. Ted could feel it. He was one of the few people there who had had enough experience to know that the concerns were more than clinical. The compassion and emotion weren't being forced. They were coming from the heart. He could see that in their eyes and hear it in their voices and in the words they chose. In what they willing to say and do for Chris and his family.

BALTIMORE

Gabe Scasino was having a hard time concentrating on teaching. Twenty young men sat at their desks staring at him with that look of expectation common to high school boys, the look that asked, "Well?"

After he had received the call from Little Brian informing him that Chris had died, Gabe had hung up the phone and sat in disbelief. Through his tears, he spoke to himself. *Oh God, no. This can't be. I'm imagining it.*

He tried to put on a brave face for his students, but it wasn't working. *How can Christopher be dead?* It had been just months before in that very classroom that Chris had stopped by for a quick visit. Gabe saw him. He saw how he moved with the confidence of a senior on the verge of graduation. Ready to take on the world. Gabe remembered the sound of his voice and his easy laugh, even the clothes he was parading around in. He was no longer the skinny sophomore Gabe had taught; he had grown into a strapping young man. Gabe felt a lump in his throat and tears in his eyes. He decided to change his lesson plan for the day.

"Guys, I have a bit of bad news to share with you."

For the rest of the day, Gabe's classes started with the news about Chris. And gradually the whole school learned of his death.

TULANE UNIVERSITY MEDICAL CENTER

Matt was sitting in the waiting room staring off into space. He was taking the news about Chris very hard. He looked like a kid who hadn't slept. Thankfully, his dad was on the way, and his presence would make the job of propping up Jenn and Colin a little easier.

A small community was forming at the hospital. Matt, Jenn, and Colin would be joined by the Beggars and Jenn's sorority sisters. Nick and Woody would be there a lot, and Rebecca, Mary, and others would come and go. It became a vigil. People sleeping on uncomfortable waiting room furniture. Blankets and pillows and coolers everywhere. It looked like a big slumber party or young people waiting in line overnight for concert tickets to go on sale.

The hope of the previous day was gone. There were no nervous jokes. No desire for comic relief. Everyone was faced with a new reality. Everything had suddenly become serious. Really serious. I could feel the emotion in the waiting room. It was difficult to accept that Chris might actually be dead. Everyone who went into his room had the impression that Chris was just sleeping. If you overlooked the ventilator in his mouth and the lead to the ICP monitor on his head, you could imagine he would open his eyes and speak. But that wasn't going to happen. It was hitting everyone hard. They were all doing what they could to hold each other up. It didn't help that the grownups, okay, I, always seemed to be crying.

Fr. Jim was genuinely concerned about Jenn. He wanted to make certain she was eating and drinking something of some nutritional value. He had given her a bottle of apple juice the day before. He was constantly asking her if she had finished it. Apple juice for Jenn. Fresh air for Colin. The Jesuit was doing what Jesuits do—meeting people where they were. And the folks in the waiting room were in a very bad place. Despite the chatter and the small talk, the sense of fear was palpable.

LAUREL, MARYLAND

The Abdo household is a noisy, joyful, riot of love and family and fellowship. There's always something happening. The lights are always on. Young people are coming and going. Doors are slamming, children are hollering, and nearly always, someone is singing.

Music is a big part of life in the Abdo household. Maureen Hasson had stopped by after hearing that Chris was in the hospital. Maureen, Mo to her friends, was like a sister to Chris, Kevin Abdo, Little Brian, and Matt Nolan. A gifted dancer and music lover, Mo was a sophomore at Catholic University in Washington, DC.

Mo thought the world of Chris. They all did. Little Brian was busy setting up a prayer service for that evening. He put it out on Facebook, text messages, and e-mails making sure that anyone who knew Chris or our family knew to come that night. Still hoping for a positive outcome, Brian called the group "Get Better Soon Chris Gregory." But on that Wednesday afternoon, a darkness descended on the Abdo house that had never been seen before.

Mary Abdo answered the phone call from Grace. The sound that Mary made that afternoon was guttural in origin, loud, absolutely primal. Those who knew her didn't think she was capable of making such a noise.

"This is death," Grace told her. "That's what they said. This is death."

Grace was crying on the phone. Hard. Until that moment, Mary had been filled with hope. As soon as she had heard from Grace the day before, she learned everything she could about brain aneurysms. Since updates from New Orleans came in bits and pieces, Mary still thought that Chris was in a coma. She and Kathy Nolan had gone to church. They sat in the empty church praying. Just the two of them. They remembered it was a place so full of memories of their children, Chris included. And so it seemed right. If God would hear anyone, he would listen to them in that place. But that was in the morning.

Mary's reaction so scared the children that they immediately left the room. Neither she nor they had known Mary was capable of making such a noise. Big Brian came running down from his office upstairs. He held his wife as they knelt on the kitchen floor sobbing uncontrollably. Mo and Little Brian took Meghan into the other room and just held her.

Kathleen was still in New York. She'd saved up to make the trip to Broadway for spring break. She was in New York dreaming about making her own mark on Broadway. It would be Friday before she returned home. Breaking the news to her would be difficult, but they decided not to tell her until she returned. It would be a very dark couple of hours as the reality set in.

NEW ORLEANS

The flight to New Orleans just couldn't go fast enough for Gerry Nolan. Matt's father sat silently staring out the window at the clouds below. On the Baltimore-Washington Parkway, in the parking garage, in the terminal at BWI, and finally on the plane. The whole way, he was frustrated at the interminably long time it took to move anywhere. Check-in. TSA. Boarding. Taxi. Takeoff. *Am I ever going to get there?*

He landed at Louis Armstrong Airport and took a taxi to Tulane Medical Center. He emerged from the elevator and headed to the waiting room. He was telling himself to be positive. *Put on a brave face. There's still hope.* He knew he had to be strong and positive for Matt and everybody else. *It's going to be okay.* The first person he saw was his son, Matt. He immediately realized nothing was okay.

The kids in the waiting room looked totally wrung out. Their hair was a mess; each was bleary eyed from crying and lack of sleep. They looked as if they had slept in their clothes. They had. Gerry thought he'd just walked into a nightmare. He felt powerless. He had come all the way to New Orleans only to realize that all he could do was share the pain. That would have to be enough.

I for one was never so happy to see anyone in my life. Of all the people to come at a time like that. Gerry Nolan was there. He always carried himself in a manner that exuded confidence and maturity. I'd never had to share a traumatic event or emergency with Gerry, but I knew his being around would be nothing but positive. He was a friend. A guy we could relate to and count on. And he was there. Some guys don't give you a chance to tell them no. They don't ask. They just post up. Something bad happens, and they're on their way. That's Gerry Nolan.

Gerry looked around and noticed Fr. Ted and Fr. Jim. He was instantly relieved by their presence. Having sent Matt to Gonzaga, he knew all about the Jesuits and was grateful to see them. There was something about their presence that said, "This is what we do." At a time like that, when one's emotional and spiritual back is against the wall, to a have a Jesuit or two on your side tends to even out the odds.

He introduced himself to Fr. Ted.

"We heard you were coming," said the Jesuit. "Do you have a place to stay?"

"As a matter of fact I don't," Gerry replied. In his rush to New Orleans, he had completely neglected to look for a hotel.

"Not to worry. We figured out something," Fr. Ted replied. "We can put you up in a dorm."

"I'm so sorry." It seemed all that he could get out as he hugged Grace.

"Thank you so much for coming," Grace said. Her eyes were watering. "You didn't really have to."

"Yes I did."

"We're pretty much just waiting for John at this point," I said. I explained that John was headed down also. I was surprised their paths hadn't crossed at one airport or another. I told Gerry about the apnea test and what little I knew of it. Basically that they would disconnect Chris from the ventilator to confirm he was truly brain dead. And that was going to be it. That was the last hope.

But Gerry Nolan had arrived. It was an emotional pick-me-up like I'd never experienced. Gerry Nolan. On my worst day. *It's like a movie. We're going down, but we're going to go down all flags flying. The cavalry has arrived.*

JACKSONVILLE

At 3:00 p.m., Jorge and Leslie Bacardi boarded the jet that would take them back to Nassau. Jorge was moving slowly. His breathing was difficult, labored. Demoralized and depressed, he was feeling the impact of his failing health. Leslie did her best to keep his spirits up.

"C'mon, Rabs," she'd say using her nickname for him. "It'll work out. You'll see."

But it didn't help. Jorge didn't want to be a burden. A proud man, he loved his wife and wanted nothing more than to be her provider and protector. But this … this was awful. He was tired of being a burden. The fight was being drained from him.

A little after 4:00 p.m., their flight landed in Nassau. Perhaps he could still go fishing with Joaquincito. Maybe he would just call Dr. Keller and take himself off the transplant list and let happen whatever would happen. He was thinking of what he had said to Reidulf, that his boat would eventually be his coffin. His mortality was coming into a focus that had never been sharper.

TULANE UNIVERSITY MEDICAL CENTER

Jenn and Matt decided they needed a change of scenery, so they went downstairs to the hospital cafeteria. They said little on the elevator. The hopeful mood of the day before had turned into something decidedly different. Nothing seemed to be working. Every time Matt or Jenn visited Chris in his room, they hoped to find him sitting up or perhaps with his eyes open. But on each visit, he remained motionless.

"Matt, do you think he can hear us?" Jenn asked.

Matt guessed that the gravity of the situation wasn't registering with Jenn. He was every bit as worried as the rest of us upstairs. Still, he chose his words carefully.

"Jenn. There's no brain activity." He watched as his friend's eyes glistened and a tear rolled down her cheek.

LAUREL, MARYLAND

Diana Adkins had met Chris when they worked at the Outback Steakhouse in Laurel. It was Chris's first real job. Chris was a senior in high school, and Diana was a student at the University of Maryland. The two hit it off right away, and despite her being slightly older, Diana became another of Chris's little sisters. Diana and Chris were assigned to the carryout service of the restaurant; they took call-in orders out to waiting cars.

Diana enjoyed Chris's sense of humor. She laughed quickly at his antics. She liked that he could lighten the mood in any room just by walking in. They became friends instantly, and their conversations always included quoting lines from movies such as *Anchorman* and *Napoleon Dynamite*.

They were Baltimore Orioles fans of course. Sometimes, they spent Friday nights with a group of friends at Orioles games, $5 student discount nights. Diana always marveled at how Chris would run into friends no matter where they were. And how people loved seeing him. Chris was easy to talk to. He could be a jokester, but he could also be honest and sincere. Most of all, Diana appreciated how Chris could take her biggest problems and instantly put them in perspective. "Oh Diana," he'd say, "stop being such a girl."

It was early evening when Diana arrived for her Wednesday-night shift. It was a part-time job that paid for some of her living expenses. She'd just settled into her routine and was filling a drink order at the soda fountain when she was approached by a coworker.

"Hey Diana, you remember Chris?"

"Chris who used to work here? Of course I do."

"Chris is in the hospital. They think he had a brain aneurysm or something. It's very serious."

Diana felt the blood drain from her face. She was stunned and couldn't concentrate. She forgot all about the order she was filling. *Chris? No, it couldn't be. There must be a mistake.* "Chris Gregory? What happened? Where is he? Did anything cause it?"

"Don't know."

Her coworker had limited information, just what he had heard from other friends.

diana and darrell

⨉

At Outback, Chris amused Diana with his efforts to maintain his self-proclaimed G-status. As in Gangsta status. "Gotta keep my G status up," he'd say. He liked hip-hop music, and it always made Diana smile when he rolled up to work with the windows down and hip-hop blasting.

The two were amazed at how often customers would phone in their orders and then remain on the phone telling the kids about their day. Total strangers would start unloading all their issues on them. Sometimes, things were funny and light, and sometimes not.

One day, Diana received a call from a woman who had ordered takeout but had gone to the wrong location to pick it up. Diana tried to explain that her order was not at the Laurel location, nor had it ever been there. The woman at the other end of the phone was not having it. She had called back three times and eventually threatened to come to the store and take matters into her own hands if she didn't get a satisfactory resolution to her problem. Diana was still a little uneasy when the phone rang again.

"Yeah, look here. I wanna takeaway," *someone said in a deep southern drawl.*

"Yessir, what do you want tonight?" *Diana asked.*

"Gimme uh … gimme uh … gimme a full rack o' baby back ribs, extra sauce. Gimme some fries. Gimme a ordera cold slaw."

"Sure. Full rack of ribs with extra sauce. Fries and cole slaw. Anything else?"

"Naw, baby that's it."

"Your name, sir?" *asked Diana.*

"Excuse me?"

There was something odd in the voice. Something Diana couldn't put her finger on. A hesitation.

"Your name, sir. What name for the order?"

"Oh yeah. This is Darrell."

"Okay, Darrell. We'll see you in twenty minutes."

"Okay, baby. So, ah, how's your day goin'?"

"Excuse me?"

"You know, how's it goin'? I done had a rough one myself. I tell you what. My boss 'bout worked my ass to death today. You ever have a day like that, girl? You know, you just workin' and workin' and the work don't seem to end. I tell ya. I had one of those today."

Darrell launched into a ten-minute dialogue about how tough his day had been. But there was something eerily familiar in Darrell's voice. Something Diana couldn't quite place.

Ten minutes later, Diana was at the drink fountain filling a cup with ice when hands covered her eyes from behind. Panic gripped her. The cup fell to the floor.

"Hey, baby, it's Darrell. Glad to finally meet you in person," *said the familiar voice.*

Diana became unhinged, but her panic dissolved when Darrell's voice cracked and then turned to laughter. Recognizing the laugh, Diana turned around. There was Chris laughing uncontrollably and completely satisfied with himself.

"You are so stupid, Chris Gregory!" she yelled.

But Chris just stood there responding with a big, goofy laugh. "So ah, Diana," he finally controlled himself enough to ask, "are my ribs ready?"

wednesday, march 26, 2008:

THIS IS DEATH (PART II)

NEW ORLEANS

Nic Whitacre was trying to relax, but he felt miserable. His angiogram was scheduled for 5:00 a.m. the next day. Something outside the box. That's what they wanted to try. Some access port somewhere in his compromised vascular system that would allow continued dialysis. He felt miserable. Nausea was sweeping over his body. The tingling in his hands and feet was ceaseless. Five seconds, his grandmother had told him. *I can endure anything for five seconds.*

TULANE UNIVERSITY MEDICAL CENTER

Jenn returned to Chris's room. In spite of what Matt told her outside the cafeteria, she wanted to speak to him. Perhaps he might hear her. She looked up and saw Grace standing in the hall speaking to Amy. She didn't want Grace to hear what she was saying to Chris. She put a hand up to her face just in case anyone in the vicinity could read lips. Not knowing if their privacy might be interrupted, Jenn bent over his bed and softly spoke to Chris. Quietly, she recited to him her list of the top ten things she liked about him.

SIX MINUTES

The doctors had to perform what's called an apnea test to determine that Chris was brain dead. It's a scientific method to determine brain death by measuring the arterial PCO_2 in the bloodstream after ten minutes of preoxygenation and then disconnection from the ventilator. It's considered the most reliable method for determining loss of brain stem function.

In laypeople's terms, they turn off the machine for six minutes to see what happens. The lungs will not function without being ordered to do so by the brain stem. If there are no respiratory movements observed, or if the PCO_2 is like 60 mm Hg, the apnea test is positive for brain death.

I still have no idea what all that science means. However, we understood that the test wouldn't be without risks. The test can induce severe hypotension, pneumothorax, hypoxia, hypercardia, acidosis, or even cardiac arrhythmia and worse. This much I do know. It was the fastest six minutes of my life.

We knew it had been ordered earlier in the day, but the doctors wanted to wait. They asked if we were okay waiting for John. The concern was that when they did the apnea test, Chris might go into cardiac arrest. Should that happen, some of his organs might be so damaged during CPR that transplanting them might not be possible. It was a fragile situation. By that time, the hope for successful transplants had become something of an emotional lifeline. Worse yet, John might not get the chance to see his brother while he was still officially alive.

We decided to wait. I had called my brother asking him to get John to the airport. I had the distinct impression that Mark didn't grasp the gravity of the situation. It wasn't that he was annoyed with being asked to get John to the airport, but there was something in his tone that told me he didn't understand the urgency in my voice.

"Mark, I don't want him driving. Please have someone get him to the airport. He needs to get down here immediately if he wants to see his brother." I didn't have to say "alive." I think Mark had gotten the point by then. Things were bad. Very bad.

"Mom wants to know if you want her to come down," he had said. I could just imagine that. And while I sincerely understood her wanting to be with us, I didn't want to subject her to the scene.

"No. Christ, if she comes down here and sees Chris in his condition, they'll have to find another bed to put her in," I replied. No, it would be better if she stayed in Maryland.

John got a flight and was picked up at the airport by Kurt Bindewald. When they arrived at the hospital, John entered the room and looked at his brother. John's the most stoic individual I know. I don't know where in the Gregory family gene pool he'd gotten that, but he's the most composed member of the entire extended family. Nothing rattles him. He never shows emotion. But seeing his baby brother lying there hooked up to a machine and tubes running from his body must have been just too damn much for him at that moment. John and Chris were usually sniping at one another, always working on getting under each other's skin. Each reveled in antagonizing the other.

131

But here was his little brother, motionless, a breathing tube and IVs attached, as if asleep.

We put our arms around each other, and for the first time since he was a child, I held him in my arms while he sobbed. We held each other for several minutes, John crying on my shoulder. Finally, he composed himself and looked at Chris. And then he did the most remarkable thing I'd ever seen him do. Nothing. He didn't say a word. He just stood there looking at Chris ... for the next five hours. He didn't sit. He didn't move at all. He refused all offers of food or drink. He didn't leave to use the restroom or stretch his legs.

I was in and out of the room a dozen times, and each time I returned, there he stood at the foot of Christopher's bed watching over his little brother. I have never asked him what was going through his mind during those difficult hours. I've prayed that whatever torment he's suffered over the loss of his brother has been eased. Of the many things that make me proud of John, that day stands out. He wouldn't leave his brother's side until the time came for the apnea test.

The test itself was administered by a neurologist, Dr. Alvernia, the same doctor we had met the previous day. He was assisted by a respiratory therapist and by Brant, the night-shift nurse. I think Brant and Chris would have really hit it off had they met under normal circumstances.

Everyone except for Grace, me, and the medical staff left the room. As difficult as it might be, we couldn't bail on Chris. I assume they oxygenated him. I wouldn't have known one way or the other. The tension in the room rose as the preparation was completed. The attending neurologist explained they would turn off the ventilator to proceed with the test. They knew their assignments and took their positions. They looked at the clock on the wall. The ventilator was turned off.

"Oh my God, I am heartily sorry for having offended thee ..."

We stood at the foot of Chris's bed. The clock was on the wall over our heads. We and the medical team were sort of facing one another with Chris between us.

"... and I detest all my sins because I dread the loss of heaven and the pains of hell ..."

We looked at Chris. They all looked at the clock.

"Our Father, who art in heaven, hallowed be thy name ..."

I've been a Catholic all my life. When the going gets tough, I know exactly three prayers from my childhood. The Act of Contrition, the Lord's Prayer, and the Hail Mary. I recited them over and over. I prayed hard. I prayed harder than I thought possible. I prayed for a miracle. I prayed that one of those inexplicable events you read about or see in the movies might happen. I prayed that Chris would respond in some hopeful way. I prayed for God to save my son. The doctors looked at Chris.

"... and lead us not into temptation, but deliver us from evil ..."

Something started beeping. I feared he might be going into cardiac arrest, which would result in the dreaded CPR, and then all might be truly lost. I recall the mechanical noises of the medical equipment. Grace and I held each other's hands very tightly. *Please God, please give me back my son.*

"Holy Mary, mother of God, pray for us sinners ..."

Coolly and methodically, the neurologist and the respiratory therapist exchanged glances and looked at the monitors. Brant looked at the clock and then at Chris. The respiratory therapist was jotting down the time elapsed and whatever relevant measurements were required.

"… but most of all because they offend thee my God, who art all good and deserving of all my love …"

I realized I was whispering. My lips were moving. I didn't care. Brant continued to look at the clock, look at the machines, look at Chris, and then back to the clock.

"I firmly resolve with the help of thy grace to confess my sins, to do penance …"

Brant looked at the machines, looked at Chris, and looked at the clock. I noticed something. Brant's movements, posture, the way he turned his head to look at the clock—they all stayed the same. But every time I looked at his face, I noticed his eyes were getting wet. In fact, the respiratory therapist was also starting to get teary eyed. To Grace and me, these were the shortest six minutes of our lives. For Brant, they were the longest. Brant would later tell me that the apnea test was like the slow-motion ending of a bad movie he had to put himself through watching.

"… Thy kingdom come, thy will be done, on Earth as it is in heaven …"

The medical staff continued in their cool, professional manner. Looking at Chris, looking at the monitors, looking at the clock. *Not yet*, I thought. *Please! There's got to be a few more minutes. C'mon Chris! Do something please.*

"… now and at the hour of our death. Amen."

And that was it. Christopher's six minutes were up. The test was over. Positive for brain death. There were no more minutes. There would be no miracle. Chris wouldn't be coming home with us. The medical team was silent for a moment. They reconnected the ventilator and turned it on. It began breathing for Chris again. Charts were notated. The time confirmed. They all had the same dejected look. There was some small measure of consolation in the fact they seemed to be taking it as hard as we were.

Brant covered Chris's chest with the sheet and straightened the blanket that covered him up. He was tucking our son in. It seemed he was taking the test harder than the others were. He looked at Grace and me with tears falling down his cheeks.

"I wanted to take a breath for him," he told us.

The big Cajun left the room, walked to the staff locker room, sat on a chair, and wept.

LAUREL, MARYLAND

The plan was for friends of Christopher to gather simultaneously for prayer in Maryland and New Orleans on Wednesday evening. About a hundred of Christopher's friends had gathered at the little shrine at Palotti High School in Laurel, across the street from St. Mary of the Mills School, where Chris and his brothers had gone to grade school. The grotto at Palotti was often used for prayer services during times of crisis or celebration. The event was organized by Little Brian through Facebook, e-mails, and old-fashioned telephone calls from friend to friend.

On Wednesday morning, Fr. Wildes sent an e-mail to the entire Loyola community with news about Chris's condition and advising all that a Mass would be held at 9:00 p.m. that night. That same night, a campus antiwar group had planned a die-in in the Peace Quad, which was between the Dana Center and the Ignatius Chapel. Realizing there would be a Mass for Chris at the same time as their protest, the organizers called it off. They probably didn't know Chris. After all, he was a freshman who had been at Loyola only since September. But out of respect for him and his friends, they saw no need to add to the pain people already felt.

Grace and I asked Fr. Wildes and Brian Abdo to tell everyone how much their prayers meant. We had only one request. We asked everyone who attended either of the events to pick up the phone and call someone he or she loved. Son or daughter. Or parents. Or a friend they missed. But please, just pick up the phone, call someone, and tell him or her they loved them.

In Laurel, Mary Abdo wanted to give Fr. Mike, the chaplain from Mount St. Joseph, an update on Chris's medical condition. She wanted to tell him about the apnea test, but she wasn't sure what to tell him. She knew Chris had suffered a brain aneurysm. She had researched online everything she could about the condition, so she had hope. She learned that if they could find the source of the bleeding, they could maybe relieve the pressure. And even if there was damage, there still might be physical therapy. Thoughts were racing in her mind faster than she could articulate them to Fr. Mike.

"Mary, I don't need to know the medical stuff," Fr. Mike said.

"No?"

"Mary, they're watching, and they're waiting, and they're scared. That's what we're praying for. We're praying for a good outcome. Whatever God's will is, our acceptance of God's will."

"Okay," Mary said. "That's what we're praying for." Instantly, Mary felt some degree of anxiety lift. For the moment at least.

Little Brian and Kevin Nolan were going to sing a song. Matt's little brother was all of about twelve years old and already a promising musician. And Little Brian had a beautiful voice. Chris was a legend in their eyes. Music was in the blood of the Abdos and the Nolans, and it was how they shared their emotions and expressed their feelings. Kevin was dwarfed by the guitar in his lap. Tearfully, Brian introduced the song they wanted to share.

"I spoke to Papa Gregory earlier this afternoon." His voice started to crack. "He asked if I would give you all a message. He said he'd like everyone to know how much they appreciate our prayers for Chris. And how much it means to them. And if there's anything we can do for the Gregorys, it's this. Before you go to bed tonight, please call someone and tell them you love them. Call a relative, or a friend, or a family member you haven't talked to in a while. And don't ask them about their grades or their cell phone bill. Just tell them how much you love them. The doctors told the Gregorys that tonight …" Brian's voice cracked. "Tonight, they're …"

Words wouldn't come. Mary Abdo put an arm around her son. Tears flowed freely throughout the group.

"They're going to do a test … to see …to see if … to see if he's really …"

That was it. Brian couldn't continue speaking. So Kevin began to play.

"There's no one in town I know … You gave someplace to go."

It was "May Angels Lead You In," a song about someone who has died too soon. It seemed appropriate for the moment. But in this case, the tragedy was too close to home. And the emotion was just too damn much.

"I never said thank you for that … I thought I might get one more chance …"

And that was it. Tears flowed like water among the group.

As the prayer service broke up, Kathy Gilmore was telling Mary Abdo all about her daughter Kelsey's brain aneurysm and her treatment and how she was recovering nicely. Mary began to feel hopeful that Chris might experience the same. Then she saw Big Brian approaching and looking at his cell phone. Her husband didn't say a word. He had tears in his eyes, and he handed Mary the phone. A text message was displayed on the screen. It was from Gerry Nolan: "Apnea test negative. Chris is brain dead."

Up until then, Mary thought maybe it would just be a long journey. She thought of how Grace had called Kevin that afternoon to wish him a happy birthday. And of all the silly, goofy things Chris had said and done around their house. And he was gone.

Many in the group, all those kids who knew Chris returned to the Abdo home. Over the next week, the Abdos' house was a command center for grieving kids. They all needed someplace to take their sorrow and suffering. Young people in particular are so unfamiliar with tragedy; they're unprepared when it happens to a close friend, especially someone they looked up to. Someone like Chris.

They told stories and consoled each other. The pulled out smartphones with cameras and e-mailed photos to each other. Then they headed to an all-night pharmacy to print photos of Chris that they glued to giant poster boards. The boards would be full of notes and messages. They ate pizza and cried and collected some two-by-fours. And then they started working on the wooden cross that would be used to mark Christopher's grave.

LOYOLA UNIVERSITY NEW ORLEANS

That night, the Ignatius Chapel at Loyola University was filled with friends, classmates, Beggars, Jesuits, faculty, and students. Some knew Chris very well. Others not at all. Many among the group came to support Colin, Jenn, and Matt. Others came hoping their petitions might be answered with good news, a miracle perhaps.

The loss of a student rocks a college campus as few other events can. On a small campus like Loyola's, everyone feels the pain. Everyone knows someone directly impacted, so the grief can be palpable at times. Colin, a junior, was well known on campus, but even those who didn't know Chris or Colin weren't immune to a sense of loss. The day didn't end for many until the community came together to pray. Pray for Chris, for Colin, for Matt, and for Jenn. And for each other.

LAUREL, MARYLAND

Diana was completely distracted, but a familiar face put her strangely at ease when she hauled a carryout order to the parking lot. It was Rose, a regular customer. She could tell something wasn't quite right with Diana.

"Is everything all right, honey?" she asked.

Diana hesitated before saying, "I got some bad news earlier."

"What's wrong, girl?"

"A friend of mine who used to work here is in the hospital. Something about a brain aneurysm. And they don't think he's going to make it!" Diana was in tears.

"Give me your hands, honey."

Diana complied. Rose and Diana prayed together. Rose forming all the words that Diana couldn't at that moment. Two people who hardly knew each other joined hands and asked God to save Chris.

It's remarkable how tragedy can bring out the very best in people. Strangers will comfort strangers as if they'd known one another for years. The natural instinct among humans is to do good for one another. To be strong for someone who's weak. To not let them suffer alone. Especially in times of crisis.

How often and quickly during those moments of weakness and strength we turn to God.

NEW ORLEANS

Ellie and her friend, Claire, walked down a deserted Freret Street. After the Mass at Ignatius Chapel, Ellie and Claire went out for a drink and ended up at Friar Tuck's. It seemed everyone from Loyola was there. All the Delta Gammas and the Beggars. The word had traveled through the Greek network, and guys started showing up. Some of the Beggar alumni showed up. Older guys who had never met Colin or Chris. Everyone knew but nobody wanted to say what had brought them all there, so they all laughed a bit too loud for fear of what they'd remember if they paused for a second.

Ellie didn't feel up for celebrating. She was hurt and confused. More than anything, she felt angry. Walking along Freret Street, she suddenly burst into tears.

"I'm so freaking mad right now!" she blurted out through her tears.

"It's okay, Ellie," Claire responded. "It's okay to be mad."

"He's so young. He's too young for this to happen. It isn't right, and it isn't fair."

Ellie had lost her grandparents in the past year. As painful as that was, it was natural. It was even expected. Young people's first exposure to their own mortality typically comes with the death of their grandparents, and then an elderly aunt or uncle, and then their parents. By the time we start burying our siblings, most of us have come to understand the linear nature of life. That's why the death of a young person like Chris hits friends and classmates so hard. It's too close, too soon. It shatters the expectations we all have of how long we have to live. At the same time, it's devastating to lose a friend under tragic circumstances. Unexpectedly, Chris was taken from Ellie. She could no longer count on his friendship, on his looking out for her, or his big bear hugs. His jokes. His late-night phone calls. Ellie rightly felt cheated and angry.

"Maybe you'll feel better if you break something," Claire said.

"Like what?"

"Here." Claire drank down her beer and handed the empty to Ellie. "Throw this."

Ellie took the bottle, looked up and down Freret Street, and threw the empty bottle as hard as she could. It landed with a crash and tinkling that echoed in the night.

"Feel better?"

"Not really."

"Try another one."

Ellie drained her own bottle and let fly with all the strength she could muster. If it were possible to express anger, sorrow, and fear in one physical movement, Ellie tried to do just that. The bottle sailed into the night and at the same time mocked Ellie's frustration and confusion.

LOYOLA UNIVERSITY NEW ORLEANS

Gerry Nolan settled into his dorm room. He was the lone occupant of an entire floor in Biever Hall, the dorm. He tried to read a paperback he'd brought with him, but the events of the day had taken over his mind. The call from Matt. He'd never heard his son so distressed. The calls he made to his wife and the Abdos. The last chance of hope before the apnea test. The flight to New Orleans that just couldn't go fast enough. The cab ride from the airport to Tulane when hope was hanging by a thread. The hope that maybe, things might somehow turn out okay. The looks on the faces of everyone he saw when he got off the elevator. The moment he realized nothing would be okay.

Gerry felt a twinge of discomfort when he thought about his initial reaction about it not involving his own son. And then finally going back to see Chris and thinking, *This is what we're down to*. He laid his head on his pillow, closed his eyes, and rubbed his head. As bad as the situation was, it would only get worse before it got any better. And so he thought about what tomorrow would bring. Exhaustion finally took over, and he fell asleep.

pushing buttons

In Chris and Kevin's senior year, Mary Abdo was hired as a teacher at a rival Catholic high school. That was an affront to God and man as far as the boys were concerned. Not only was Mary teaching somewhere other than Mount Saint Joseph, she was teaching at a coed school. Oh the scandal! And so, one Sunday in the fall of their senior year, Christopher arrived at the Abdo residence to watch a Washington Redskins football game. As usual, Mary was elbow deep in grading papers.

"So Miss Abdo, congrats on the new teaching job," Chris said.

"Thank you, Chris."

"But I do have to ask you a couple questions."

Mary looked up quizzically as Chris opened their fridge.

"Tell me, just how many of your students are pregnant?"

Mary nearly fell off her chair, but Chris maintained a dead-serious expression. Little Brian, Kevin, and Matt Nolan were listening intently.

"None," Mary replied.

"Well, I mean, you do work at that co-ed school and all. And, I mean, I was just wondering, you know? Like how many of them are on drugs?"

"Christopher!"

The boys watching from the other room were laughing. Chris knew what buttons to push and what Mary's reaction would be. He loved her largely because he could get away with such imprudence for the sake of a laugh; Mary Abdo would never hold it against him. He wasn't being disrespectful at all. He was just pushing the limits of getting a laugh.

"I have papers to grade, Chris. The school where I work is a good place. Those are good students who go there. You know them."

"You keep telling yourself that, Miss Abdo," Christopher responded as got himself a can of soda and looked at the television. "You sent your boys to Saint Joe for a reason. And now you're a traitor."

Chris loved Mount Saint Joseph. He loved the fellowship and the camaraderie. If anyone was filled with school spirit, it was Chris Gregory. "What some people won't do for a paycheck."

The boys had abandoned the football game. They were shaking their heads in disbelief and laughing uncontrollably.

"It's work, Christopher. It's a job."

"Yeah, but there are certain standards." He shook his head in disappointment. "But really, Miss Abdo, how many of your students are pregnant?"

xavier major

Xavier Major has the heart of a fighter. He should, for he'd been a boxer. But no longer. Now, he's a Jehovah's Witness. He hails from Leonville, Louisiana. It's a short drive on Route 93 from Grand Coteau to Arnaudville, one of the oldest towns in St. Landry Parish.

Turn left, cross the bridge, and continue north on Main Street, and Route 740 becomes Oscar Rivette Road. It runs parallel to the brown water of Bayou Teche and leads to Leonville. Hardly a town at all. It's more an intersection with a couple of abandoned country stores. There's the Washington State Bank and the Classy Cuts hair salon but little else in the way of commerce these days. Xavier Major grew up there.

Despite the proximity of Leonville to the Jesuit seminary in Grand Coteau, Xavier Major hadn't been named for the great Jesuit saint but for an older cousin. Xavier's mom liked the name, and that was that. Nor does he speak the dialect of those French-speaking Cajuns whose ancestors migrated from Canada in the eighteenth century. Xavier is African-American.

As a child, he spent his days outdoors not fishing or hunting but playing basketball and riding bikes with his friends. In the 1960s in rural Louisiana, one had to make one's own fun. There was no Internet, no cable TV, no cell phones, no video games. But Leonville was small enough that a boy could walk or bike wherever he wanted to go. Xavier enjoyed growing up there.

Four children—two boys and two girls—ran around the Major household. Xavier was the oldest of the boys. Growing up, he was a big fan of rhythm & blues. It was the sixties, and R&B was never better. Summer nights were sliced open by the sound of an AM car radio. Motown, Aretha Franklin, the Four Tops, Sam and Dave. The Temptations were Xavier's favorite. The world was experiencing seismic changes in attitudes and lifestyles. In Leonville, life pretty much remained simple. Quiet, honest, hard-working neighbors. There were school dances where he and his friends could meet up and socialize and be flirted with by the local girls. The dances provided some excitement in a small town, and he and his friends attended them until he turned sixteen or seventeen.

The US involvement in the Vietnam War was winding down. There were fewer than twenty-five thousand American troops still in Southeast Asia in 1972. Still, that same year, as soon as he turned eighteen, Xavier enlisted in the army.

He went to basic training and advanced infantry school at Fort Leonard Wood, Missouri. He then attended and graduated from the army's chaplain's school in New York as a Chapel Activities Specialist. His duties included typing correspondence for the chaplains and preparing churches for Catholic and Protestant services. Xavier fully expected to make a career of the army. He was assigned posts in New York and at Fort Hood, Texas, and he was sent to Germany twice. For six years in the army, he was an amateur boxer. He competed in flyweight, featherweight, and bantamweight divisions. A bulging disc ended his boxing career, but a more serious condition ended his military career.

During his time in the service, Xavier ate something toxic. To say it disagreed with him would be an understatement of epic proportions. Whatever he ate made him so sick it ended his military career. Whatever virus or bacteria he contracted stayed inside him undiagnosed for years. The most likely culprit was some form of E. coli bacteria. In 1981, Xavier left the army.

Xavier and his first wife had four children—two boys and two girls. That marriage ended. He had another child with his second wife. That marriage ended as well. Then one day when he was home alone, there came a knock at the door. Xavier opened it to a pair of Jehovah's Witness missionaries. He invited them in. He was separated from his second wife at the time. Something was missing in his life, and he longed for something more.

He is now a Jehovah's Witness. It was through the church that he met his third and present wife, Pam. Xavier and Pam met at a friend's house. As it turned out, Xavier and Pam enjoyed one another's company. A relationship grew, romance blossomed, and they were married shortly thereafter. Pam brought a stepdaughter to the marriage, and together, they have a son, Matthew.

Xavier loves his children and stays close to them all. They see each other frequently. Sadly, Xavier is no stranger to tragedy himself. His older sister had died when she was twenty-five. His son, David, was murdered in 1997 at age eighteen.

In 1995, Xavier realized he was going to the bathroom a lot. His kidneys had begun to fail. It may have been the condition that ended his military career. While he was placed on the list for a kidney transplant, his organs continued to function well enough to keep him from ever reaching the top of the list in terms of need for a transplant. He always had at least 25 percent function in one or both kidneys.

Then, in 2002, he was diagnosed with kidney cancer.

According to the Mayo Clinic, 54,000 Americans are diagnosed with kidney cancer every year and 13,000 die from the disease. The kidneys are part of the body's urinary system. They remove waste, excess fluid, and electrolytes from the blood. They control the production of red blood cells and help regulate blood pressure. Blood travels through the kidneys, where the waste is filtered out and flows from the kidneys through the ureter, into the bladder, and out the urethra in the form of urine.

Xavier's doctors had discovered a mass growing on his kidney. And so in 2002, he started dialysis three times a week. At the time, he was living in Baton Rouge. His dialysis center was across the Mississippi in Port Allen. It wasn't a convenient commute, and the dialysis itself took a lot out of him as it does with most kidney patients.

Shortly thereafter, he started treating at the Veterans Administration hospital on Perdido Street in New Orleans. From the VA, his care was transferred to Tulane University Medical Center. The doctors at Tulane performed a biopsy on the mass on his kidney. Only then was it discovered that in addition to cancer, Xavier had hemolytic uremic syndrome (HUS). His physicians told him that the need for a kidney transplant had just become more urgent, so his care was transferred to Ochsner Medical Center in New Orleans.

There are two types of HUS. The most common is Typical-HUS or STEC-HUS. This represents 90 percent to 95 percent of all HUS cases and is caused by E. coli bacteria. E. coli bacteria is often found in healthy humans and animals. Some strains of E. coli are responsible for food-borne infections. This is the type most commonly found in cases of children stricken with HUS.

There is also atypical HUS or aHUS, which accounts for 5 to 10 percent of HUS cases. Adults who develop this form of hemolytic uremic syndrome may have the disease as a result of certain medications such as quinine or possibly chemotherapy. Adult HUS has also been known to be genetic in certain cases. But in many cases of adult HUS, the cause is simply unknown.

HUS results from the premature destruction of the body's red blood cells. The damaged red blood cells clog the kidneys and prevent normal kidney function. Symptoms include abdominal pain, vomiting, bloody diarrhea, fatigue, and blood in the urine. HUS can lead to stroke, high blood pressure, end-stage renal failure, and death.

In January 2008, Xavier received his first call for a possible transplant. He and Pam made hurried arrangements to get to New Orleans and to stay there for a while during Xavier's recovery. Fortunately, their church community provided a very accommodating support system. The Majors hurried to New Orleans, checked in to Ochsner, and began the pre-op testing.

Their hopes were dashed, however, when blood tests revealed that Xavier's potassium levels were too high to proceed with the transplant. They returned to Baton Rouge, and the wait continued. Then in March, he received another call.

the selfless truth

$\times\!\!\!\times$

I've seen my fair share of selfless people in my life. However, many people's selfless acts go unnoticed. They simply live their lives to help others; they put themselves second to everyone else.

Chris Gregory was one such individual especially when it came to what he did for me. At the end of the summer of 2003, I started freshman year at Mount Saint Joseph High knowing no one except Chris. Coming from a middle school where it had taken me three years to establish myself, I was more than a little intimidated by the idea of starting all over at a new school in a foreign atmosphere. I was naively convinced that to establish myself right out of the gate, I needed to try out for the freshman football team. I thought, What better way to make friends than to make friends with guys who would someday be the big men on campus?

Before tryouts began, I found out that Chris, the only guy I knew, was trying out as well. Just having him there during those few hot days gave me more confidence than I could have imag-

ined. Chris had played organized football in middle school and was a classmate of some of the other guys trying out.

I had no experience, and I knew only Chris. Making the team would be a stretch. When the final cuts were posted, Chris had made the team and I hadn't. I was crushed. What Chris did next caused me to appreciate him more and more as our friendship developed. As I weighed my uncertain future, I thought about track and maybe running cross-country. That would help me get in shape.

"That's all right," he told me. "Let's go out for cross-country instead."

Giving up his spot on the football team was the most selfless act I had ever received from a friend. He had given up his spot on the football team for the sake of showing support to a guy he had just gotten to know! I was not able to truly comprehend Chris's gesture until my sophomore year when I began to thrive as a runner.

While I moved up to the varsity squad, Chris continued to grind out some tough miles on a sore knee he had injured in middle school. He never made it past junior varsity. He might have had just as much trouble with the knee had he played football, but I doubt it. Football is a game geared more toward strength and heart. I know Chris would have made a great football player and a solid teammate. Sacrificing that to make certain I wasn't alone trying out for another sport was selflessness in its truest form.

Chris flew under the radar throughout most of our high school years, but his selflessness continued. Whether giving back to his community through Scouts or participating in summer service retreats in Washington, DC, he was always there when needed. The most beautiful thing about Chris during those years was the complete absence of accolades he ever got for his gener-

osity. He never wanted recognition for what he did. He just did it. His big and generous heart I have found to be a rarity these days. Chris's selfless acts have inspired me to live my own life less selfishly. I never got to thank him for all he did until now. Thanks, Chris. Love you, buddy.

Kevin Abdo

thursday, march 27, 2008

(PART I)

TULANE UNIVERSITY MEDICAL CENTER

There comes a day in everyone's life when all the money and power and prestige in the world has no value. For some, that day comes on the last day of their lives. If you're fortunate, that day comes early and without pain. But that day comes. Pity the soul who lives an entire life in pursuit of wealth and honors only to realize it will all be left behind. It has no value. For us, that day was Thursday, March 27, 2008.

That Thursday will always be marked as the day Chris officially died. He might have been gone before we ever got there. But that's the date on his death certificate. So how do you tell people about the day your son died?

Well, we got up early on Thursday and made our way to the hospital. Chris was just where we had left him. He hadn't moved, and despite my best hopes, he wasn't going to either.

But Grace still spoke to Chris as any mother would speak to her son.

"Hey, bud." Her voice was cheerful despite his condition. Chris looked calm and peaceful. It was tough to wrap our minds around the fact that his life as we had experienced it with him was over. Maybe his calm appearance allowed us more time to try to accept his death. I kept waiting for him to open his eyes, yawn, and maybe ask for breakfast.

Brant was on duty. He greeted us warmly. ESPN was on TV. He and Chris had been keeping up with the sports world.

"Look at your boy," he said. "He's doing that all by himself." What Brant meant was that Chris was maintaining his own body temperature, blood pressure, and heart rate. He needed no outside medications to remain stable, just the basic medications to keep his organs perfused. Brant had a determined look. He had worked through the night to reduce the medications Chris was on. He knew his patient had a mission now. He would help Chris claim a victory from his ultimate defeat. Of course, there was no brain activity; Chris couldn't breathe for himself. But the effects of the vasopressors were gone. He was by any other measure a perfectly healthy human being. It's just that his brain didn't work anymore. It was that simple. A damn blood vessel in his brain had ruptured, and the increasing pressure caused him to lose all brain stem function. He could no longer breathe on his own. But his organs could be perfect match for someone.

Brant had long abandoned his earlier suspicions. Somehow during those several nights, he had connected with the young man in his care. They watched ESPN. The NCAA Men's Basketball Tournament was on that week. Brant wondered whom Chris might have been pulling for, and he offered his own opinion. Chris was not unlike Brant at that age. Had he been able to speak, Brant figured they probably would have hit it off.

Chris had made an impression on him during those few short nights. He seemed to remind Brant of many of his own friends growing up.

The big Cajun was flooded with memories during the nights Chris was in his care. So much so that he had difficulty sleeping when he got off work. After the apnea test, Brant thought about his high school football coach. His coach's daughter had been struck by a car. Coach had stayed by her side during her apnea test. Brant thought about her a lot that night.

"Look at that heart beat," Brant said pointing toward the EKG. "Whoever gets his heart is gonna feel like a million dollars soon." Except it came out as "dollas" with a strong hint of a Cajun accent.

Since there was no need for gowns or gloves, we were permitted as much intimacy as we wished. Grace stroked Chris's head and held his hand. I was so proud of her. She never lost her composure except for the day before when Dr. Posey had broken the news, "This is death." Grace's poise and demeanor during Chris's stay in the hospital were the most dignified I ever had the privilege to witness. I say that not because she is my wife or the mother of our children but because she really continued to live as an example of what a decent human being can be. No anger. No bitterness. Just a quiet dignity and compassion for everyone around her.

OCHSNER MEDICAL CENTER

The day had started early for Nic and Michelle. At 5:00 a.m., the staff at Ochsner planned an angiogram to determine the condition of Nic's renal arteries in hopes of finding a viable access for continued dialysis. An angiogram is an imaging test of the body's blood vessels. By inserting a needle and catheter through his femoral artery, Dr. Britt Tonnessen, the vascular surgeon, would be able to inject an iodine dye into Nic's bloodstream and take X-rays to determine where their next attempt at establishing an access point would be. The test was expected to take several hours, so they left their home in Slidell at ten after four that morning and hoped there would be no delays on the drive to New Orleans.

Nic recalled his conversation with Dr. Tonnessen when they discussed the angiogram. "Let's find someplace, any blood vessel that will work." That was the goal. Find a vein still strong enough to support a port that would allow Nic to continue dialysis until a donor match could be found.

At 8:00 a.m., Dr. Tonnessen walked into the recovery room. Nic was eating a snack. He noticed tears in her eyes, and she wouldn't look directly at him. *This can't be good*, he thought.

"I'm sorry," she said. "I'm very sorry. There's nothing I can do for you. Your veins are like eggshells."

She explained that despite their efforts, they simply couldn't get access to a vein. The diabetes had calcified Nic's arteries to a dangerous degree. Without access, the dialysis technician couldn't connect Nic to the machine. Nic's prognosis had just become grim. Michelle burst into uncontrollable crying and was led from the room by a nurse. Nic and the doctor discussed his fate.

"How much time do I have?" asked Nic. He heard his hysterical wife in the hall.

"I don't know," Dr. Tonnessen replied. "Maybe six weeks. Maybe six months. No longer than that. You need to get your affairs in order." She paused, took a deep breath, and said, "No one deserved it more than you."

Britt Tonnessen was beyond disappointed. As Nic's attending physician, she was his last chance. She was young in her practice, having received an MD from the prestigious Mayo Clinic Medical School only a few years earlier. This wasn't supposed to happen. Not saving the life of her patient was proving difficult to accept. Especially in Nic's case. Years later, Dr. Tonnessen would tell me that Nic was always positive and upbeat. Always a pleasure to be around. And even in that terrible moment, Nic actually consoled her.

Nic began to question what his grandmother told him when he was near death months before: "You can do anything for five seconds." And Nic had often been forced to live his life five seconds at a time. Endure pain and nausea five seconds at a time. Be uncertain and in doubt five seconds at a time. Feel fear and loneliness, discomfort and agony, blindness and neuropathy five seconds at a time.

All the while, he watched his wife endure the dread of the impending heartbreak with stoic resolve. And now? Now he began his own mental checklist. All the little details he had to get right and into Michelle's hands—bank accounts, insurance policies, passwords, PIN numbers. He started through his own mental inventory as if he were preparing to leave his house in the care of a house sitter. Except there would be no coming home for Nic.

TULANE UNIVERSITY MEDICAL CENTER

John and I ate breakfast with Brant in the hospital cafeteria. I wanted to thank him for all he'd done for us and for the way he treated Chris. What a great guy. Brant told us he was getting married in a couple of months. He was excited at what the future held for him. But he was also a little nervous.

"No more late-night poker games," he said.

"Have a family," I told him. "You won't ever regret raising children. There's nothing better than having a houseful of kids running around."

As Brant and I chatted, John pushed his food around his plate. Brant, on the other hand, was consuming his breakfast like a man who had just worked all night. He poured Tabasco sauce on his eggs and explained he was from a small town not far from Avery Island, where the McIlhenney Company manufactures the red condiment that's ubiquitous throughout the state.

I took a liking to the guy. He made us feel very comfortable with the care Chris was getting. His respect for Chris was more than apparent. He showed it to Grace and our whole family. But he was always respectful with Chris even when it was obvious the boy wasn't going to leave with us. Nobody ever treated Chris like a commodity. Though he was kept on the ventilator for the purpose of donating his organs, neither he nor we were ever treated with anything but the utmost respect. It was obvious that Brant came from a good, loving family who had done a great job of instilling in him the same values we wanted our sons to have.

After breakfast, Brant stood to say good-bye. I knew it might be the last time we'd see him. Before he left, he wrote down his cell number.

"Mr. Gregory, I'm sorry about your boy," he said. "Here's my phone number. If you want someone to talk to, feel free to give me a call."

At ten minutes before ten that morning, my cell phone rang.

"Hey sir, whaddya know?" It was my old boss, Ken Rittman.

"Nothing new, man. I wish I had something good to share."

I had made a couple of observations about myself during that week in New Orleans. I found that I could be an emotional train wreck one minute and half an hour later be completely lucid and carry on a professional business conversation. I had taken my work cell phone along since I had left in a hurry and certainly didn't expect to find what we had upon our arrival. So I was getting calls from family and work all the time. I might be sobbing on one phone, and the other phone would ring, and my mind would clear, and everything would seem perfectly normal.

I also found that it was entirely possible to cry until there were physically no more tears to shed. There may be a physiological explanation for that. I don't know. But it happened. There were times when I didn't need to cry, and there were times when I couldn't. And for what it's worth, 100 percent cotton handkerchiefs are much more absorbent that any poly blend. And they dry in your pocket. I'm just saying.

Ken was only three weeks into a new assignment. He had just relocated to Houston and was still learning who was who in his new post. Someone had called him from up north. Someone we both worked with. That person had known little. Just that Chris was in the hospital and it wasn't good. Ken had needed to hear no more. He cleared his schedule and called his boss. "I'm going to New Orleans," he told her. His friend was in trouble.

"Well, I'm on Interstate 10, and I think I'm supposed to take the Canal Street exit. Do you know what parking's like at that hospital?"

I couldn't believe what I was hearing. My friend—he used to be my boss—had left his house at four that morning and had driven six hours from Houston to New Orleans. If ever there was a voice I welcomed, it was Ken's.

"Can't say. We took a cab from the airport, and our hotel is right across the street."

"Okay. Well, I should be there in about thirty minutes," he said and hung up.

Of all the people I expected to see in that hospital, I'm not sure Ken Rittman and Gerry Nolan would have been the first two. But they were. I always tell people that God didn't make me go through that ordeal alone. He sent angels to hold me up. One was Gerry Nolan. The other was Ken Rittman.

I saw Ken as soon as he stepped off the elevator. He is not a tall man or a thin man. And you see his smile before you see the man behind it. He's a Mormon. If he'd ever decided to sell used cars, the only thing he'd need would be a bright-plaid sports coat. We had worked together for several years before UPS reassigned Ken from Philadelphia to Houston. The fact that he had made such a drive speaks volumes about the man. He's a wonderful human being, and I'm fortunate that he's my friend. I was crying before he got to the waiting room.

"My heart is broken," I blurted out as I buried my face in his shoulder.

Ken threw his arms around me and held me. "I know, bud. I know."

Ken's just one of those guys who as soon as he shows up changes the whole mood in any room. Whatever's wrong suddenly isn't so wrong any longer.

"I can't believe you made the trip," I said wiping my tears.

Ken kept an arm around me as we walked toward the waiting room. He was at first struck by how big and cold the place was. Later, though, as he got to know the people who made up

Christopher's family and friends and were filling that space, the hospital wouldn't be as big or as cold.

"No, Mr. Gregory, there's no way I could be this close and let you be down here by yourself," he replied in his Texas drawl.

God wasn't going to make me go through this alone. He'd sent me angels.

Amy was the nurse on duty that day. Dr. Posey had declared Christopher's time of death to be 9:30 a.m. There was a discussion about an additional neurological exam to confirm the results of the apnea test. Dr. Posey seemed protective of us. He insisted that it wasn't necessary. When he came in on Thursday, he had completed a thorough secondary neurological examination. He had already declared my boy dead. But the additional exam was necessary in order for Chris's organs to be donated. It was like checks and double checks. It was necessary that a second physician come to the same conclusion to satisfy the legal requirements of the Uniform Declaration of Death Act. It was a necessary verification to assure LOPA, the Louisiana Organ Procurement Agency, and us that Chris was really brain dead. And so, later that morning, a different neurologist assisted by a resident and Amy performed a more comprehensive neurological exam.

When they checked his pupils' reaction to light. Grace said, "That's the last time I'll ever see those beautiful green eyes." I looked at his feet as the neurologist squirted water in his ear, and for just a second I thought maybe I'd seen his toe flinch. It was only my mind playing tricks on me. They poked, they prodded, and they poked some more. The doctors completed their examination, and the neurologist looked at us.

"My examination is complete. And it confirms the diagnosis of brain death. I am very sorry," he said.

I walked out to the waiting room. Gerry Nolan, Fr. Ted, Fr. Jim, Ken Rittman, Matt, Jenn, Colin, and John were there. They looked at me as I walked down the hall. My dejected posture must have said it all. I just shook my head no. I couldn't speak. No one else did either.

The air conditioning in the hospital was working overtime, and it left us cold at times. Grace wanted to go outside. We walked onto the terrace, just the two of us. We sat there on a bench holding hands and said nothing. It was warm and humid. Hot almost. We stared at the puffy white clouds and the blue sky. We let the sun warm us and let our minds go blank. It was just too much to deal with. Too goddamn much. We just couldn't think, and we needed a break. So we sat there, tilted our heads back, closed our eyes, and let the sun shine on our faces.

bedtime with brian and mary

✕✕✕

It was a typical Friday night in Laurel, Maryland. As usual, the Abdo house was full of kids. Kids from the neighborhood, kids from church, and kids from school. Meghan and Kathleen had their own friends, and the boys were hanging together. Food and sodas were being consumed, and every TV in the house was on. The boys would be watching sports if they watched at all, and the girls would be watching ... Well, most likely they'd be talking with the TV providing ambiance.

Brian and Mary Abdo had worked all week and were exhausted. They had headed to their bedroom as the clock approached midnight. They finally found some peace and quiet from the riot downstairs. They had turned on the TV in their room and settled comfortably into bed when they heard a knock at the bedroom door. It was Chris.

"What's wrong?" Mary asked. She couldn't understand why Chris would need to come in unless there was a problem downstairs.

"Nothing," Chris answered. He said nothing more. Instead, he took three steps toward Brian and Mary's bed, leaped into the

air, and landed right in between the startled adults. Immediately upon landing, he tucked one arm under Mary and the other under Brian.

"So, what are we watching, kids?" he asked in a dead-serious tone.

A mortified Mary said, "Christopher, get out of my bed."

"Oh I've seen this before!" Chris announced. "This is a great movie."

"Christopher, get out!" But Mary was trapped under her blankets and the hulking man-child who had just joined them.

Brian was laughing hysterically. "No, you don't have to leave."

The novelty of the scene was beyond amusing. The audacity of the act was at once shocking and funny beyond belief. Like a great gag line in a stand-up comedy routine that prompts the stunned audience to ask, "Did he just say that?" There was a twinkle in Christopher's eye as he looked at Brian and started to rub his head.

"How's it going, man?" he asked.

Mary started laughing uncontrollably too. "Christopher," Mary shouted, "get out of my bed!"

But there he stayed, all six foot four and nearly two hundred pounds. It was his senior year, and he had spent much of it in the weight room. As he lay there on top of the covers, he had pinned the Abdos under their blankets. There was no escape for them, and so there they lay. The three of them. Watching television. Chris engulfing Mrs. Abdo with one arm and gently massaging the head of Mr. Abdo with the other as if it were just normal Friday night behavior. And there they stayed until another knock was heard at the door.

"Come in," said Chris in a loud voice. And there stood Little Brian frozen temporarily in disbelief staring at the bizarre scene.

But in an instant it all made sense. Only Chris could have pulled off such a stunt and gotten away with it.

"Well, obviously there's no room for me," he said. He closed the door and left.

thursday, march 27, 2008

(PART II)

METAIRIE, LOUISIANA

There's a standard protocol for hospitals to comply with when identifying potential organ donors across the country. Since 1998, every hospital in the United States has an agreement with its state or local organ procurement organization (OPO) and tissue bank. Some states such as Arizona and Louisiana have only one OPO. Others including California have several. The standard is set up by the federal government, and it's necessary for hospitals to remain in good standing with the joint commission. Ask anyone who's ever worked in a hospital what it means to be recertified by the joint commission. It's a big deal.

Prior to 1998, hospitals were encouraged to notify their local OPO if there was a potential donor, say, a young person killed in a motor vehicle accident. Now, it's required. OPOs now have hospital liaisons who spend a lot of time educating hospital staffers and administrators on the requirements and mechanics of notification.

If a patient reaches a vegetative state or worse, the OPO must be notified. The primary criteria for determining this neurologic state is the Glasgow Coma Score, which assigns a value to a patient's response to about twelve different stimuli: pain, light, etc. The test measures motor response, verbal response, and eye opening. Patients who are alert and can obey commands receive the highest score of fifteen. If they're completely nonresponsive to all stimuli, they get the lowest score, a three.

In Louisiana, any time a patient scores five or less, the LOPA gets a call. Chris had scored a three. When LOPA got a call from Tulane, people there notified a family advocate and a recovery coordinator. Under national protocols, LOPA had two hours to respond to Tulane's notification about Chris. The recovery coordinator who got the call was Joe Guillory.

Joe called Tulane and spoke to Amy, who gave him the same report she had given Brant on Chris's first night in the hospital. She added the details about the failed apnea test and the more comprehensive neurologic examinations that confirmed Christopher's condition. Amy also offered what they knew about Christopher's toxicology screen, liver numbers, and blood work. By the time they hung up, Joe knew that Christopher was an excellent organ donor candidate. He called the LOPA call center, which dispatched Margot.

OCHSNER MEDICAL CENTER

If Nic had thought Michelle looked bad when she had left the recovery room, she looked a hundred times worse when she returned. She took his hand and sat down by his bed. They said nothing. For the next two and a half hours, they sat in silence contemplating an uncertain future.

Nic was on borrowed time. He was numb, in shock. Nic looked at Michelle and thanked God he wouldn't have to see that look on her face much longer. The sorrow, the desperation, the grief. How many years had she stood by him as he retched his guts out? How many trips to emergency rooms in the middle of the night? How much pain and uncertainty had she had to bear? *She hasn't signed on for this*, Nic thought. *And soon, it'll all be over.* And yet he prayed for more time. *Maybe there'll be a miracle. I can do this for five more seconds.* But at that moment, Nic needed to be alone for a little while.

JONESBORO, LOUISIANA

Shortly after 2:00 p.m., Mac Jackson arrived at work. He wasn't really going to work. There was a cookout to commemorate 30,000 Safe Work Days at the plant. There would be burgers, hotdogs, and grilled chicken. It would be a chance to catch up with the guys he hadn't seen much of since he'd been so sick.

As it turned out, Mac was late. Real late. Like they were cleaning up and the day shift was back at work; that's how late. However, Mac was one of the guys, and the bosses asked him to return later that afternoon. "Come back at six and celebrate with the swing shift" he was told. So Mac left the plant and returned home.

TULANE UNIVERSITY MEDICAL CENTER

Margot answered her cell and took down the information from the LOPA call center. The potential donor was a nineteen-year-old college student. He appeared to have suffered a fatal brain aneurysm. Margot postponed whatever she had planned for the afternoon and headed downtown to Tulane Medical Center. Like all professionals in the organ donor and transplant community, Margot understood deep in her own DNA that the task immediately ahead was more important than anything she had hoped to accomplish that day.

When she arrived at Tulane, she met with the medical staff in the SICU—Dr. Posey, Dr. Alvernia, and Amy. "Tell me about the patient," she asked. The medical team confirmed that Christopher had sustained brain death. "How's the family?" she asked. She learned we were doing as well as could be expected. It was clear to them that we had accepted the fact that Christopher's condition was irreversible, fatal.

It was important for Margot to determine that Chris was in fact brain dead and that we, his family, had accepted that. In many cases, families aren't willing to accept that their loved one isn't coming home. If a family is telling the medical staff they want the patient moved to another facility, that's a good indication they shouldn't be approached about organ donation. That's not a negative reflection on the family or the hospital. Families who have just learned of the death of a loved one, especially an unexpected death and especially the death of a child, are confused, shocked. They're trying to deal with an absolute overload of information and emotion. Trust me. I know.

It's for this reason that registered organ donors should tell others of their wishes to be organ donors. It's not enough just to sign the donor card or check the box when getting a driver's license. Once people register as organ donors, they're identified in the state where they registered, but they may not be identified as donors in another state. Chris was identified as an organ donor on his Maryland driver's license, but that didn't necessarily identify him as an organ donor in Louisiana. So Margot was uncertain about his status when she approached us.

We were ushered into another conference room and introduced to Margot. She was polite, respectful, and to the point. Would we consider donating Christopher's organs? We didn't hesitate. "Yes," we said at once. We'd been asked that the day before. We knew then that we'd donate his organs. Grace reminded me of the discussion she'd had with Chris only a week earlier in Arizona. It was after dinner, and the conversation had turned to organ donation. Grace asked Chris if he'd registered as an organ donor when he got his driver's license.

"Of course," he'd said. "I'm an organ donor. What good would they do me when I'm dead?" he asked her. And then as only Chris could, he said, "I mean, come on, who wouldn't want this body?"

Margot was going to walk us through the steps of authorizing our son's organs to be donated to people we might never hear from. But it a strange way, it seemed to offer some measure of hope. Of what we weren't certain. But hope. Maybe.

"I can tell you one thing," I said to Margot. "The biggest thing you'll find inside that boy is his heart."

LOYOLA UNIVERSITY NEW ORLEANS

If the mood on Loyola's campus wasn't discernable to the average bystander, among those who knew Chris and Colin, it was suspenseful. The situation at the hospital was known.

The apnea test the night before had determined brain death. There was still the neurological examination this morning, and everyone was waiting. People pretty much expected the worst. Nothing could be done but wait.

Kevin Drohan ran into Woody and Dan Z on campus. They started chatting. Had anyone heard anything? It was perhaps the most asked question at Loyola that day. No. Nothing. The three walked on until they ran into Colby Carpenter and Adam Meyerson. Had they heard anything? No.

The five young men stood staring at one another, the ground, and the buildings. Chris was dead. How could that have happened? They had just seen him a couple of days ago. They'd heard his laugh. They'd shared jokes. They'd enjoyed his company. And now. It was too much. One of them began to sniffle and broke into sobbing. Before long, the five of them were in tears. There were no words exchanged. They just stood there and cried for a while. Finally, Colby spoke up.

"Let's go to the chapel."

The chapel was empty except for a woman who was cleaning and arranging chairs. The sight of students visiting the chapel during the day wasn't unusual. Loyola was after all a Catholic university. But five at once? That was not something she saw every day. Especially not five young men. Still, she gave the group their space and worked as quietly as possible. To the boys, her presence was just that. A presence. They were aware of her without knowing who she was beyond the fact she obviously worked there. She could just as easily have been a butterfly that somehow managed to find itself lost in the same space.

Each of the boys was lost in his thoughts and prayers at first. The tears started rolling again. They offered up no specific, collective petitions. They didn't recite any age-old prayers or say the rosary. They just sat and wept. The Jesuits would call it contemplative prayer. Just being aware of God and of God's presence and wanting to share in that presence. And perhaps by getting close to God, somehow trusting that God would know what was in their hearts, there would be no need for words.

No sound beyond the sniffles and sobs. Until quietly the door opened and then closed. Jon Villien entered and sat in the row of chairs behind them. They all sat there quietly in the chapel. Each alone with his thoughts.

TULANE UNIVERSITY MEDICAL CENTER

Colin had to be interviewed by Margot as part of the life-style screening necessary to protect possible recipients from harmful lifestyle behaviors that Chris may have engaged in. There was none. He smoked cigarettes and drank beer, but that was about the extent of it. I stressed to Colin the need to be as candid with Margot as possible. We excused ourselves to make sure.

We returned to the waiting area where the crowd on duty included Kurt Bindewald and Fr. Wildes. We told everyone about the process of screening Chris for a possible donation. They had mentioned the possibility of a directed donation. A directed donation occurs when a donor family identifies the recipient and directs the donation of their loved one's organs to that individual. I asked Kurt and Fr. Wildes if anyone at Loyola knew of a family member waiting for a transplant. They could ask the vice president of student affairs, but they knew of no urgent need immediately. I turned to Fr. Wildes.

"Is it even the right thing to do?" I asked.

"The holy father has said that organ donation is among the highest expressions of love and generosity possible," he replied.

I guessed that was the kind of answer one should expect from a priest.

He put his arm around my shoulder. "Listen. Nobody deserves to go through what you're going through. You shouldn't even have to make such a decision."

It was a difficult moment. In hindsight, that small gesture provided tremendous support. It was an affirmation that we were doing the right thing. That Chris was doing the right thing.

The past couple of days had left us feeling as if we'd somehow wandered into a pitch-dark room. We couldn't see, so we didn't know where to turn or where to go. We couldn't find an escape from the darkness. But after being asked to consider donating Christopher's organs, there seemed to appear a pinhole of light. Not very big, but a light nonetheless. It was different from the rest of the space. If we looked away, all was darkness, but when we looked back, the light was still there. It offered something we could not fully understand at that moment. It offered hope.

JACKSONVILLE

Dr. Keller was in his office thinking about the conversation he'd had with the Bacardis the previous day. *If only the Mayo Clinic had a hospitality house on campus.* As it was, patients had limited options before and after their transplants, and those included two hotels. For most patients, they might be acceptable, but the lungs are the only human organs in direct contact with the environment. Hotel rooms carried too many germs and bacteria left over from prior guests. As much as the cleaning staff might try, they'd never live up to the standards required by the recipient of a lung transplant.

The doctor hoped his patient would take his advice and wait out his transplant in Jacksonville. It seemed to him that Jorge had finally realized the urgency of his situation. It's not uncommon for people listed for transplant to fall into a state not quite of denial but not a complete understanding of the immediacy of their situations either.

Jorge's appointment the day before was a routine outpatient visit. Those visits are scheduled with greater frequency as patients' conditions decline. Jorge's condition had declined to the point that the need for a transplant was urgent. It was his only option. Keller feared that if Jorge got any sicker, he might not be in any condition to make the trip from Nassau to Jacksonville. It seemed that Jorge may have just had an epiphany. He may have finally realized how sick he was.

Keller's cell phone rang. It was the transplant coordinator at the other end. A set of lungs had become available, and patient Bacardi was number two on the list. Keller scribbled notes furiously.

LOYOLA UNIVERSITY NEW ORLEANS

The six fraternity brothers quietly got up and left the chapel. They walked the few steps down the hall to the Office of Mission & Ministry. They entered and asked if they could speak with Kurt Bindewald. They had decided to conduct a memorial service for Chris. None of them had ever arranged such an event. Would Kurt be willing to offer some suggestions?

Their idea was not only appropriate but laudable in Kurt's mind. Yes, they could use the chapel, and yes, whatever they required was theirs for the asking. The Beggars had an outlet for their emotions. Their confusion began to fade as they began expressing ideas for the sendoff they planned for their friend and brother. There would be music. Fr. Jim could help with that. And there were more than a couple of music majors among them. Dan Z could sing. Nick Payne would play the keyboards. There would also be reflections by Chris's friends. A way for everyone to remember him and celebrate his life, not just dwell on his death.

Yeah, they thought. *Let's do this.* They were no longer confused and scared college boys caught up in circumstances beyond their control. They were fraternity brothers, and they had a job to do for themselves and Chris and his friends and family. Most important, they had an outlet for their grief. A means to turn it into something less destructive. Hope was rising again.

NASSAU, BAHAMAS

At 4:00 p.m., the phone rang at the Bacardi residence in Nassau. It was Dr. Keller.

"I am placing you on standby," he said. "There's a set of lungs that is a match and that has become available. But there's one person ahead of you on the list." Leslie's heart skipped a beat. She whispered a quick prayer of thanks and hoped it would be her husband's opportunity for a new lease on life. But there was one person in front of Jorge.

Dr. Keller explained that there could be any number of reasons the patient in front of Jorge might not actually get the lungs. There might be concerns about the donor lungs, the recipient ahead of Jorge might be too far away, or maybe they couldn't locate him or her. Jorge thought of the conversation he and Keller had had a day earlier about relocating to Jackson-ville.

"But if it's you, we may not have a lot of time," Keller explained. "That surgery may have already started by the time we get the call." Both men understood by then that sometimes, the donor site had to move on. Patients much sicker and in more-desperate circumstances could be waiting.

"You have to prepare to be away from home for three months," Dr. Keller said. They had known that for some time. It was just a fact of life when you're on the waiting list for a transplant. Leslie knew she could get someone to help her get whatever she needed to Jacksonville. But she had to be certain that the bills and salaries of their employees would be paid, that the house would be cared for, and that they were prepared to live away from home for an undetermined length of time.

First, they had to get back to Jacksonville. She called Hop-A-Jet in Ft. Lauderdale. Barbara Ann Weeks was the director of customer relations. She had come to Hop-A-Jet from the medical ambulance industry, and her experience in this kind of mission would be valuable. Yes, they could have an aircraft and crew available. Yes, they could come to Nassau on a moment's notice. Yes, they would make arrangements to be on their way.

In fact, the relationship between the Bacardi family and Hop-A-Jet went back some time. All of Jorge's family had used the charter service at one time or another. Jorge's sister, Carmen, was famous for making rum cakes for the crew when-ever she flew. Joaquin, Alberto, and their children were familiar faces to the pilots. The Bacardi children, like their parents, were always absolute ladies and gentlemen. The staff held the Bac-ardi family in high regard. Knowing what this mission was all about was on the minds of the entire organization. They had committed to always having a jet ready when the call came for Jorge's transplant. And it was time.

SHREVEPORT

Carolyn Harrell was waiting in front of Willis-Knighton Medical Center in Shreveport. She had just been discharged and was waiting in the warm sun for her husband, Horace, to get the car. The sixty-four-year-old grandmother and retired office manager suffered from liver disease. Oddly enough, she'd never drunk alcohol. She was thirty-nine months into her wait for a liver transplant. She was startled when she heard her name called from the front door of the hospital. Even more so when she recognized the woman calling to her was Dr. McMillan's nurse. The first thought that entered her mind was that she had forgotten something. The urgency in the nurse's voices said something else.

"Miss Harrell! Dr. McMillan wants you to come back upstairs right away!"

It was soon apparent that she hadn't left her purse in the doctor's office.

NEW ORLEANS

Mary Claire Trant drove the two hours from Grand Coteau shortly after the morning rush hour. Her baby was hurting, she could tell. And she was close enough that the drive was a small inconvenience compared to the trauma Ellie was feeling. They went to brunch at La Madeleine on the corner of Saint Charles and Carrollton Avenues. Ellie just wasn't able to go to class. She and Chris had formed a genuine friendship in the few short months they'd known one another. After a leisurely brunch, mother and daughter took a long walk around Audubon Park. It was a glorious spring day, a little humid but warm and sunny.

They walked arm in arm. Ellie and her mother had always been close. She was Mary Claire's youngest child and her only daughter. The anger from the previous night was gone. In its place was a deep sorrow. Chris had always told Ellie that she reminded him of his mom. Their affection for their mothers was important to them, a cornerstone of their friendship. Ellie and Mary Claire talked little, and when they did, it was mostly small talk. Most of the time, Ellie just sobbed.

The two crossed Saint Charles Avenue as a green streetcar rumbled past. It was the middle of the day, so only a few passengers were aboard. As they headed across campus, Ellie saw Fr. Ted as he prepared to head back to the hospital.

"I guess you heard about Chris," Fr. Ted said.

"Yes," she replied. She could feel the emotion well up inside.

"There's a Mass scheduled for tomorrow night. Will you be there?"

"Of course."

"How would you feel about speaking?" Fr. Ted asked. "I know you and Chris are good friends."

"Yes," Ellie replied. "Thank you. Thank you for asking me."

TULANE MEDICAL CENTER

Before he returned to Houston, Ken Rittman needed to stop in the Walgreen's on the corner of Tulane and Loyola Avenues. Grace and I walked with him. The corner was a bustle of rush-hour activity. The sidewalk was crowded, and cars honked impatiently as they drove up Tulane Avenue toward Interstate 10. The world continued to turn it seemed. I must have had a dejected look on my face. Ken knows me pretty well.

"Cheer up, bud," he said.

"I don't know, man. I just don't know," I replied. "It's just ..."

"It's just what?"

"It's just that there was so much I look back on. There are so many things I wish I'd done differently. I feel like there were so many times when I was angry or I lost my patience with him. I let him down. He looked up to me, and I let him down. And now I can never make it right."

Ken looked at me. On came the tears again. Right in the middle of a busy New Orleans rush hour. Except for when my father had died a decade earlier, I'd never cried in my adult life. Ever. And I couldn't seem to stop then. I didn't seem to care.

"Let me ask you something," said Ken. "Was there ever a time in your life that you ever said something to any of your sons that wasn't from the love in your heart?"

Remorse, embarrassment, and shame fell like a ton of bricks on my heart when I thought of at least once when I'd let my frustration get the better of me.

"Let me ask you this," he continued. "Was there ever a moment in your life when you didn't love your children completely? And unconditionally?"

"No," I replied. "I just wish I'd have shown it more often. I should have been more a part of his life. I just feel like I look back and see so many times when I was so selfish with my own time. I should have spent more time with Chris. I should have been more patient. I wish I'd never lost my temper."

"Nobody's perfect," Ken replied. And he smiled. "Nobody's perfect, and there's no doubt in my mind that you love your boy. And he's in heaven right now, and trust me, he knows it

179

too. And he knows that you did the best you could when he was here. He knows it. There ain't a doubt in my mind."

"I hope you're right," I said.

"It's gonna be okay. One day, you're gonna have that final interview with the man upstairs, and he'll look over the life you provided for Chris and the love you showed him, and he's gonna be okay with it. So don't start beatin' yourself up."

I just cried and nodded.

Ken smiled again and gave me a big embrace. He hugged Grace, who was wiping away tears. Such poise. Such courage she showed. What can you say about a friend willing to drop everything at a moment's notice and drive six hours just to be there? As he walked off to the parking garage, Ken turned and paused for just a second.

"By the way," he hollered above the din of the traffic. "If those Catholics upstairs ain't getting' you what you need, just gimme a call. I'll have a busful of Mormons here in half an hour!"

My friend waved good-bye and started for the garage. I never doubted that he wasn't joking. Angels. God sent me angels.

Grace returned to Christopher's room. She was struck by the scene. An image as tender and bittersweet as any mother could witness. Colin was seated in a chair next to Christopher, his head resting on his brother's bed. He was sound asleep. Grace knew just how he felt. The process of donating a loved one's organs is not quick, easy, or painless. Once Chris had been given the prognosis that his condition was not "compatible" with life, there were many steps that had to be completed. None could be avoided or skipped. The process became something that had to be endured. During the ordeal that lasted a little more than three days, sleep had been snatched in short naps, so everyone was exhausted. Yes, Grace knew exactly how Colin felt. She too wanted to stay as close to her boy for as long as she could. And at that moment, she had to fight the urge to crawl into bed next to Chris.

Despite the fact that he looked like a strapping, powerful man, he was her baby. And she wanted to comfort her baby. Grace stayed with Chris constantly, rarely leaving his side. Every possible moment during those short few days, she talked to Chris, held his hand, studied his features, and tried to commit all the little details of Chris to memory. She counted his freckles and studied every eyelash. She memorized every contour of his handsome face. She visualized its shape when he was smiling or when he was in deep thought. He could be pensive at times, and when he was, there was a seriousness to his features that gave the appearance of concern and revealed a maturity in the boy that far exceeded his years. It was as if he knew something the rest of the world didn't.

She studied his lips and remembered the countless kisses they had delivered and how they had shaped his smile. His was a most genuine face. She could recall specific moments when his mouth formed smiles that were sincere, or carefree, or mischievous. Her boy and his most beautiful face. She was determined to memorize its every feature. To sear it into her consciousness. In her own way, she was saying good-bye. And the whole time, she continued to pray for a miracle.

Grace had always wanted to be a mother. She was very close to her own mom and had always admired and respected my mother and grandmother. She looked up to them as role models and always tried to emulate the very best they had to offer. Patience, caring, and a sense of humor. As soon as she found out she was expecting, Grace dove headfirst into motherhood. She read every book on parenting she could, and she tried her best to get me to read them. And God, how I wish I had.

When she was pregnant with each of our boys, she was absolutely beautiful. I mean she glowed. She just carried herself in a way that let everyone know she already loved her children and would be a great mom. She made a huge emotional investment in preparation for motherhood. When each of our sons was born, she was prepared physically and emotionally for the job.

She took to the role of motherhood with great joy. She carried the boys and fed them and clothed them and washed them as if those tasks were always pleasures rather than chores. She laughed with them, praised them, and cried with them. Their joys and disappointments were hers as well. Grace lived for her sons. She was never too tired to read to them, cook for them, or stay up at night when they were sick. Countless mornings found an extra little boy in our bed between us. She taught me the most important lesson of my life: the best things in life aren't things.

And so she had to gaze on her children as one lay dying and two had to watch it happen. Their hearts were breaking before her eyes. God knows I've never done anything in my life worth bragging about, but goddam it, Grace didn't deserve this! It just wasn't fair. How do you square that? How could this ever be made right? She'd done everything she was supposed to do and then some to raise her family and make sure her boys turned out all right. She had every reason to look forward to growing old and watching Chris grow up and have a family of his own. And then she could spoil his children someday. But someday would never come. Not now.

She knew it was only a matter of hours before she'd have to say good-bye to Chris for the last time. She could feel the seconds ticking away. Like a prisoner on death row, she anxiously wished for time to stand still. And while she waited, she tried to absorb as much of Chris as she could while he was still in the world with her.

A thousand memories flashed through her mind almost at the same time. She remembered the distinctive, sweet smell of a little baby's wet hair as she wrapped him up in a towel after a bath. She felt his smooth skin while she clipped his little fingernails. She heard him giggling as she changed his diaper. She saw the look of concentration on his face while she read him a bedtime story, his thumb in his mouth and his forefinger wrapped over his nose. She saw the brightness in his eyes when he was excited to see her pick him up from school. She heard the sincerity in his voice as he told her about his day. She heard the innocence in a question he'd ask her. She saw him in his baseball uniform sitting with his friends on a warm summer day. She even heard him complain about his brothers.

She saw him on the altar at Saint Nick's trying to stay awake during 8:00 a.m. Mass. She saw him first in his Cub Scout uniform, and then in his Boy Scout uniform, and then standing tall as an Eagle Scout. She saw the confidence in his gait as he confidently walked to the car and the smile on his face as he waved out the window driving away. She heard him practicing his guitar.

A million memories came rushing back all at once and yet one at a time. And if she just closed her eyes, she could still feel his breath on her neck while she rocked her baby to sleep.

"We have a match."

Joe Gillory was the recovery coordinator sent by LOPA to the SICU suite. He is a registered nurse, a father of two, and one of the most decent human beings I've met. Ever since Dr. Posey informed us of Christopher's condition, the opportunity to save someone else became our own lifeline. If we could just get one piece of good news, maybe something could be salvaged from the wreckage that the ordeal had become. We had held our breath throughout the apnea test, the neurological exam, all the blood work, and the personal history evaluations. If we could just initiate a successful transplant, at least he wouldn't be dying for nothing. At least something could come of this. If we could just get a match.

So LOPA sent Joe Guillory to Tulane to work with the doctors and nurses to keep Chris's body in good enough shape to transplant his organs. Somewhere, somebody needed his organs, and Joe would be the key player in making that happen. Chris's race on earth wasn't done just yet. Joe would get him over the finish line.

Recovery coordinators work side by side with bedside nurses at the donor hospital. Amy and Brant had their own documentation they were required to maintain, and Joe did the same for LOPA. Amy, a bedside nurse, couldn't perform certain LOPA protocols; only Joe could. However, some tasks she could perform for Joe such as drawing blood for LOPA using LOPA's tubes. Or Joe would monitor Chris's vital signs, blood pressure, heart rate, etc. using Tulane's equipment. LOPA cannot take over total care of the patient. A Tulane employee still had to oversee all the Tulane rules for patient care.

But Amy and Joe would work together throughout that afternoon and into the evening to make certain Chris would remain a suitable donor until the United Network for Organ Sharing (UNOS) could identify appropriate recipients. If Joe missed an infection, the result for one of Chris's recipients could be catastrophic.

"We have a match for a liver in Shreveport." Joe tapped his pen on his paperwork like a drumstick. He was sitting on a stool outside Chris's room. A counter served as his desk.

"Louisiana?" I asked.

"Yes. A woman in Shreveport is a match for Christopher's liver."

On national television one day, a panel was discussing the recent liver transplant of Apple founder Steve Jobs. One of the panelists remarked, "Steve Jobs should have the right to negotiate for those organs." Thankfully, that isn't the case in the United States. That one poorly expressed, ill-timed comment on national TV did little for the cause of organ donation. Strict federal guidelines exist for the equitable distribution of organs. Since 1986, the Organ Procurement and Transplant Network (OPTN) has provided the framework for this process. The OPTN is managed by UNOS, a nonprofit organization under contract with the federal government. There are fifty-eight organ procurement organizations (OPOs) in the United States. The Louisiana Organ Procurement Agency (LOPA) takes care of that state. These agencies perform extraordinary work and are staffed by individuals with remarkable dedication and compassion. Joe Guillory is one of them.

Joe's job was to monitor Christopher's condition and to communicate with the LOPA placement coordinators in Metairie, outside New Orleans. The fifty-eight OPOs are linked by a sophisticated computer network. Information on patients in need of transplants is communicated from the recipient hospitals to UNOS. It involves a scoring process that's handled by a committee of medical professionals who evaluate the condition of each person on the transplant list. The sicker you are, the higher you are placed on the transplant list in your region. When Chris's organs became available, the recipient coordinator accessed the UNOS database to find the most suitable match and contacted that patient's treating physician.

Because organs to be transplanted can't be more harmful to the recipient than their present organs, donors are monitored very closely. Besides that, the size of the donor organs becomes an issue. Chris was six four and weighed nearly two hundred pounds. You can't take a Cadillac V-8 engine and drop it in a Volkswagen Beetle. And after flying an organ three hundred miles is not the time to find out it isn't a good match. So coordinators such as Joe Guillory go to the hospital where deceased donors are, monitor their vital signs, tests, etc., and communicate with the LOPA placement coordinator. Hearts, livers, and lungs are matched by blood type and body size. For kidneys and pancreas transplants, tissue typing aids in identifying the best genetic match.

Once the donor information is received, potential recipients are identified in that region. Most people don't have the means to travel immediately across the country, and organs cannot practically be transported long distances and remain viable.

Potential recipients are identified through a separate scoring system that includes medical urgency, tissue match, location of the patient, and how long they've been waiting for a transplant. The OPO placement coordinator will then contact the transplant center of the potential recipient identified as the person on the top of the waiting list for that organ in that region. Transplant surgeons can accept an organ, accept it conditionally, or decline it. If their patients aren't available or if the donor's age or social history is problematic, they may have to decline the organ. Christopher's liver would be transplanted into a then-anonymous woman in Shreveport.

JONESBORO, LOUISIANA

At 5:30 p.m. in Jonesboro, Louisiana, Mac Jackson dressed again for the cookout at work. The telephone rang.

"Mr. Jackson?" she asked.

"Yes ma'am."

"Mr. Jackson, this is the Ochsner Transplant Center in New Orleans. We have a match for you, Mr. Jackson. How far are you from New Orleans right now?" The woman's voice at the other end was crisp and efficient.

"I'm about six hours away by car, ma'am," Mac replied. Mac suddenly remembered what he'd said the last time he'd gotten the call. *Mac, you better watch what you say*, he told himself. Mac said he'd leave right away.

"We'll be expecting you."

MIAMI

Sonia Bacardi was in her daughter's bedroom helping her pack for their trip to Nassau. The telephone rang. She recognized the voice immediately.

"Que pasa, querida?"

"Hola, Tio! Donde estas?"

"There's a set of lungs that has become available, so we're preparing to go to Jacksonville." Jorge sounded nervous. "There's one person ahead of us on the list, so if that person isn't within range, I'm up. Dr. Keller has put me on standby. We've already called the Hop-A-Jet people. They can have us there in little more than an hour."

"Oh my, Tio! Buena suerte. We'll be praying for you."

"Gracias, amor. Un abrazo para su familia. Hasta pronto, si?"

"We love you, Tio."

Sonia turned to Joaquin, who was standing in the doorway of Carolina's room. They were excited and nervous. Unsure of what to do next, they knew that packing was no longer necessary. It looked that they wouldn't be going fishing with Jorge and Leslie.

NEW ORLEANS

We decided there was little to be gained by sitting around the waiting room. Besides, everyone was hungry. Fr. Ted could tell everyone had had it. The looks on their faces said it all. The tremendous weight of Christopher's death was sinking in. The future didn't look bright. For now, there were all the tests being done in search of organ recipients. Then the transplantation process. And then they all had to endure a funeral. As bad as things were at present, they were just getting started.

"Let's go," Fr. Ted spoke up. "Dinner's on me."

There was a restaurant in the Holiday Inn where Grace and I were staying. It was only a year and a half since Katrina, and much of the city was still in ruins. As we walked the two blocks to the Holiday Inn, we passed abandoned office buildings that reeked of mold and decay.

Dinner was a great idea. Not that anybody ate much. But the change of scenery was enough to break the tension that held everyone in an emotional vise grip. As the waitress took drink orders, John produced his thickest possible Baltimore accent and asked for a National Bohemian beer.

"Hey, hon," he started, "Y'all got any o' dat Natty Boh?"

The table erupted in laughter. Maybe we were punch-drunk or just exhausted. Matt fell into hysterics laughing uncontrollably. Sometimes, when you're enduring extreme stress and in a deep emotional hole, the smallest things suddenly become much funnier. The evening was a welcome relief.

NASSAU, BAHAMAS

At 6:00 p.m., the telephone rang again. Leslie's heart stopped.

"I'm sorry." It was Dr. Keller. "It appears the other recipient is a good match. He's in easy travel distance, and they're accepting the transplant. I'm so sorry to have put you through all of this."

"No, no," Jorge responded. "This was okay. This was a good exercise." At least Jorge had gained a better understanding of the process and some measure of control over what was happening. The false alarm was not all that bad a thing, he felt.

Leslie's heart, once pounding with the nervous energy of victory, sank. Having been so close, they now seemed a million miles away. She hung up and allowed Jorge and Dr. Keller to continue their conversation.

There are many more people on the waiting list for transplants in the United States than there are organs available. So the OPOs will contact several potential recipients to avoid losing the opportunity to transplant precious organs.

Leslie called Hop-A-Jet and told them the bad news. The pilots would be genuinely disappointed. Not because they needed the business but because the Bacardis were longtime and well-liked clients. Everyone at the jet company knew what this particular mission was all about, and they were anxious to pull this one off with bells on. The pilots would be told to stand down. She called Sonia in Miami again.

"Hi Sonia. It's Leslie." Her voice was calm and soothing. It masked the disappointing news she had to deliver. "Well, it was a false alarm."

"I'm sorry," replied Sonia.

"No. It was a good drill," said Leslie. "It was a good exercise. There are so many things we thought we had taken care of but we hadn't. So it was a good exercise."

Sonia and Joaquin were equally disappointed. The initial call had them excited about a second chance for Jorge even though it was only a standby call. They felt the disappointment along with Leslie, but they also felt certain that when the phone rang a second time, their tia would be telling them they were headed to the airport.

The trip to Nassau was back on. Sonia and Joaquin had dinner, loaded up their remaining clothes, and headed to the marina.

TULANE MEDICAL CENTER

Amy had completely embraced the community that had formed around Chris. Anybody can go to work and collect a paycheck. But her profession requires more. It requires compassion and caring especially in such a sensitive situation as the death of a young man. Chris was not just a patient with a medical record in room 3. He was a boy with a family and friends.

He was a real person. The fact that he couldn't communicate made it so much harder for Amy.

She had met John, Colin, Jenn, and many of Chris's friends. We had shared stories about Chris. Amy learned about his Eagle Scout project, and the sports he played, and that he'd been an altar boy. We showed her pictures from his Eagle Court of Honor. In the midst of our tears, we told her all about our vacation the previous week in Arizona. Amy was a presence and a witness to the slow-motion good-bye that was happening in the SICU. We were holding our own private memorial in that room while we waited for Joe to find a match.

Jenn bent over Chris to give him a kiss on his cheek and suddenly recoiled. "Whoa!" she exclaimed. "What's that smell?"

"Oh honey, that's just from the ventilator," Amy explained. The room filled with chuckles because everyone knew Chris would have been aghast to be found anything but pleasing in appearance or scent.

"Oh my God," Jenn said. "You smell bad."

Amy thought back to when she had just been accepted to nursing school. Her grandfather was an old-school, black-bag carrying, house-call making family doctor. He had long since retired, but Amy wanted him to be the first to know. She expected him to offer some advice about studying, or anatomy, or maybe even something philosophical. Her grandfather told her, "Amy, treat every one of your patients as you would want your family treated and you'll do just fine."

Amy had been stunned herself the first morning she met Chris. It was easy for her to identify with our family beyond the Loyola connection. A year earlier, Amy had reported for work only to find that her patient that day was the older brother of a boy who went to high school with her son. The boy survived albeit with many disabilities. That case had hit particularly close to home. Apparently, Chris was hitting close to home too. So she was doing what her grandfather had taught her nearly twenty years earlier. She was taking care of us as if we were her family.

SLIDELL, LOUISIANA

It was nearing 7:00 p.m. in Slidell. Nic was in a chair in his living room feeling sorry for himself, feeling angry, feeling dejected. It had been a long, silent, forty-five-minute ride home from Ochsner. Michelle was on the back porch talking to her sister, Stephanie.

"Michelle, you have to get ready to say good-bye to him," Stephanie said. Michelle could offer little in response. Her world was in free fall. Tears flowed. She had pretty much spent the afternoon calling all their friends and relatives from Louisiana to California. She told them that if they wanted to see Nic alive, they'd better start making arrangements to come. Soon.

Nic was still in a state of shock. Physically, he was numb. Like the feeling professional athletes experience when with seconds left in a championship game the opposition scores to end the game with a walk-off. Stunned, numb, and unable to process just what has happened beyond the blunt realization that the worst possible outcome had come to pass. Nic was not in pain or discomfort oddly enough, but his ego had gotten the better of him, and he was getting angry.

On the dining room table was an array of insurance policies, bank statements, bills, and so on. Nic wanted to be certain that everything was available to Michelle. Account numbers, passwords, and PINs. He worried that she'd be burdened with having to figure out how to keep their household afloat by herself. Theirs had been a happy marriage despite his illness. Michelle's life would not necessarily be made any easier in Nic's absence. If anything, he feared it would become more complicated. Nic felt the frustration build inside him.

Shut the hell up! he told himself. *Don't waste the next three months. No, ego, shut up. Shut the hell up.*

His cell phone rang. The voice at the other end was terse and direct.

"Can I please speak to Nic Whitacre?"

"Yeah, this is him."

"This is the Ochsner Transplant Center. We have a match for you."

JONESBORO, LOUISIANA

Carl Jackson was quite surprised to see his brother's Chrysler 300 pull up in his driveway. It was after 7:00 p.m. The sun had set. "What you doing, Stat?" Carl asked his brother as he walked into the house.

"I need you to go to New Orleans with me," Mac replied.

The two men entered Carl's living room.

"What's going on?"

"The hospital called. They found another heart for me. So I told them I could be there about eleven. And they said c'mon."

"Let me get some things and we'll get going," Carl replied.

Twenty minutes later, the two pulled out of Carl's driveway and headed south toward New Orleans.

TULANE MEDICAL CENTER

Joe Guillory was writing notes. He tapped his pen on the paper and paused. He looked into Chris's room. Amy was checking the IV and attaching a bag of some fluid. The wheels were in motion. Nothing was within our control any longer. We were just along for the ride.

As Christopher's parents, we were left trying to hold up his friends and brothers. The best we could do was to put on brave faces. My son was dying or dead in a hospital bed, and all I could do was watch. We could hold his hands, stroke his face, speak softly to him. But little else. His fate was in the hands of a logistical apparatus I didn't understand.

Amy adjusted Christopher's pillow and tucked in the sheet that covered him. He couldn't feel it. He couldn't know Amy was mothering him. But she did it anyway. The neurological tests all confirmed he had no sensation. He could feel neither comfort nor discomfort. And yet his nurse was making an effort to make him comfortable.

"How we doin', Joe?" I asked.

"Pretty good, Mr. Gregory," he replied. Joe looked at his notes, looked into Christopher's room, and looked into my eyes. "Mr. Gregory?"

"Yeah, Joe?"

"Mr. Gregory, there's gonna be planes flying all over the country tonight because of your boy."

BATON ROUGE

Mac's Chrysler pulled off the interstate at the first Baton Rouge exit. He was nervous. He asked Carl if he would pull off the highway so he could visit a few friends. Spur of the moment. It was half past eight when they pulled up in front of Bill Jackson's house. Bill was surprised but pleased to see the two men.

"Whaddya say, stranger?" asked Bill Jackson. No relation to Mac. The two had been fraternity brothers at Southern University. Phi Beta Sigma. That would be the same Phi Beta Sigma that is the home of Jerry Rice and Emmitt Smith.

"Not too much, not too much," replied Mac. "How you been?"

The two old friends engaged in little more than small talk. Mac decided against telling his friend the purpose of his trip to New Orleans. After a twenty-minute visit, Mac and Carl departed.

OCHSNER MEDICAL CENTER

Nic's head was spinning as Michelle pulled up to the ER at Ochsner Medical Center on Jefferson Highway. After his failed attempt at an angiogram that morning, Nic's status had been elevated to 1A. Top of the list. Nic and Michelle were nervous. *What if it's a false alarm? What it doesn't work? What if …?*

But they couldn't dwell on the negatives. If ever there was a time to have a positive mental attitude, this was it. Still, physically, Nic felt horrible.

BATON ROUGE

Mac and Carl's next stop was to an old sorority sister, Verna. "How's Oliver?" Mac asked.

"He's doing fine, Mac. How's your family?"

"Kids are growing like weeds."

It was nothing more than small talk.

"I was in the neighborhood visiting Bill Jackson. It just wouldn't have been right not to stop by and say hello," said Mac.

"Well, give everyone my love, hear?"

"Okay, darlin'. We best get going."

Mac knew exactly what he was doing. He was stalling for time. He thought he might never see these folks again.

Carl Jackson describes himself as a man who walks next to the Lord. Not in an arrogant way but as a humble servant of God who tried to live his life in a way that would meet with God's approval. As the two drove to New Orleans, Carl said, "Stat, I gotta tell you something."

"What's that?"

"Three days ago, I had a vision that you don't need a new heart. All you got is asthma, man. You don't need a new heart. You just need to get tested for asthma."

"Carl, I already been to see three doctors, and they all said I needed a new heart."

"Listen, man, I'm not kidding. I had a vision, and I'm serious about this. Something bad may happen if you go through with this." Carl was nearly scolding his older brother.

Mac listened to his brother intently. He knew the science. The doctors had all told him he needed a heart transplant. He'd nearly died several times waiting and during the testing. But he also knew Carl was a man of deep faith who had committed himself to his church and God. Carl wouldn't have said such a thing if he hadn't truly believed it. Doubts began to stir in Mac's mind as the car hurtled down the freeway.

LOYOLA UNIVERSITY NEW ORLEANS

The Manresa Den was a large room in Bobet Hall on Loyola's campus. It was a space where the campus community could come to grieve, share, and reminisce. Students and staff had been encouraged to write some words on and sign a blanket bearing the Loyola New Orleans logo. Chris's classmates and friends could write their reflections in a journal. As was happening in Maryland at that moment, photographs were being glued to poster boards and Chris's friends were writing good-bye messages. The Manresa Den in Louisiana and the Abdo residence in Maryland were places that night where grief could find a constructive outlet.

Ellie knew she had to think of something to say at Mass the next day, but she hadn't a clue just what that would be. Words weren't coming easily. She paged through the journal and read the sentiments others had left there. Amazing, genuine, true friend, your too short life. The words and phrases were repeated throughout the journal.

Halfway through one of them, Ellie could take no more. She buried her face in her hands and sobbed. She cried for Jenn, who'd been so happy to be with Chris. She cried for Colin knowing how close siblings could be having been blessed with three older brothers herself. She cried for Grace having not even met her but loving that Chris said Ellie reminded him of his mother. She cried for herself. But mostly she cried for Chris. It wasn't fair that he should have to die so soon. He should have had so many more years. He had so much to offer the world and had asked for so little in return. She felt sorry for him and for his family, and at the same time, she felt angry. Ellie's heart ached.

Having cried her eyes out for two hours, Ellie knew what she wanted to say at Chris's Mass the next night. She composed a letter to Chris. Friend to friend.

The approximately 125 transplant centers in the United States don't have a uniform process for notifying transplant patients. In all cases, a transplant coordinator such as Joe Guillory from LOPA responds to the hospital where the potential donor is being treated. The vital statistics and medical information is put into the national or regional database, and a potential recipient is identified. An e-mail is sent to the organ procurement coordinator (OPC) of at the potential recipient's hospital.

The OPC notifies the medical or surgical team. At the Mayo Clinic, the call goes to the medical team, which knows its patients better because its members see them regularly. The transplant surgeon may meet a patient only once and not see him or her again until the day of their transplant. The typical call to the team included the age of the donor, the cause of death, bronchoscopy description, and any other relevant medical information including possibly chest X-rays sent by iPhone. Ultimately, the physician responsible for the care of the transplant recipient must ask, "Is this donor suitable for my patient?"

If the medical team is satisfied, someone on it calls the head of the surgical team and discusses the specifics of the donor. If the surgical team concurs, a call is placed to the recipient.

Since the OPO determines the time that the donor will be taken to the operating room, all potential recipients are told what time they must be at their transplant centers. If the recipient cannot make it in time—perhaps they've removed themselves from consideration to go fishing with a nephew—the

OPO at the donor hospital is notified and the physician responsible for the next recipient on the list is contacted.

JACKSONVILLE

Dr. Keller couldn't believe his ears. For more than twenty years, he'd been a member of the lung transplant community and had seen the practice evolve from near science fiction in the 1980s to the advances he himself had been a part of in the present. He'd gone from studying the possibilities of lung transplantation, when saving one life in ten was considered significant, to his present position as the head of lung transplantation at one of the most prestigious hospitals in the world. But nothing in his professional career had prepared him for the phone call he'd just received.

Patient Bacardi had become number one. A set of lungs was available. The second set of lungs in the same day. They looked good. Real good. Blood type, blood gasses, age. A nineteen-year-old male. Everything was good. Keller scribbled notes. He'd have to try to get hold of Jorge. If only his patient was in Jacksonville. Keller had one final question. *Where was the donor?*

New Orleans.

NEW ORLEANS

Friar Tuck's Bar was a seedy college bar on Freret Street not above serving an underage college kid or two. It was the kind of place you can find near most college campuses. The place that no college career is complete without visiting. A visit to Friar Tuck's marked the quintessential rite of passage at Loyola.

By 10:30 p.m., the backroom had been taken over by the crowd from Loyola. Everyone who knew Chris or Colin was there. The room was packed. The noise was deafening. Someone had purchased a keg of beer and was dispensing its contents freely. The only liquid flowing more freely were tears.

John and Colin showed up. It was the first time many of them had met John. Everyone was struck by how much Chris looked like his oldest brother.

"You look so much like Chris," Jenn and Ellie told him.

"Hey, look!" John replied. "I'm the oldest, okay? I was here first. *He* looks like *me*, got it?"

The bar was packed even for a Thursday night. All the Beggars were there. They had to post up for Colin and for Chris. As were the Delta Gammas. Jenn was a DG, as was Ellie. Those gathered did their best to comfort one another. Someone like Chris, young and physically strong, was never expected to die so suddenly and from such a freak occurrence. Such tragedies have such a different impact on young people. Their methods of coping are different from what they will be later in life. So on that night, Tuck's was packed with Christopher's friends who were grieving the only way they knew how.

Off to the side, Matt, Nick, and Kevin Drohan were discussing what they knew would happen later that night at the hospital.

"So they're gonna take him to the operating room to recover his organs at about four thirty," Matt said. "But they said we could come back and say good-bye."

The three looked at one another. The fear and horror were gone. They were in a new place. At last they could do something. Even if that something was nothing more than just showing up.

Because in some circles, in some places, there's great power in just showing up. You don't have to fix anything, you don't even have to say anything. But you have to show up. Sometimes just showing up means a lot.

"Who's going?" Kevin Drohan asked.

"My dad. Jenn's gonna go. John and Colin are gonna go," Matt said. "I just don't know if we have enough room to fit everybody in a car."

"You go," Kevin Drohan told Nick. "You haven't been to see him yet, and I've been there already. You go in my spot."

"No. Bullshit," Matt said. "We're all going. We'll figure it out."

NASSAU, BAHAMAS

Jorge was in his office at home reading e-mails and pondering the day when the phone rang. The false alarm had been a good drill. A good exercise Leslie kept calling it. *So many things we thought we had prepared for still need to be tightened up,* he thought. By education and training, Jorge had perfected the art of attention to detail. Yes, it was a good exercise. He looked at the clock. Eleven forty-five. Call it a premonition, call it confidence, or call it one of those inexplicable things that happen sometimes, but Jorge knew with a certainty who was calling him. Dr. Keller.

"You're not going to believe this," Dr. Keller said. "I'm having a difficult time believing it myself."

"What it is it?" Jorge heard footsteps running down the hall toward him. Leslie entered the office out of breath.

"Another set of lungs has become available. We have a donor with perfect lungs. They're yours if you still want them."

friday, march 28, 2008

(PART I)

MIAMI

Sonia Bacardi woke with a start. It was one in the morning and the phone was ringing. The past few hours had been difficult, and it seemed she'd just fallen asleep. She was on an emotional roller-coaster. First, the anticipation of the fishing trip with Jorge and Leslie. Then the excitement of the first transplant call. Then the disappointment of the false alarm.

After dinner, Sonia and Joaquin had taken the remaining clothes and supplies to their boat. Their captain, John, would take it to the Bahamas later that morning. Sonia would take their children to school while Joaquin went to work at the office. They would all take a flight to Nassau later that afternoon and meet up with their tio and tia for a week of fishing, swimming, snorkeling, and sharing the love and fellowship of family.

Since their travels by boat would take them far beyond the range necessary to get to Mayo in time, Jorge would have to notify Dr. Keller and temporarily remove himself from the transplant list. He was still wrestling with the moral consid- erations of even accepting a transplant. Spending time with family trumped everything.

"Hi, Sonia." It was Leslie. Her familiar voice again soothing and calm, nearly matter of fact. "We're at the airport in Nassau. We're heading to Jacksonville in a few minutes. Another set of lungs appeared."

"What? You said what?" Sonia was astonished. Her husband had bolted awake and was sitting upright, his eyes and mouth wide open. "How can another set of lungs appear so quickly?"

Leslie told her niece about the late-night call from Dr. Keller. The Bacardis were standing in a nearly empty airport terminal. They'd soon board a plane for Florida. The two said goodnight and hung up.

"Who was that?" asked Joaquin. "Who was that?"

"Your aunt," Sonia replied. "They're on their way to Jack- sonville. Another set of lungs has appeared."

Sonia and Joaquin stared at each other in disbelief. Another set of lungs. They were in shock. Their excitement, however, was restrained. No jumping for joy. No laughter. No shouts. Just quiet disbelief coupled with nervous excitement. Miraculously, another set of lungs had appeared.

NASSAU, BAHAMAS

As she returned her cell phone to her purse, Leslie noticed that Jorge's breathing was labored and difficult. She'd called Hop-A-Jet shortly after receiving the miraculous call from Dr. Keller about the second set of lungs. She got the company president, Barry Ellis, on the phone. Barry told her the plane would depart Florida just as soon as the crew was contacted.

Fortunately, the pilots, Brooks Coleman and Christopher Steele, lived near the Fort Lauderdale airport. They were surprised but excited when Barbara Ann Weeks called them at midnight. They hurried back to the Fort Lauderdale International Airport where the jet was still mission-ready. Thirty minutes after Leslie called, the two had the Lear 55 airborne and headed east over the Atlantic.

Leslie was told that it would take the plane less than two hours to get to Nassau. The pilots ended up making the flight in forty-five minutes. Coleman and Steele knew the Bacardis as well as any pilots who'd flown them. They were excited the mission was on again.

As the plane headed over the dark Atlantic, Barbara Ann made more calls to the Bahamas to alert the handler at Odyssey Aviation who would contact the Bahamian customs authorities and arrange the helicopter to shuttle the Bacardis from the airport in Jacksonville to the hospital.

Customs and immigration still had to be cleared, but the nearly vacant state of the Lyndon Pindling International Airport worked to their advantage. However, getting Jorge to the airport proved to be slightly more complicated. After getting assurances from Hop-A-Jet that a plane was en route, Leslie called Jorge's brother Alberto to advise him of their leaving. "Good luck," was all he'd said. "We'll see you in Jacksonville."

She knew a taxi was out of the question at that hour in Nassau. Leslie called their friends, Nick and Pam Klonaris. Shortly before 1:00 a.m., their friends arrived to take them to the airport ten minutes away.

The customs and immigration staff worked feverishly to complete the necessary documentation for their departure. Just before dialing Sonia's number, Leslie looked out the window and saw the Hop-A-Jet pilots dashing across the tarmac. The race to save Jorge's life was on.

SOMEWHERE OVER THE ATLANTIC

Jorge and Leslie held hands but said nothing the entire flight. They had that nervous feeling we all get when life's great events are at hand. Call it stage fright, butterflies, or whatever. That was the sensation both felt as the Lear 55 descended in the darkness and touched down at the Jacksonville airport at 2:45 a.m.

As they taxied to the terminal, they realized that someone had called ahead to prepare the airport for their arrival. Uniformed officers from US Customs and Border Protection ran to the plane once the wheels were chocked but before the engines were stopped. Coleman, the copilot, kicked open the door and unfolded the stairway for the CBP officer, who clambered aboard.

"Good morning, folks. How're we doin'?" the excited officer asked.

"So far so good," replied Leslie. "We're here for his lung transplant at St. Luke's."

St. Luke's Hospital had recently been acquired by the Mayo Clinic.

"Yes ma'am, so we were told."

The pilot, Captain Christopher Steele, had contacted the tower at JAX and notified the personnel there to prepare CBP for their arrival. This had been deemed a medical emergency. The CBP officers were on top of their game.

As the customs officer reviewed the Bacardis' passports and stamped their entry into the United States, his younger uniformed partner climbed into the cabin, grabbed a suitcase in each hand, and hustled down the steps of the aircraft. Both men were happy to be involved in a break from the normal routine of admitting tourists and business travelers returning from tropical vacations and business trips. This inspection was like the high-priority task it was. No time to waste. As the officer completed his paperwork, an eerie light illuminated the tarmac.

Exiting the plane, Jorge and Leslie heard a high-pitched whine of an engine coupled with a rapid *whop-whop-whop* of rotor blades as a helicopter settled onto the concrete nearby. As they carefully descended the stairs, Leslie saw the helicopter door open and the pilot exit before the rotors stopped. The helicopter pilot ran over to the Hop-A-Jet pilots, held a brief conversation with them, grabbed some luggage, and started running for his chopper. The scene at the airport was nothing short of poetry in motion. A ballet. The most experienced logisticians would marvel at the intricate machinery at work in perfect sync that night.

Joe Guillory was right. Planes were indeed flying all over the country. This was just one scene in a single act of a very detailed and intricate drama. But in this performance, the audience couldn't be disappointed. In this play, if the actors and stagehands didn't perform flawlessly, the critics didn't write scathing reviews. People died. So the pilots, ground crew, and customs officers all pitched in, grabbed bags, and took them to the helicopter.

The helicopter pilot introduced himself as they met on the apron. He guided them to their seats, assisted in buckling them in, provided them with headsets, and took his place at the controls again. It wasn't far to Saint Luke's. During the brief flight, the Bacardis learned that their pilot had many years of experience in lifesaving flights such as this. He'd started his flying career rescuing wounded GIs from the battlefields of Vietnam.

The helicopter landed. The helipad was eerily empty. Unlike the orchestrated chaos at the airport, no reception committee was there to greet them. No ground crew, no doctors, no nurses, only an empty landing pad. Jorge and Leslie exited the helicopter and slowly made their way up the hill to the hospital entrance.

As Jorge struggled up the hill, he was observed by another group departing Saint Luke's. Dr. John Odell and his team were headed to the Jacksonville Airport where a jet was waiting to take them to New Orleans. There, they'd be taken by ambulance to Tulane University Medical Center. Dr. Odell would lead the team that would recover Christopher's lungs. As he observed Jorge from a distance, Odell noticed how labored and difficult the climb was for him.

Dr. John Odell was South African by birth. Before going to the Mayo Clinic in 1993, he held the prestigious Chris Barnard Chair of Cardiothoracic Surgery at the University of Cape Town. Dr. Barnard, famous for performing the first heart transplant in Cape Town, had retired in 1983. In 1990, Dr. Odell was appointed head of the department Dr. Barnard had built. As a result, Dr. Odell worked with Barnard's team including the same scrub nurse, perfusionist, and anesthesiologist who performed that first heart transplant in 1967.

Odell's team would meet Joe Guillory and the other surgeons in Tulane's OR and begin the complicated task of removing Christopher's organs for transplant around the country. Each transplant center has its own protocols for organ recovery.

Once the organs were accepted, the recipient team can visit the donor and confirm the results that were communicated. In this case, it meant Dr. Odell and a small team from Mayo would inspect Christopher's lungs to be absolutely certain they were suitable for transplant. Once in New Orleans, Odell would look at the X-rays, review the documentation relating to brain death, the blood group (twice), and the serology of any communicable disease. He would review the latest lab results and chest radiographs. Finally, he would bronchoscope Christopher and look into the lungs that he would explant and return with to Jacksonville. The sight of Jorge struggling to the ER gave Odell a vivid and lasting reminder of his purpose this night.

senior year

If ever a young man starts to truly come of age, it's during his senior year of high school. Boys' emotional maturity escalates rapidly between ages seventeen and nineteen. They set aside their childish ways and begin searching out their identities not as the boys they were but as the men they seek to become. Chris was no different. It was then that he reached his full potential and was ready to take on the world.

Despite the close relationship Chris maintained with the Abdo family, he and Kevin had a major falling out during their senior year. It was never anything he discussed with me or Grace. In fact, he didn't even talk about it with Mary and Brian Abdo. But they knew. They saw it more than we did. We were still as affectionate with Kevin whenever we saw him, but we realized we were seeing more of his little brother, Brian. Whenever we asked, Brian always explained that Kevin was off on some service project with XBSS, the national organization of Xaverian Brothers Sponsored Schools. It was a high honor to be asked to join XBSS. Kevin had been asked to join. Chris had not.

Kevin excelled academically and athletically in high school. After Chris gave up his place on the freshman football team, he suffered from a nagging knee injury that and finally gave up running after two years on junior varsity. Kevin went on to earn accolades and honors up and down the East Coast running cross-country, indoor track, and outdoor track. Chris stayed just below the radar throughout his high school career. He was not one of Fitz's Boys, those young men closest to Saint Joe's principal, and the resentment wore on his relationship with Kevin.

Kevin's little brother, Brian, looked up to Chris, and during senior year, the two spent a lot of time together. Having no little brothers of his own, Chris took Little Brian under his wing. If Little Brian was having difficulty with someone, and it did happen, Chris had no problem stepping in and making his presence known. If Chris didn't like someone, that person learned it. And he was a big believer in loyalty. Such was the case with one particular kid. Chris's mere physical presence served as a sufficient deterrent.

At the tender age of sixteen, Little Brian was smitten with a girl who lived on his street. Brian had to suffer the embarrassment of being broken up with. But if that wasn't bad enough, the girl's father had to get into the act and reiterate his disapproval of Little Brian. Injury on top of insult. But Chris refused to let his friend suffer alone, so he made himself available for the emotionally restorative powers of fast food and movies. The two bonded over cheeseburgers and Friday and Saturday nights at the movie theater.

And then in March, while Chris and Little Brian were watching HBO, the phone rang at the Abdo house. It was Big Brian's brother Mark with news that their brother Joel had died. It was a suicide. When Mary and their daughters heard that, they were hysterical. The raw emotion was overpowering, and at age eighteen, Chris found himself in the middle of a family crisis. At first, he stepped back from the scene, but he didn't leave. These people were not just friends; they were like family, and at that moment, they were suffering a terrible trauma. Chris grabbed Mary, wrapped his arms around her, and held her for the longest time while she sobbed uncontrollably. And then he grabbed the girls in his big arms and did the same for them. Rock is the word the Abdos use to describe Chris that terrible night.

Eventually, Chris asked Big Brian if he thought he should leave. Brian told him he didn't have to leave but he didn't have to stay if he didn't feel up to it. Chris stayed with the family until Fr. Mike and Mr. Fitz arrived from Mount Saint Joe. He stayed until after midnight. Eighteen years old but already so emotionally strong.

Kevin eventually returned home. He didn't attend his uncle's funeral. Instead, he elected to be with his classmates at senior retreat. It was there that Kevin and Chris reconciled their differences, offered one another sincere apologies for taking their friendship for granted, and over several cigars experienced the most emotionally powerful moment of their young lives. Kevin didn't realize the significance of his decision to attend senior retreat instead of his uncle's funeral until a year later.

friday, march 28, 2008

(PART II)

><><

OCHSNER MEDICAL CENTER

By the time Carl pulled his brother's Chrysler 300 up to the ER at Ochsner, it was well past midnight. During the drive, Carl had pretty much done his best to share with Mac his concerns about the transplant. He was sincere in his doubts. The vision he'd had three days earlier convinced him that perhaps a transplant wasn't what his brother needed. Perhaps what he really needed was a second opinion. Maybe the doctors were wrong. It wouldn't have been the first misdiagnosis in medical history.

Mac got out of the car. His breathing was labored and difficult. The plan was that he would go upstairs and tell the medical team that he was refusing the transplant. Carl would wait for him in the car.

It seemed to Carl that his brother was full of surprises that night. When he returned to the car, Mac opened the backdoor and retrieved his suitcase.

"Go ahead and park. Come on in," he said to his brother. Mac had made up his mind to proceed with the transplant.

"You sure you're gonna go through with this?"

"Yeah, I'm sure," Mac replied. "One way or the other, something's gotta change. I just can't live like this anymore."

JACKSONVILLE

The Bacardis finally reached the entrance to the ER. The nurse on duty asked if she could help them. When Leslie informed her that they were there for a transplant, the nurse called Dr. Keller at home.

"That's impossible," he exclaimed. "I just spoke to them. They cannot have made the trip so soon. It can't be him."

The nurse handed the phone to Leslie.

"Hello, Dr. Keller. We're here," she said.

Dr. Keller was still incredulous. "How did you get here so quickly?" It had been only three and a half hours since he'd called to tell Jorge to come to Mayo. The flight, which should have taken an hour and a half, had taken less than an hour. An amazing feat. The entire trip had been an exercise in professionalism and execution performed flawlessly by public and private entities working in unison with a sense of purpose. A demonstration of what was possible. Murphy's Law had been suspended for the night.

"You can ask the pilots about that. We told them we were in a hurry, and boy, did they step on the gas," Leslie explained.

Fortunately, both pilots lived near the airport. It was one of many strange coincidences that night. Somehow in an odd twist of fate, when the real call came just before midnight, they were at home in Ft. Lauderdale. Since the flight plan was already filed and the plane was ready, all Steele and Coleman had to do was fire the engines and take off.

She looked at Jorge, who was breathing with great difficulty after the walk from the helicopter. Forms and paperwork awaited them. Among the reams of forms and releases to be signed was one that puts every transplant recipient on edge. It was an acknowledgment that Jorge's lungs were to be removed before Christopher's arrived from New Orleans. It was a common release signed in transplant cases—part of the informed-consent protocols. It's especially important in cases in which the organs must travel great distances. It means that if the plane carrying the donor organ crashes, the recipient dies too.

TULANE MEDICAL CENTER

Joe Guillory told us that the plan was to take Chris to the operating room about 4:00 a.m. That plan got pushed to 4:30 a.m. In the transplant process, the donor center determines the time the donor is taken to the operating room. All the recipients are then advised when they must be in place. It all goes back to the ischemic times, the viability of donor organs, and the incredible challenges to move them great distances. We said we wanted to say good-bye to Chris before he was taken to the OR. Joe told us whenever we got there would be fine. "You're his family," he said. "We'll wait on you."

So we all agreed to return to the hospital between 4:00 and 4:30 Friday morning. In spite of the urgency in addressing the health needs of the donors who were being prepared at other places, the team at Tulane was willing to give the boy's family the chance to say good-bye.

We had no idea what to do or say. Grace and I walked into Christopher's room. Grace took Chris's hand in her own. Words became more difficult. What could she say? A mother's worst nightmare come true. She stared at her boy still desperately trying to commit to memory every detail of his face. Tears filled her eyes. I was speechless. Even had I known what to say, I doubt I could have formed the words.

Gerry Nolan walked in with a large cup of coffee from McDonald's for me. Everyone pretty much arrived at once. John and Colin, Colin's girlfriend, Fiona, Jenn, Matt, Woody, MG, Fr. Ted, Kevin Drohan, and Nick. Matt and Kevin Drohan were on their way to the hospital when they asked if there was anyone they should pick up along the way. Even in the middle of the night, they immediately said, "We gotta bring Nick." Chris and Nick were really close, and the boys knew that Nick wouldn't handle it well if he didn't get an opportunity to say good-bye. So they'd called Nick, detoured to pick him up, and headed to the hospital.

There was a new nurse on duty. I don't recall her name. She shared with us that this was her final shift before she retired. *Well, this is one to go out on,* I thought. She continued to monitor Chris's vital signs. And of course Joe Guillory was there.

I had no idea what we should do or say. Fortunately, Fr. Ted was well qualified to take charge at moments like that. And so chrism and consecrated hosts were produced. I took Joe Guillory off to the side for a quiet moment.

"So what do we have matches for?" I asked.

"All the thoracic and abdominal organs are moving tonight," he said. "Heart, lungs, liver, pancreas, kidneys. Everything."

"Man. That's something, isn't it?" I said.

"You have no idea how big a deal this is. Five people are waiting on your boy. He's saving five people tonight."

"Joe, would you mind stepping inside and telling everyone about that? Please? I think it would mean a lot to everyone if they knew," I said.

We entered Chris's room. Everyone stood around his bed. *This is what defeat looks like*, I thought. It was a roomful of the most desperate, dejected, broken-hearted bunch of people one could ever see. The fear and hope we'd seen on Tuesday had turned to shock on Wednesday. By Thursday, sorrow had begun to set in, but everyone had done his or her best to hold one another up. But it was Friday morning. The look on everyone's face was one of defeat and dejection. Those not actively crying had tears welling up. It was obvious no one had slept. It was an alien environment for everyone except maybe the priest. The rest of us were whipped. Just whipped. *This is defeat. The game's over. We lose. Sorry, Chris.*

"Everyone, I asked Joe here if he would tell you about where we are donating Christopher's organs."

Joe took over. "His liver is going to a woman in Shreveport, the lungs to Florida. The heart, kidneys, and pancreas will stay here in Louisiana. A lot of people will get second chances tonight."

The news didn't seem to matter too much at first. Everyone looked at Chris and then at Joe. John and Colin never took their eyes off their brother. I knew it meant nothing to them. It was hollow news as far as they were concerned. But a couple of the kids, MG in particular, looked at Joe and kind of cocked their heads as if pondering an unanticipated turn of events. Something they still couldn't comprehend but could sense anyway.

MG, the EMT, understood perhaps better than any of Christopher's friends the importance of what would happen over the next several hours. *Stuff is flying out of here tonight*, he thought. He'd known it since he first saw Chris intubated on Tuesday. He knew what the outcome would be; he just couldn't admit to himself or anyone else and be of any assistance to any of us in the hospital. But now it was coming to pass. If none of Chris's other family or friends recognized it, MG certainly did.

Nor did the news that Joe just shared come as a surprise to MG. To know that Chris was an organ donor. He was one of the most giving people he'd ever met. As much as he knew that tragic deaths could shatter families, MG knew that organ transplants touched the lives of people far beyond those who received them. *There might be a silver lining to this week after all*, he thought. Such a giving person, and there we all were to witness his final gift.

Fr. Ted asked everyone to join hands. I expected Joe to say what he had to say and leave the room. Instead, he took Grace by the hand. Fr. Ted led us in the Lord's Prayer and the Hail Mary. He distributed communion to the group, including Joe. I had begun to sense during the hours leading up to this that something remarkable was unfolding. Fr. Ted had felt it too. The Jesuit later said he could feel a sense of grace descending on the people gathered there. Not just us and Chris's friends, but everyone. Even the doctors and the nurses. Something tragic had happened for certain. But from that tragedy, something of great decency was emerging. Out from all the badness, something of great goodness was coming. And whatever it was, it was being recognized.

Maybe that's why Joe stayed in the room. It was touching that he did. Small gestures at a time like that can mean so much. Ted anointed Christopher's forehead with chrism again sealing his commitment to God as a Catholic. He hugged Grace and me and left the room.

Slowly, one by one, those in the room said good-bye to Chris. They embraced Grace and me on their way out. I looked at Matt and couldn't comprehend the emotions he was experiencing. He had known Chris since grade school. They had grown up together. Yes, they had attended different high schools and for a while traveled in different circles, but he was his friend. He knew he would never see him again. Never share a beer, or a cigarette, or a laugh, or a story. They had pledged the same fraternity.

Matt and Chris had driven together from New Orleans to Laurel during the breaks that first semester. They'd often made the seventeen-hour drive straight through. Never again. Whatever plans for life they had made during those long road trips, Matt would have to do without Chris. Chris wouldn't be there to share their remaining college years. He wouldn't be there for the laughter and friendship the next three years would bring. He wouldn't be there to share the joy of graduation. Even though his own father had just left the room, Matt became like our son that night.

Matt, Jenn, MG, Nick, Kevin Drohan, Brant, Amy, certainly Fr. Ted, and Fr. Jim. Any of the people who shared that experience were now family. Jenn had a look of agony on her face. She leaned over Chris, held his face in her hands, and tenderly kissed him on the cheeks and forehead. My heart was broken, but the scene simply shattered it if that was even possible. In her own misery, she was so tender. Tears streamed down her cheeks as she stroked Christopher's face. *She loves him*, I thought. *My God, she really loves him.*

Colin, John, Grace, and I were alone. We remained silent as we looked at Chris. It was our last moment together as a family. And it had to be like this? He just lay there motionless. The only sound was the mechanical rhythm of the ventilator and the beeping of the electrocardiogram. I still recall the image of him in that bed.

As the boys said good-bye, they each mussed their brother's hair. Swirls is what they called it. They would sneak up on each other, mess up the hair of the unsuspecting victim, and proclaim, "Swirls!" Colin took Chris by the hand as though he were shaking it.

"Save a spot for us over on the other side, kid." He hugged Grace and me and walked out into the hallway.

Grace kissed Chris on his cheek. "Goodnight, sweet boy. Mommy loves you very much." She walked out of the room. I was alone in the room with my boy. He was so much like me. His hair had a cowlick in the exact spot where mine once did. He and I were the same height after nineteen years. We loved so many of the same things. We had so much in common. We had a relationship that was different from those I had with his brothers. I can point to those moments when I could tell he was really trying hard to be like his dad. In Christopher's life, there had been moments, jokes, stories, opinions he shared because he wanted to be like his dad. He wanted so much to please me, and at that moment, I couldn't help him. I couldn't protect him. Or stick up for him. I could do nothing for him. Still, I was just not ready to say good-bye.

I leaned over his bed one last time and kissed his forehead. I wanted to hold him in my arms and cradle him. But all the wires and tubes scared me. I didn't want to disconnect anything vital. I was afraid to hold him too close. I wish I could say that I'd told Chris, "It's not your time yet. Please come back." But I didn't. I didn't think to say that. I'm sorry. It just didn't enter my mind. Not on Friday morning, not back on Tuesday when we first arrived.

And I wish I could tell you that when I prayed, I implored God to return Chris to his family and take me instead. But I didn't, and I'm ashamed. I'm sorry, but I didn't think to ask that. In hindsight, after hearing about other people doing so under similar circumstances, I wish I had. But I didn't. "I love you, son," was all I could say over and over. "I love you, Chris." Tears welled up in my eyes again. What I did say was what I'd said to him two days earlier. "Put your hand in God's hand, Chris. Put your hand in God's hand." I prayed that God would open heaven's doors to him. I prayed that God would do for him what I couldn't. Maybe God would hear me and meet Chris halfway.

Grace was waiting for me when I left his room. I looked to the nurse's station across the hall. Three or four women in blue scrubs stood there staring at us and crying because they knew what we'd been doing in Chris's room. Saying good-bye to the handsome young man who had been there since Tuesday. A nurse was standing in the hallway next to Joe Guillory wiping tears from her eyes.

Instead of returning to the waiting room, everyone had collected at the end of the hall just steps from Chris's room. Matt, Nick, Kevin Drohan, and Chris had formed the core of a collection of friends. And at that point, it was just the three of them in the hallway. The boys were crying. Jenn joined them. They wrapped their arms around each other. They were experiencing something not every set of friends had to go through. It was killing them all. My heart was breaking for them.

Something was happening in the SICU that night. Something important and dignified though tragic. Nurses talk. They help with each other's patients. By Friday morning, the whole floor had learned that Chris was a donor case. Everyone on duty in the SICU that night knew what was happening in that room. They knew of Christopher's sacrifice and that he was being accorded the utmost respect. He, his mother, his family, his friends wouldn't leave until it was time to go. They knew what was happening in his room, and they could see what was happening in the hall, and it was having an effect on the whole floor. And so the entire nursing staff had stopped what they were doing. They were standing in the hallway crying.

senior retreat

><><

Every school has a culture that's created largely by all the members who buy into the mission of the place. Ours relied heavily on a senior class that understood who we were and what we were about besides math and English. Ours relied on the gospel story that to many seemed a fairy tale, but to us, it was a tale to live by, a tale to give us strength and courage and hope.

Schools also have ceremonies that celebrate culminating events in the lives of their students, and we had those as well. Graduation, Baccalaureate Mass, assorted Masses and dinners with parents and grandparents, a recognition dinner, and so on. One event, though, stood out from among the rest, and if you were to poll the seniors at graduation, they would tell you that Senior Retreat was the most memorable event of their four years, and most would be able to elaborate why in profound ways.

Chris's senior year was no different in their assessment. What was different was the number who chose to partake. For the first time on this retreat, we had well over half the class there all taking part voluntarily. The program was to talk a little bit about why you chose to come and then plow into a reflective look at the past four years. The retreat built on earlier retreat expe-

riences at the school that examined the three key relationship structures in our lives—self, others, and God.

The program builds up to a service on the last evening called reconciliation. The introduction to this piece involves a major story of forgiveness from the presenter's experience, and then the seniors are invited to sit for a minute and think about what they'd like to say to each other perhaps by way of forgiveness before they go their separate ways. With 160 young men, that could take a long time, so we encouraged them to think about what they wanted to say and then practice "economy of language" as they expressed it.

Chris was a figure in his class who commanded genuine respect in ways that allowed you to feel comfortable about yourself. He kept his friends close, and they meant a great deal to him as did his family. If you knew Chris, you knew his family and you knew his friends.

We were sitting in a candlelit chapel in Buckeystown, Maryland, the last night of his Senior Retreat when after a brief pause in the sharing, Chris stood to speak. Heads turned to him. Some straightened up in their chairs while others leaned forward to hear what he would say. In a style that was pure Chris, he asked everyone in the room to appreciate the sanctity of the moment, a moment "we will never, ever have again," and to tackle whatever it was that might be keeping them from each other. Life is too short, he would intimate, to get stuck in an obstacle. Let's all of us "seize this moment now" so we won't walk back in the halls next week regretting a missed opportunity. And then he spoke directly from his heart to those he needed to address. The rest remained between Chris and them, as it should.

I remember most the look in his eyes that night. It was commanding without putting anyone off. It was sincere and challenging at the same time, and it demanded a response, a response from the heart. I believe he got that.

I pray every day for the young men who have died "in my care," those guys at the two schools where I have served who have died way too young all in different ways, all special to me in some way or another. Chris is one of those I mention each day by name. Lately, he's come into my mind as I reread a poem by Marie Howe about the Annunciation of Mary, the Mother of God. The poet writes:

> Even if I don't see it again—nor ever feel it
> I know it is—and that if once it hailed me
> it ever does—
>
> And so it is myself I want to turn in that direction
> not as toward a place, but it was a tilting
> within myself,
>
> as one turns a mirror to flash the light to where
> it isn't—I was blinded like that—and swam
> in what shone at me
>
> only able to endure it by being no one and so
> specifically myself I thought I'd die
> from being loved like that.

Chris Gregory was so specifically himself that no one ever doubted the depth of his caring. As I see his face in my memory of Senior Retreat, I take some small solace in feeling that God saw that same look as Chris was swimming toward the light that only God can shine on all of us. I can only hope that Chris died from being loved just like that.

—Barry Fitzpatrick

friday, march 28, 2008

(PART III)

TULANE MEDICAL CENTER

The mood among Christopher's friends changed as they began to depart from the hospital. It must have started soon after Chris was wheeled out of his room and to the elevator. The tension had to be broken.

"Well," Kevin Drohan spoke up first. "If Chris owes anyone money, they're shit outta luck now." The laughter and the stories started. It wasn't long before even the irreverent tales were told with some measure of gusto. Even Gerry Nolan couldn't resist getting into the act.

"Look at this fuckin' guy, will you?" he said as we passed a portrait of some very WASPish, patrician physician. "You can just tell he went to Tulane."

Punch-drunk, the group made its way out of the hospital. Like a team that just lost the Big One. Heads held high but earnestly swearing never to return to the premises again. Shaking the proverbial dust from their shoes.

Dr. Odell and the recovery team from Mayo Clinic arrived and introduced themselves to the surgeons assembling in the operating room at Tulane. It would become a very crowded and busy space in the next several hours. In addition to the team from Mayo, another team would arrive from Willis-Knighton Hospital in Shreveport to recover Chris's liver, and separate teams would transport his heart, one kidney, and pancreas to Ochsner Medical Center in New Orleans. A final team would transport Christopher's other kidney to the LOPA office until final crossmatching could identify the next recipient in line.

There's a necessary order to the departure from donor sites—the heart and lungs leave first, and the abdominal organs leave last due to the ischemic time of the various organs—how long they can survive without blood flow even if they're literally on ice and in preservation fluid. The goal for a lung transplant is four hours or less for the best outcome. Four to eight hours is acceptable. Beyond eight hours, the recipient will likely pay a price, possibly an irreversible price.

Six to eight hours is acceptable for a heart, eight to twelve for a liver, and upward of twenty-four hours for a kidney. The team assembling at Tulane would ultimately determine the time the operation on Chris would start, and Jorge, Mac, Carolyn, Nic, and Xavier would be contacted and told how quickly they had to be at their respective transplant centers. The ballet was about to begin.

Odell introduced himself to the OR nurse and the anesthesiologist. It was important for him to remember their names since he'd be communicating with them more than with any others in the room. He looked at the chest X-rays again. He reviewed the lab work and the serology. He inserted a bronchoscope, a thin tube with a camera attached, into Christopher's airway.

OCHSNER MEDICAL CENTER

Nic and Michelle sat quietly in their hospital room. Nic had been hit with a battery of questionnaires and surveys since being admitted hours earlier. Had he had a fever? What had he had to eat? Had he had a cough? How was he feeling at present? They probed and poked. They drew twenty vials of blood.

The transplant team at Ochsner had called in two other possible candidates in case Nic wasn't a suitable match. Just in case. Organs are precious and are never to go to waste if at all possible.

There was paperwork and releases and authorizations to be signed. Insurance information to be verified. Blood pressure, temperature, pulse, ad nauseam. Nic sat pondering his future and Michelle's should they be sent home again. The door opened, and a team in surgical scrubs pushed a large gurney into the room. "It's you!"

OCHSNER MEDICAL CENTER ICU

Mac also sat alone in his room thinking about the deteriorating state of his marriage as well as his health. He hadn't been washed and scrubbed for surgery this time as he'd been at the previous false alarm months earlier. He thought about Stefi, Ashley, and Chris. What would their lives be like without him? Had he done enough for them? All his life, he had worked hard. Too hard maybe? Did he spend enough time on what was important in life? Did his family know just how much he loved them? An awful lot was going on in his head.

Mac was deeply concerned about what Carl had said on the way down. Was a transplant truly necessary? It was true he hadn't been tested for asthma, but he'd had a stress test that had nearly killed him. All the doctors told him he had congestive heart failure. None of them mentioned asthma. Maybe Carl was just worried. Maybe he was misinterpreting the vision he'd had three days earlier. Carl was a deeply God-fearing man, and Mac knew he wouldn't have tried to convince him to get an asthma test first if he didn't believe it. No, Mac knew his brother's intentions were true, but he trusted Dr. Ventura.

Mac had been admitted through the ER since he had arrived in the middle of the night. He was given a bed in the ICU where he would return after surgery. He'd undergone some monitoring of his vital signs, and his final blood work was complete. A tall physician in green scrubs and a white lab coat entered the room and introduced himself to Mac.

"Hi. I'm Doctor Parrino."

Dr. Patrick E. "Gene" Parrino had grown up playing sports. A knee injury had put him in an ER and then in an OR when he was in high school. Gene Parrino knew then and there that he wanted to go to medical school. The Georgia native attended the University of Virginia as an undergrad. While attending medical school at the Medical College of Georgia, he developed an interest in cardiothoracic medicine. He returned to Charlottesville to complete residencies in general surgery and cardiothoracic medicine. From UVA, he traveled to the Cleveland Clinic, where he was a clinical associate for heart failure and transplantation. As a thoracic surgeon, Dr. Parrino performs lung as well as heart transplants.

Transplant surgeons are not as intimately familiar with recipients as are the patients' treating physicians. They're more like experts able to operate on any patient at any moment. Hector Ventura is an expert on Arthur "Mac" Jackson; Gene Parrino is an expert on heart and lung transplants. He happened to be on call that Thursday when Mac received word that a donor heart had been found.

Four heart transplant surgeons are at Ochsner in New Orleans; a fifth is based on the north shore of Lake Ponchartrain. The surgeons of the thoracic transplant team travel to the donor site to recover donor organs. As Dr. Parrino and Mac chatted in the early morning hours, one of Parrino's partners accompanied by a transplant coordinator would be at Tulane working with Dr. Odell, the Mayo Clinic surgeon, to remove Christopher's heart and lungs.

"So how are we doing?" Parrino asked.

"Nervous," Mac replied softly.

"That's to be expected."

Mac was immediately put at ease by the confident demeanor of the younger man.

"Everything is ready to go. The team's waiting, the operating room's ready, and all we're waiting on is a call from the donor hospital. As soon as we know everything is good, we're going to take you downstairs and do your transplant."

It sounded so matter-of-fact that Mac had no reason to be worried.

And as a practical matter, it was. Dr. Parrino had performed such operations for four years at Ochsner, several years at the Cleveland Clinic, and at the University of Virginia before that. Ochsner hospital is one of the busiest transplant centers in the nation. They perform twenty-five to thirty heart transplants each year. Parrino had arrived shortly before Hurricane Katrina. In the storm's aftermath, he was the only faculty physician to remain performing heart transplants. In the year after Katrina, he performed twenty-eight transplants. Mac was in very good hands.

In fact, all Parrino was waiting on was the call from the Ochsner transplant coordinator who had accompanied the recovery team to Tulane. Once they received confirmation that Christopher's heart was healthy and on the way, they'd take Mac to the operating room. It would be as the entire night was turning out to be a highly complex exercise in timing and logistics with the desired outcome being that Mac's heart would be ready for removal just as Christopher's arrived.

The anesthesiologist entered the room. Mac had already had an IV inserted when he came into the room. The anesthesiologist took the cap off a syringe and inserted the end into the IV.

"What do we got here?" asked Mac.

"Just a mild sedative," the young man responded while looking at the IV.

Mac felt a warm sensation come over him. He suddenly felt very comfortable. He forgot all about Carl. The discussion about asthma faded away. He was peaceful, relaxed, and comfortable. The last thing he remembered was the touch of warm blanket against his neck and shoulders.

TULANE MEDICAL CENTER

The surgical team in the OR at Tulane busied themselves cleaning and draping Chris while Dr. Odell scrubbed and gowned. Odell and the thoracic team conferred with the abdominal recovery team and agreed on a time for cross-clamping Christopher's aorta. From that moment on, a new clock of sorts would start running. Once the aorta was clamped, there would be no blood flowing to Chris's organs. This is what is called ischemic time. A time out of sorts took place to be certain all necessary instruments were present, antibiotics had been administered, and yes, that the correct person was on the table. Before proceeding, Joe Guillory asked for a moment.

In some operating rooms, there's music. In others, there may be playful banter. A joke might even be shared. But not in this operating room. Not that night. As crowded and as busy as the room was, there were no jokes, no music. Nobody dared laugh. Doctors and nurses are sworn to promote life. It's more than a job. It's a calling. A vocation. In the OR at Tulane Medical Center on that night, the tone was hushed like a church. There was something akin to reverence in the air.

Joe Guillory took control of the room and called the doctors and nurses to attention. "Can we all please take just a moment. This young man's name is Christopher. He's nineteen. His mom and dad and brothers are upstairs. We should take a moment to respect his sacrifice. And pray for his family."

The room fell silent.

It's now standard operating procedure throughout Louisiana that recovery operations don't begin without a moment like that. The transplant community has a profound respect for deceased donors and their families. Medical professionals have an inherent compassion and respect for human life. This is never more apparent than among those engaged in the life-saving work of organ transplantation.

JACKSONVILLE

On the day of his transplant, Jorge and Leslie Bacardi had been married for 12,527 days. During all that time, Leslie had cared for Jorge and encouraged him and made certain he took his medications and watched his diet. They lived and loved and cared for one another as only a truly committed married couple could do.

For 12,527 days, ever since that ceremony in the flower-filled garden in Nassau, Jorge wore the gold wedding band given to him by Leslie. At 7:50 a.m., Jorge slid the band from his finger and handed it to his wife. The significance of that simple act overwhelmed her. For his part, Jorge had nothing to lose. He knew he might not awaken from his surgery. Fully cognizant of the risks, he had the confidence of a condemned man. He knew that without the transplant he would be dead anyway in a matter of months if not weeks. One way or another, his fate was not in his own hands, and he was resigned to that fact.

Tears filled her eyes and rolled down her cheeks as Leslie grasped the ring and Jorge's hand in hers. Neither said a word. Leslie kissed his cheek, said a prayer, and stood all alone in the hallway.

TULANE MEDICAL CENTER

Satisfied with what he saw, Dr. Odell turned to Tiffany, his surgical technician.

"The lungs look fine. Tell everyone back home they can proceed with the operation on Mr. Bacardi." The technician walked outside and placed three calls. The first was to Dr. Keller informing the team in Jacksonville they could proceed with operation to remove the first lung from Jorge. A second call informed the ambulance driver outside that the operation was underway and would be completed shortly. The third call was to the pilot of the jet waiting at Louis Armstrong International.

After Odell separated the main pulmonary artery from the ascending aorta, he assisted the abdominal team. He was a serious student of the human anatomy and was always fascinated to observe it in a fresh state. Assisting the abdominal team would quicken the pace of the surgery and permit the team from Mayo to return to Florida sooner.

Once the abdominal team had completed the dissection, the anesthesiologist intravenously delivered 30,000 units of the anticoagulant Heparin. One of the technicians from Mayo hung a bag of preservation fluid on an IV pole. Odell sutured the main pulmonary artery, stabbed it with a small knife, and inserted a cannula into the artery. Satisfied that the tubing from the bag of preservation fluid was adequately connected to the pulmonary artery, Dr. Odell was prepared to begin in earnest.

Six to seven liters of cold preservation fluid would be injected into Chris's body, which already had five liters of blood in circulation. Replacing those fluids could be a messy task if not handled carefully. He inserted a suction tube into the inferior vena cava, the large vein that returns blood to the heart. After clamping the ascending aorta, the cold preservation fluid was allowed to flow from the IV bag to the lungs through the just-inserted cannula. He checked the fluid exiting the atrium and saw that it was clear, indicating that the preservation fluid was adequately perfusing the lungs. Ice and slush were placed inside Chris's chest cavity to cool the organs.

The team next moved to remove Chris's heart. His heart was injected with potassium chloride to make it stop beating. Wanting to make the transplant easier, they took care to save as much of the left atrium and pulmonary artery as possible. The heart was taken to a side table where it was prepared for transport. Like his lungs, his heart would be packed in ice, bagged, and bagged again. It would be a short drive across town along Claiborne Avenue to the Ochsner Medical Center on Jefferson Highway. There, Dr. Parrino and the heart transplant team were awaiting the arrival of Christopher's heart and had begun prepping Mac for surgery.

Dr. Odell concentrated as he began the delicate process of removing Christopher's lungs. After severing the esophagus, he asked the anesthesiologist to inflate the lungs. Satisfied that there was no danger of atelectasis—collapsed lung—Odell severed the trachea and carefully removed both lungs. On a side table, they flushed the lungs with sterile preservation fluid.

The abdominal teams began in earnest to explant the abdominal organs. Odell and his technician placed the lungs in a large plastic bag containing a cold saline solution and tied off the opening. They placed that bag inside another. And then another. The surgeon attached a sticker to the outermost bag that contained a donor ID code. He gently placed the triple-bagged organs inside a Tupperware-like container and placed that in an ice-filled cooler.

After signing a copy of the operation note, Odell bade his colleagues good luck and departed the operating suite. The Mayo team hurriedly undressed and then hustled out to the waiting ambulance. The ride to the airport was quick. The ambulance traveled with lights going and siren wailing just as the ambulance carrying Chris's heart was as it raced to Ochsner across town. Once Chris's organs were in an ambulance, the situation was deemed a medical emergency.

At Louis Armstrong International, the private jet that would take them to St. Augustine was already spinning up its engines. Organ transplant flights receive special priority over every other aircraft in the country except for Air Force One and Two. The rush-hour traffic was coming into New Orleans as O'Dell and his team headed in the opposite direction. The physician looked at his watch and then the traffic as they raced west on Interstate 10 toward the airport and the jet.

OCHSNER MEDICAL CENTER– OPERATING ROOM 10

The heart transplant team at Ochsner that night consisted of Dr. Parrino, an anesthesiologist, an anesthesia resident, an anesthesia fellow, a perfusionist to operate the heart-lung machine, a nonsterile circulating nurse, a sterile scrub nurse, and Dr. Parrino's surgical first assistant, Chris Medina. Medina is across the operating table every time Dr. Parrino operates. They have been together for ten years; they often spend more than thirty hours a week in surgery. It's fair to say that during some weeks, Parrino spends more time with Medina than he does with his wife.

It would be a large team, but the ORs at Ochsner can accommodate large teams. The real work is at the operating table, where the first assist and the scrub nurse huddle close. There are a total of twenty-six operating rooms at Ochsner. OR 10, where they would be this night, is a marvel of technology. Flat-screen monitors display Mac's vital signs. OR 10 is designated for heart surgery, so all the equipment and supplies needed for a heart or lung transplant are there. It makes no sense to have a heart-lung machine in an OR where a kidney transplant would be performed. Every detail down to the sutures and staples is planned in advance and available to the doctors and nurses.

The operating table itself is surprisingly small in the large space of the operating room. It's not nearly as wide as a basic hospital bed. The rule with Dr. Parrino's team is that the height of the operating table is set for the tallest person in room, often Parrino. The short people are welcome to stand on step stools. You don't want surgeons performing such delicate work hunched over patients and getting prematurely exhausted.

Something that's rarely discussed outside the community of surgical teams is the choice of music in the OR. Yes, music. Academic papers have been written on the subject. It's not so much about the effect a particular musical genre might have on a particular group of surgeons or how doctors react physiologically; rather, it's a statement about management styles. NFL coaches and corporate executives might take note.

Surgeons have different personalities. Some are so high strung that they can't deal with music during surgery. However, that high-strungness can affect the entire surgical team. During an organ transplant, it's critical that everyone in the room feels comfortable in his or her role. The best outcomes result with a surgical team that's cool, calm, and collected. The surgeon is like the head coach or the CEO. If the others there are scared the surgeon might snap and start screaming at them, they won't do as good a job as they would if they were relaxed. A person who listens to music is typically someone people are more comfortable working with. Music makes for a more relaxed environment. And during a heart transplant, you definitely want a relaxed, confident team.

Parrino is that kind of leader in the operating room. And as was his custom, Dr. Parrino deferred to the junior member of his team to make the choice of music. As long as that choice wasn't Italian opera, Parrino could live with it. Tonight, that awesome decision fell to the guy running the heart-lung machine.

HOUSTON

After receiving the call from the organ transplant coordinator at Ochsner, Nic called his father in Houston. The elder

Whitacre, a former pastor in the Church of Christ, was accustomed to calling upon the Almighty in times of crisis. As a pastor, he was often the one whom families in crisis looked to for guidance and spiritual direction. He'd led countless families in prayer during times of illness and calamity.

And his own son's life hung in the balance. He turned to God and asked him for another chance for Nic. Another day with his son. After making his own petition, the elder Whitacre began calling his lifelong friends. Before long, he had a prayer chain started; many people were asking God to intercede on Nic's behalf. Praying that God would keep Nic strong enough to survive the complicated surgery. Praying for the skill of the surgeons to be sharp and their training and experience to give them the confidence they'd need that day. Most of all, he prayed that God would let him see his son again. Alive.

OCHSNER MEDICAL CENTER– OPERATING ROOM 10

By March 2008, the medical profession had forty-one years of experience in the field of heart transplantation since Dr. Christiaan Barnard performed the first in Cape Town, South Africa, in 1967. Mac's transplant team at Ochsner waited for a call similar to the one Dr. Odell made to the team at Mayo.

When Dr. Parrino received the call from the recovery team at Tulane that Christopher's heart was healthy and suitable for transplant, they took Mac to the OR. He was placed under general anesthesia. Intravenous antibiotics were administered to prevent infections at the incision sites. Immunosuppressive drugs were given to prevent Mac's immune system from responding to Christopher's heart as a foreign object.

The operation commenced with a sternotomy. Mac's chest was opened up, and his sternum divided, exposing his diseased heart. The tubes for the heart-lung machine were inserted. The plan would be to prepare Mac to go on the pump and wait for confirmation that Chris's heart was en route. The great vessels of Mac's diseased heart were transected. The superior vena cava and the lesser vena cava, which carry deoxygenated blood to the heart from the upper and lower body respectively, were separated from Mac's heart with a sharp scalpel. He was then connected to the heart-lung machine.

The heart-lung machine is just that. The technical term for the device is a cardiopulmonary bypass. The body's blood vessels are detached from the heart and attached to the heart-lung machine. The heart-lung machine, sometimes called the pump, oxygenates and circulates blood throughout the body mechanically outside the body.

In some cases, after connecting the patient to the heart-lung machine, the operation may be placed on hold. Usually, the transplant operation team will wait for confirmation that the donor heart has landed at the airport before removing the bad heart. In some tragic circumstances, aircraft delivering donor organs have crashed taking their precious cargo with them. That's one reason why transplant centers are getting away from the use of helicopters; they aren't that much faster than ambulances are from airports to hospitals.

In Mac's case, there were no aircraft involved since Chris was only a couple of miles away at Tulane. So after a short pause, the heart-lung machine was turned on and Mac's diseased heart was removed.

Just as the team was removing Mac's heart, the ambulance carrying Christopher's turned off Jefferson Highway and pulled up to the ER entrance. The recovery team hustled through the hallway and took the elevator to the second floor. It was a short walk from the elevator to OR 10.

Once in the operating room, Parrino's team had to verify that the heart they had received was the one assigned to Arthur Jackson. It's a detailed but not elaborate process to ensure that the heart received is the same one they'd discussed earlier. Satisfied that the identifiers matched, they opened the cooler and removed the bags from the ice. Removing his heart from the bags, Dr. Parrino looked the organ over. It was easy to inspect in its inert state; 10 to 15 percent of all people are born with small holes in their hearts called an atrial septal defect. Had he found one, Parrino would have repaired it before proceeding.

Working as fluidly and expeditiously as possible, they began implanting Christopher's heart into Arthur Jackson. "Never rush—always hurry" is an old saying among surgeons. Their actions weren't spastic or disorganized but more like a well-rehearsed symphony, each member of the team knowing his or her role and executing it flawlessly. Once Chris's heart was in place, Parrino began connecting the blood vessels. The left atrium first, then the inferior vena cava, followed by the superior vena cava, and then the pulmonary artery.

"John, what are we flowing at?" Parrino asked the perfusionist running the heart-lung machine.

"Five and a half," he replied, meaning five and a half liters per minute.

"Okay, here we go." Parrino completed the final suture in the aortic connection, the final blood vessel to be connected to the heart. Once complete, the anesthesiologist administered a big dose of steroids. Dr. Parrino removed the clamp from the aorta, and blood began to flow into Christopher's heart. At that moment, the lives of two men who had never met came together.

JACKSONVILLE

The helicopter pilot waited patiently as the chartered jet made its final approach into St. Augustine Airport. The jet landed and taxied to the area of the tarmac where the helicopter waited. By the time the jet was within walking distance, the helicopter's engines were running. The door to the jet opened, and Dr. Odell and the recovery team exited it. The sun was rising over the Atlantic as the small group walked briskly to the helicopter. They carried a normal-looking Igloo cooler. The helicopters blades were turning before the last of the party was buckled up. It would be a short hop from St. Augustine to Saint Luke's Hospital in Jacksonville.

The helicopter landed at the helipad outside the ER, where Jorge Bacardi had entered only hours before. The team and their precious cargo headed directly to the OR, where Jorge was under general anesthesia. The recovery team had maintained contact with the surgical team from Mayo, so by the time Odell and his group arrived, Dr. Richard Agnew and Dr. Ali Sadeghi had already begun operating on Jorge. One of his lungs had been removed.

Despite Odell's presence and the fact that Christopher's lungs had never been out of his possession, the necessary check of all donor identifier codes was completed and verified. Odell excused himself to scrub and gown. He would assist in the operation to implant Christopher's lungs.

OCHSNER MEDICAL CENTER– OPERATING ROOM 10

Mac's new heart still needed time to flush out the potassium chloride that had been used at Tulane to stop it from beating. And it needed time to warm up. Mac was still on bypass; the heart-lung machine was still performing its job.

The nature of the equipment is more like a dial than a switch, so once blood started filling the heart's chambers, Parrino wanted to see how the organ would respond. If it didn't start beating spontaneously, the team had equipment that would administer just enough of a shock to establish a rhythm until the heart started to beat on its own. Nobody would scream, nobody would panic; they'd just connect the electric pacer, and the pacer would get the heart pumping.

"John, why don't you come down to three and a half," Parrino instructed the perfusionist.

Mac's blood coursed through Christopher's heart flushing the potassium chloride from the organ. For a moment, all eyes focused on the new heart. The team held its collective breath and waited. And then it happened. Almost miraculously, Christopher's heart began to beat all by itself. Parrino looked up at the overhead monitors and saw a pulse and blood pressure. The team let out a collective breath and smiled. Parrino was satisfied and amazed. This is why he went to medical school in the first place.

The anesthesiologist in particular was interested in the monitor. They needed to get a sense of how Mac's new heart would perform. They especially needed to know what his blood pressure would do once they came off bypass. If the heart wasn't beating, they'd have connected the pacing wires. If it was beating but not squeezing well, they'd administer drugs to make the heart squeeze better. Or if it was beating but the blood pressure was really low, they'd administer drugs to improve the blood pressure.

Once they were satisfied the heart was beating well enough on its own and the blood pressure was sufficient, they reduced the heart-lung machine from three and a half liters per minute to zero. Mac's new heart took over and was beating on its own.

MIAMI

Sonia Bacardi attended Pilates three days a week. That Friday was no different. Except that it was. The events of the past twenty-four hours were obvious on her face and in her voice. That the second call happened at all was itself unusual. Mayo Clinic had been trying for some time to reach Jorge. Being unsuccessful in their efforts, they called Dr. Keller, who had immediately called Jorge's cell. Thus, the news of her uncle's trip to Jacksonville was no small matter in itself.

Before leaving to take her children to school and then go to her Pilates class, Sonia called her mother, Manuela, in San Juan, Puerto Rico, with news of the phone calls from Jorge and Leslie the night before. Manuela is of a generation of women around the world whose faith is unshakable. Sonia knew her mother would activate her "prayer people" who would quickly start praying for Jorge's transplant to be a success.

"What happened to you?" a friend asked her. It was obvious to her friends that Sonia was deeply troubled. After receiving Leslie's call at one that morning, she and Joaquin spent the remainder of the sleepless night tossing and turning. They decided to say nothing to their children because so much was still up in the air. Joaquin was at work at the Bacardi offices in

Miami. Their children were blissfully unaware of the great-uncle's present disposition, and so Sonia was alone with her emotions. She was still in shock. She couldn't feel her fingers. But the company of her friends was comforting.

"Nothing," Sonia replied.

"You don't look yourself," her friend said. "You're *not* yourself. Is everything all right?"

"I'm sorry," said Sonia. "It's nothing."

Sonia couldn't contain herself. Her friends had all known about Jorge's condition for some months. "It's Joaquin's uncle!" she finally blurted out. Gasps filled the air.

"Your uncle? What happened?"

"He's undergoing surgery right now. I'm extremely anxious. Nervous. I want all of you to say a prayer with me."

Sonia and her husband are people of great faith. They got that from their parents. During times of difficulty, the Bacardi family always turned to their faith. Two of her Pilates friends were Jewish, but that was of no consequence. The women joined hands, bowed their heads, and asked God to give Sonia's uncle a second chance at life.

OCHSNER MEDICAL CENTER– WAITING ROOM

The surgical waiting area at Ochsner is a huge space that seems to run the length of the building. Huge picture windows look out over Jefferson Avenue and the warehouses and neighborhoods to the north. Carl Jackson looked up from his newspaper and saw a young man in surgical scrubs looking at him.

"Are you with Mr. Jackson?" the man asked.

"Yes sir," Carl replied. "I'm his brother."

"Mr. Jackson, how are you holding up?"

"I'm fine. How's it going in there?"

"Everything's going normally. Your brother is still in surgery, but everything's going as planned."

An uneasy feeling suddenly descended on Carl. Something inexplicable yet familiar. Carl rubbed his eyes. He heard a voice. "Arthur just died … Arthur just died, but he's going to be okay." Carl jolted upright, looked around the waiting room, and felt the blood rush from his face. He was alone in the room. The young man in surgical scrubs was gone.

OCHSNER MEDICAL CENTER

Dr. Tonnessen heard a familiar *thump-thump-thump* coming from the operating room. The transplant boys were at it again. She couldn't tell if it was Led Zeppelin or the Four Tops. She was working on yet another angiogram. There was a transplant happening next door. Britt Tonnessen held the transplant surgeons at Ochsner in high regard. They were heroes who worked long hours performing their lifesaving work. She had seen surgical teams work around the clock. She herself had known the physical limits that were routinely surpassed by these talented physicians, nurses, and technicians. She decided to stick her head in on her noisy neighbors. She saw George Loss and Umberto Bohorquez.

"Hi guys, whadda we got?" she asked.

"Hey there, Britt. How are you?" one of the masked surgeons asked. "Doing a little kidney and pancreas today."

She knew the patient. Nic Whitacre. She'd been copied on an e-mail alerting everyone remotely connected to Nic's care at Ochsner that he was undergoing a transplant.

Dr. Tonnessen marveled at the scene. *These guys are amazing*, she thought. *So many patients, and they are all complicated. And they're all so near death.* Then their lives intersect with doctors like Umberto Bohorquez and George Loss, and suddenly they're redeemed. They're given another chance to live.

She felt very excited. Almost giddy. There was the same man she had sent home to die the day before. And now his future was literally in the hands of the two men she knew could guarantee him a future. If anybody was capable of saving his life, Bohorquez and Loss were the guys. *Amazing*, she thought. The youthful man whose body had been ravaged was getting a transplant. She left the room with an uncontrollable smile on her face.

OCHSNER MEDICAL CENTER–
WAITING ROOM

Michelle Whitacre was extremely nervous. So when Dr. Loss entered the waiting room, her heart sank.

"How're you doing Michelle?" he asked.

"Okay. How's Nic?"

"We're having some complications. His vascular system is severely compromised. We're having trouble getting blood to the pancreas."

He explained that the pancreas was such a fragile organ that even a healthy one like Christopher's had to be handled with a mesh bag.

"It's like this," he said. "Ten percent of the pancreas produces insulin. And ninety percent produces enzymes that will break down whatever they come in contact with. And if that were to happen, those enzymes would get loose inside Nic's abdomen and we'd have a real mess on our hands. So you don't want all that other stuff leaking around."

Michelle just nodded.

"But that isn't the main problem. Right now, we're having difficulty connecting the donor pancreas to Nic's blood supply."

Dr. Loss explained that most type 1 diabetes transplant patients are under age fifty as was the case with Nic. Michelle nodded again. Most of them don't have too much calcium in the arteries that the doctors have to deal with. Nic was different. The years of living with his disease had left many of his arteries as brittle as eggshells. That's why the angiogram of the previous day had been unsuccessful. Usually, the surgeons could find at least a small part of the circumference of the artery to tie in the blood supply to the pancreas. They were still searching for that soft spot in Nic's very calcified circulatory system.

"You'll keep trying, won't you?" Michelle asked.

"Of course," he replied. "As long as it takes."

She watched the surgeon return to the OR. She was alone with her thoughts.

HOLIDAY INN–NEW ORLEANS

I woke up to Grace's typing on her laptop. It was just shy of noon. Grace was sending an e-mail to someone at home. For a while, we'd been measuring time by events, not by a clock or calendar. It was Friday, March 28, 2008, about 11:00 a.m., but in our new reality, it was the day after Chris had been pronounced dead. The new measuring stick of our lives would consist of all the tasks and events that would occur during the days, weeks, and even months ahead. There was the call we got from Colin Tuesday morning. Then there was the news from Dr. Posey.

Then the apnea test. Then he was pronounced dead. Then they took him to the OR for the explant of his organs.

The days and months and even years ahead would be measured in the same manner. We had to fly home. We had to meet with a funeral director. Chris's body would come home. Then the funeral. Then all the benchmarks of a normal life except that Chris wouldn't be there to share them. Graduations and weddings and reunions and anniversaries.

Maybe, just maybe, there might even be a chance to hear from one of his organ recipients. Maybe, we would get a letter that said thanks to Chris, someone was living a life that would not have been possible otherwise. That of course would be in the future. For the time being, we calculated what time it was by considering the tasks involved in putting Christopher to rest. The next task was to head to Loyola and clean out his dorm room.

OCHSNER MEDICAL CENTER–ICU

Mac opened his eyes, looked up at the lights, and wondered when the surgery would begin. Aside from the anesthesiologist speaking to him a short while ago, he had difficulty remembering any details.

He slowly became aware of his surroundings. He sensed others in the room with him. Lights and motion seemed fuzzy at first, and then gradually, his brain started processing the sights and sounds. He wondered when the operation would start. *They sure seem to be taking their time.* He sensed he wasn't in the same room where he'd fallen asleep, where he'd felt the warm blanket pulled up to his neck. It was busier there, more people. A woman in a surgical gown looked at his eyes and moved to him.

"Mr. Jackson?" she asked.

Mac's throat was dry and slightly sore. "When are we going to get started?"

"Excuse me?"

"When ..." Mac nearly whispered, "... are we going to get started?"

"Why Mr. Jackson," the nurse smiled. "Mr. Jackson, you have a new heart."

Mac wasn't so much surprised as he was curious. *The operation's over?* Contributing to his curiosity was the fact that he was experiencing no pain. None at all. Certainly the medications he was on may have contributed to that, but the real reason lay in the human anatomy.

The human sternum, the breastbone, is broad and flat. To get to the heart, the sternum is separated right down the middle. The ribs attach to the sternum but can swing open. As the lungs inflate, the ribs swing much like a bucket handle but the sternum stays in place. After Christopher's heart was implanted, Mac's sternum was wired back into place. It's a much less painful incision than perhaps what's necessary for operating on lung cancer or even an abdominal incision.

All other transplant incisions cut cross muscle. During heart transplants, the incision was between the pectoris muscles. So during Mac's recovery, as he moved around, there was no incision through the muscle pulling at the incision and causing him pain. It's not uncommon for heart transplant recipients to experience little pain.

OCHSNER MEDICAL CENTER– WAITING ROOM

It was midafternoon when Dr. Loss appeared again in the waiting area. By that time, Michelle had been joined by her sister as well as Nic's mother and sister. Michelle was obviously tired, but she perked up immediately upon seeing the surgeon. She hoped for the best, but the look on Loss's face betrayed his own frustration.

"We're still having difficulty with the pancreas," he said.

"Do you think you'll be able to do something?" Michelle asked.

The difficulty with finding a suitable point to suture Christopher's pancreas to Nic's blood vessels had been met so far only with frustration. A typical kidney-pancreas transplant procedure takes about three to five hours from the first incision to the last staple. Nic had been in surgery for nine, and they still hadn't overcome the challenges presented by his compromised vascular system. Time was running out.

"Look, Michelle, we'll give it one more try, okay? But if we don't find something soon, then …" His voice trailed off.

Michelle was again gripped with fear. She knew as much about Nic's medical condition as anyone. She had witnessed firsthand so many of her husband's close encounters with death. Every time, he'd pulled through and returned to her. The long-awaited transplant had arrived and with it a second chance at a normal life. But it might be lost anyway.

"Please do something," she pleaded in a soft, measured voice.

"We can't stay in there forever." He paused. "We can give it one more try."

The surgeon returned to the OR.

JACKSONVILLE

Jorge awoke to a mild gagging sensation in his throat. He was still intubated. He looked around the room but couldn't immediately see anyone. He heard the rhythmic cadence of the heart monitor and the mechanical sound of the ventilator. He heard voices coming from the hall. He heard a doctor being paged over the PA. When he saw a nurse in the room, he realized he had survived surgery.

He wanted to alert the nurse that he was awake, but the tube in his throat prevented him from making any noise. He wanted to wave or reach for her, but his arms wouldn't move. They'd been strapped to his bed to prevent him from instinctively yanking out the breathing tube. However, it felt as though he could wiggle his toes. And so he wiggled them as mightily as he could. It was a slight wiggle but enough to make the blanket move and catch the nurse's eye. She saw Jorge looking at her.

"Well there you are!"

Jorge didn't respond. He couldn't. Despite the anesthesia, he wanted desperately to tell her to please get the tube out of his throat. His efforts to point at his mouth with his hands continued to be frustrated by the restraints. Jorge almost started feeling panicky. But that was short lived.

The nurse picked up a telephone. "Dr. Keller, your patient is asking for you." She turned to Jorge. "Dr. Keller will be here in a few minutes."

Jorge immediately relaxed. He'd survived the surgery. Cesar was on the way. Everything would soon be well. He relaxed and immediately thought of Leslie. And then he drifted back to sleep.

OCHSNER MEDICAL CENTER–ICU

Nic opened his eyes and stared at the ceiling. He was aware of an odd sensation just below his hips. The nurses helped him sit more upright in bed. He was still groggy from the anesthesia. He wiggled around in his bed. He looked down at the bag tied to the end of the bed and saw a most satisfying sight. Yellow fluid. Urine. His new pancreas was at work. He leaned back and smiled. *Still here. Still alive.*

Nic looked at the clock on the wall. It was after 4:00 in the afternoon. An operation that routinely took three to five hours had taken Loss and Bohorquez nearly ten.

The pancreas proved to be the difficult part of the operation due to the brittle nature of Nic's arteries, but the task had been accomplished. Swapping out kidneys, on the other hand, had been almost as routine as swapping out car batteries.

The anesthesia was wearing off. The cobwebs were clearing. Everything felt different. Everything. He was soon able to focus, and he began thinking clearly. He looked around the room for Michelle. *Five seconds, just like Granny said.*

Sometimes, it had been for only five seconds at a time, but he'd survived.

BATON ROUGE

By midafternoon, Xavier Major had fully recovered from that morning's dialysis treatment. He felt exhausted during the drive home from the dialysis center in Port Arthur. He always did. But he always recovered and regained the strength to continue as normal a day as he could. He was fixing a glass of ice water when the phone rang. It was the organ procurement coordinator at Ochsner. The call was similar to the calls Nic Whitacre and Mac Jackson had received.

"May I speak to Xavier Major, please?" The voice was sharp and quick.

"This is he," Xavier replied.

"Mr. Major, I'm calling from the Multi-Organ Transplant Center at Ochsner Hospital. There's a kidney that has become available, and you're at the top of the list."

Xavier was very excited and nervous. Not the imminent danger kind of nervous; more like the first-date kind of nervous. The coordinator asked how long it would take him to get to Ochsner. He replied that his wife was at work but that he thought no more than a couple of hours. Very well, he was told. They'd be expecting him in New Orleans in a few hours.

He called Pam. The Blue Cross office where she worked wasn't far. She hurried home to pick up her husband, pack some bags, and start the drive to New Orleans.

LOYOLA UNIVERSITY NEW ORLEANS

The sun was bright. The air was warm and humid even for March. We climbed aboard the streetcar. It began its noisy rumble down St. Charles Avenue to Loyola's campus uptown. We had to clean out Christopher's room and box up his belongings. I just stared out the window at the mansions that line St. Charles Avenue. A couple of young women had struck up a conversation with Grace. It was the first time she would have to struggle with telling someone our son had died. The conversation was as awkward then as it is today. It never gets easy to tell a stranger your child died. The conversation simply doesn't flow. You struggle to tell them in a manner that allows you to maintain your composure. They of course immediately look for a way to change the conversation.

A thousand memories came back as we walked across campus to Kurt Bindewald's office. Sights and sounds brought memories of campus tours and orientations. We'd been on campus before Katrina and the semester after the storm. We'd grown to love New Orleans and the people who lived there. Kurt, the director of university ministry, was his typical kind, generous self. He explained there would be a memorial service for Chris later that evening in the Ignatius Chapel.

Walking across campus, we soaked in the memories of Colin's first years there and Christopher's arrival as well. Chris's roommate was nowhere to be found when we arrived at Biever Hall. We sorted through the pile of clothes on his bed. Some were even clean. Souvenirs from Mardi Gras were mixed in with textbooks and the odd syllabus. Photographs of our family. Every item brought back a memory. Every paper and notebook that had his name or handwriting on suddenly became of tremendous value. Old, familiar T-shirts even if in need of washing were tangible connections to Chris. While we were busy cleaning and packing, my phone rang. It was Joe Guillory, the organ recovery coordinator.

"Mr. Gregory, how y'all doing?"

"Hey, Joe. What can I do for you?" I thought maybe there was a missing piece of information he needed. There wasn't.

"I just wanted to tell you how sorry I am about your boy."

"That's really kind of you, Joe. We appreciate everything you did last night. You're a class act, man. I mean that."

"Mr. Gregory, I hope you don't mind me sayin' this, but I gotta tell you I'm a father myself. I have two little boys. I can't imagine having to go through what y'all are going through. But if I ever have to, I sure hope I'll have the courage to do it with as much class as y'all did."

I wasn't sure how to respond. Joe was one of those guys who shows up during the absolute worst moment in people's lives and gives them something to believe in. We'd instantly hit it off when he arrived at the hospital to begin coordinating the donation process. He was naturally caring and competent. He's one of those born leaders everyone rallies around when the going gets tough. The previous day, it couldn't have been tougher.

"Seriously though, if you ever want someone to talk to, you have my number," he said.

"What a nice guy," I told Grace. He didn't have to have said that. But as had so many other people that week, he genuinely cared. He cared about the recipients who would get Christopher's organs. But he cared very much about Christopher as well. And he cared about us. It was a really touching moment.

I came across a tiny, round piece of metal. On its face was a slash like a lightning bolt. It was a pledge pin. Like Colin, Christopher had pledged the Beggars. The Beggars are a fraternity unique to Loyola New Orleans. They're not found at any other college or university. Chris adored his big brothers and wanted to be just like them. Even when they were picking on each other, he loved them. He wanted to be like them so badly it hurt. It had hurt that he didn't get into Gonzaga. It had hurt that he'd tried three years in a row. But he'd gone to Loyola with Colin and pledged the same fraternity, and that made everything all right.

He'd looked forward to spending his college years hanging with his brother and then whatever the future held. They would remain close. He'd had that stolen from him by an unforeseen medical catastrophe that was no fault of his. He'd been cheated in the worst possible way. He hadn't gotten a chance to say good-bye. Remembering what Dr. Posey told me the day before about keeping his son's rock in hands for a year, I slipped the pin into my pocket.

JACKSONVILLE

By 4:00 p.m., the waiting area at St. Luke's was crowded with the Bacardis' friends and relatives. After seeing Leslie alone in the hallway, Dr. Keller called his wife, Ingrid, who drove to the hospital to keep Leslie company.

Dex and Ann Crotts, longtime friends of the Bacardis, had been among the first to arrive that morning. They had been in North Carolina, and after receiving Leslie's call that Jorge's transplant was imminent, they couldn't sleep. So they'd packed in the middle of the night, drove home to Atlanta, and took a flight to Jacksonville that morning.

They were followed shortly by Leslie's sister, Joy Tobin. Joy was in her kitchen in New York when her phone rang just before midnight. "Are you going?" is how she answered the phone.

Jorge's brother, Alberto, and his wife, Mari, were soon joined by their older children, Juan, Christina, and Maya. Sighs of relief greeted the news from Dr. Keller that Jorge's transplant had been not just a success but a textbook example of how perfectly it could be done. Things were looking up. The mood was completely opposite from what it had been just a few days earlier when Jorge's life was in jeopardy.

Smiles were the uniform of the day. The visitors arrived, embraced Leslie, and greeted one another. The briefest news was exchanged before the same question was asked, "How is he?"

Alberto and Dex went to Jorge's room in the ICU and were amazed by his transformation. Their reports to the family in the waiting room made the mood only brighter. Hands were shook. Backs were slapped. *Abrazos* were exchanged. Laughter finally permeated the air. The sense of concern was replaced by relief and then triumph as each visitor to Jorge's room reaffirmed the good news. The operation had been a success.

Leslie called Joaquin and Sonia in Miami.

"Hello, Leslie. How is he?" Joaquin asked.

"Your tio's out of surgery. Everything went well. He's in the ICU recovering. Everything went the way they expected," Leslie replied.

Joaquin heard the relief in Leslie's voice. He too felt tension leave his body and be replaced by a warm sensation of compassion and gratitude.

"Great. Is there anything you need? Anything we can help you with?"

Joaquin was torn between throwing some things in a bag and heading to Jacksonville right then or driving up later. He wanted to be there. He wanted to be with his aunt and uncle. Joaquin's father often told Jorge, "He's more your son than he is my own." Jorge and his nephew shared an especially close bond.

"Everything is fine," Leslie replied.

OCHSNER MEDICAL CENTER

Xavier and Pam walked into the ER as it was getting dark. They checked in at the admitting area and were asked to take a seat in the waiting lounge. They said little as they watched TV and noted the ER patients coming and going. Hospitals are remarkable places to people watch, but Xavier was too preoccupied to do that. His thoughts were on whatever the next few hours would hold.

He heard his name over the PA. As requested, he picked up the courtesy phone. The caller instructed him to take the elevators to the third floor.

Xavier and Pam were excited and nervous as they exited the elevator and walked into the ICU. The staff was waiting for them. He was taken to a room. He changed into a hospital gown and hopped into the bed. Blood work was done, blood pressure taken, and an IV was inserted.

LOYOLA UNIVERSITY NEW ORLEANS

We finished packing up Chris's belongings and cleaning his room. I tried to imagine what his roommate would think when he returned. It was as if Chris had never been there.

At the memorial Mass that evening, the first thing that struck me was that all Chris's and Colin's friends were dressed up. Grace and I were still in the clothes we'd worn when cleaning out his room. We looked like a couple of train wrecks.

The service had been entirely arranged by the Beggars. It was at once somber and uplifting. Fr. Jim and Fr. Ted were there. Fr. Wildes, the president of the university, participated. Beggars who were music majors offered the musical pieces of the program. A big screen carried a slide show with images of Chris and his friends. Images we had never seen before. All of them with smiling faces and eyes bright with youthful optimism. It was nice to know Chris had been well loved by those who knew him.

Matt Nolan told a few stories of their long road trips back and forth between home and New Orleans and of Christopher's desire to stop at every fireworks stand. At one such stand, they discovered an aerial bomb that required the separate purchase of a launching tube. Chris tried desperately to get Matt to buy just the aerial bomb. Matt asked, "Chris, how do you plan to launch this thing?" Chris smiled. "Dude! We can always find a mortar launcher!"

Ellie Trant spoke of the strapping youth who had befriended a homesick girl and became her best friend. Besties they called each other. She read the letter she'd written to Chris and reminded him of a promise he'd made to find her a good man.

Nick Magnello offered an irreverent account of meeting Chris during freshman orientation. "I'll never forget meeting Chris. It was during freshman orientation. I kept noticing that during all the different presentations, two guys were always off to the side smoking cigarettes. Finally, I just said, 'Shit! I'm going with those guys!'"

Nick spoke about how he, Matt, Chris, and Kevin Drohan had become friends by skipping all the freshman orientation events. The room erupted in laughter. Even the Jesuits got a kick out of the tale.

I was numbed by the experience. I couldn't wrap my head around the idea that this was Chris, our Chris, at the center of everyone's attention. It seemed surreal. I was going through the motions. After sending three kids off to college, I pretty much knew what to say and how to act in the role of a college parent. But these were different circumstances, and I suppose, like everyone else, we just sort of stumbled through the events as best we could.

As I would in the following week, I offered up a few words of gratitude for all the support we'd received during those days when Chris was in the hospital. I shared with those in the chapel what my family meant to me. That if my whole life was lived on an island and it consisted of just Grace and me and the boys, I'd have been happy with just that. But so many other people were a part of that life at that time, and for that I was grateful. I said that if I'd been told twenty years ago I could have a child but would lose him after nineteen or twenty years, I'd have said okay without hesitation.

The service was a huge success. It was indeed a celebration of Chris's life. And while tears were shed, there was also laughter. I sat next to Gerry Nolan after the program was over and just took in the scene. Grace and some of the girls were watching the slide show while Toto sang "Africa." It had somehow became an anthem for Chris after he and Matt bought a tape during one of their long drives home.

LAUREL, MARYLAND

Brian and Mary Abdo knew that breaking the news to Kathleen wouldn't be easy. She had saved a long time to go to New York for spring break. Kathleen had loved performing in plays and musicals at her school as well as at Christopher's school, Mount Saint Joseph. She dreamed of performing on Broadway one day. Her trip to New York was a dream come true, and so when the news about Chris hit the Abdo household, they decided to wait until she returned home to tell her.

Their plan was to pick up Kathleen, pick up some pizza for the kids who were at their house, and return home. There was no way they could let Kathleen walk into a house full of grieving kids. So they decided to break the news in the car in front of the pizza place. Kathleen's reaction was a combination of shock, horror, and disbelief.

"Why are you lying to me?" she screamed.

The three of them burst into tears.

"I'm sorry, honey," was all Mary could say.

"You're lying!" Kathleen's scream was loud, high pitched, almost childlike in its agony. "He's not dead! Why are you saying this? Why are you lying to me?"

The pain that Brian and Mary felt over losing a boy who was like a member of their family was bad enough. But to experience the effect it had on their own children made it only that much worse. They could offer no response. It would have done no good anyway. And so they sat there for the next half hour holding Kathleen as she and they sobbed uncontrollably.

OCHSNER MEDICAL CENTER

Pam smiled at Xavier when he looked at her. He hoped everything would go all right. After what seemed like endless lab work was over, they were left alone in the room. Every now and then, another nurse would check on them and try to keep them as relaxed and comfortable as possible. There was nothing else for Xavier and Pam to do except exchange idle sighs and the odd chitchat. Mostly, they just waited. They looked at the clock and watched the second hand sweep around its face.

NEW ORLEANS

The mood at Friar Tuck's was significantly different from the previous night. Instead of the awkward, "Please God, don't let this be happening," it was a full-on Irish wake. The Beggars were in their glory. One of their own had gone ahead, and they would damn sure send him off in true New Orleans style. Someone purchased a keg, and the number of sober denizens could be counted on one hand.

Shots were ordered. Toasts were raised. Songs were sung. Stories were told. Tears were shed. The hope that maybe, just maybe, they'd all meet up again on the other side was given voice. Nothing shocks the heart and soul of a young person as does the death of another young person.

But for a few of them, they remembered what Joe Guillory had said. Planes were flying. Chris was performing miracles. Right as they were drinking away their sorrows. While they cried and sang, Chris was going off to do something remarkable. He'd make his mark on the world in ways they still couldn't wrap their heads around. They might never know the full power of what he had done that night. Dozens of doctors and nurses they would never meet had worked through the night and into that day, and lives had been transformed. Families had been saved from the very tragedy that was enveloping them. "They'd better appreciate it," the Beggars said to one another.

Unable to fully understand or accept what had happened, they turned to each other in their grief. But there was something out there. Something not easily understood. Chris had checked a box and someone had gotten a liver, someone else new lungs, someone else a new heart. Surely that meant something. Perhaps in years they would know more. Perhaps not. For the present, they just needed to know they were alive.

my dearest chris,

⤬

I remember the day I met you. It was the beginning of last semester, and I was struggling with a lot of homesickness and having trouble making new friends. You and I had a class together, and I had seen you around campus a few times, so one night at our beloved Friar Tuck's, I worked up the courage to introduce myself to you. You'd think I would have been too intimidated to march up to a man your size, but I was just so drawn to your ever-smiling eyes and your great, big, old laugh. Our connection was immediate. Our friendship blossomed from then on. You and I soon became what you so lovingly called besties.

One of the things I loved most about you was your kind and loving nature. I soon realized, however, that you could use that irresistible boyish charm of yours for manipulation. I'll never forget those late-night phone calls from you, Nick, and Kevin pleading with me to drive you to McDonalds. In the beginning, you'd call Caroline or Cesca first, but they would usually tell you no. You soon figured out that the one person who could not resist your borderline-desperate pleadings of how hungry you were was me. And when I would walk downstairs with an angry look on my face fully intending to tell you off for how mad I was that you made me get out of bed, all my irritation would melt away when I saw that old smile of yours.

You and I would often talk about your family, and I fell in love with them through your stories. I couldn't stop laughing when you told me stories about you, your brothers, and your hilarious dad. I actually got to meet you oldest brother for the first time last night, and one of the first things I told him was, "You look just like Chris." He immediately corrected me, stating that he had been born first and that it was you who looked like him. Of course, a brother of yours would say something like that. I'd also love hearing you talk about your beautiful mother, and I'd get so thrilled when you would tell me I reminded you of her. I am so happy I've gotten meet her.

You touched so many people's lives in huge ways, but I think it's the little things we're going to miss the most. I know Andrew will never forget the hours you two would spend watching episode after episode of Cops. Cesca will never be able to look back on the time that she went to give you a hug and accidentally bit your nipple without rolling on the floor laughing. Also, I know that even though Caroline pretended to hate giving you back massages, she secretly loved it. And I know that Sarah, Jay, and Haley will always remember that adorable little girl voice you would adopt when you were so excited about something! I could go on listing things for days.

The one thing I'll miss most about you is your great, big, old, embracing hugs. I never felt so safe as when I was wrapped in one of those famous embraces.

Oh, and one more thing. Don't think I've forgotten about your promise to find me a good man, Christopher Gregory. You're not *off the hook. I still expect you to deliver. You've changed the lives of everyone you have ever met for the better. So rest in peace, my sweet friend. And know that we'll be besties forever.*

I love you,
Ellie Trant

friday, march 28, 2008

(PART IV)

TULANE MEDICAL CENTER

The OR at Tulane was nearly empty save for the young man lying on the table and a technician putting away equipment and cleaning up. The room was eerily silent. The bustle of a few hours earlier had left with the last ambulance. There was no longer a sense of urgency in the space. Just Chris.

Airplanes were racing toward Jacksonville and Shreveport. Ambulances had already arrived at Ochsner Hospital only miles across town. The nervous energy that had once filled this room at Tulane was filling operating rooms at other hospitals. Instead of one very busy operating suite, there would soon be five.

Quietly, another technician entered the operating room. He had been sent by the Southern Eye Bank to recover Christopher's corneas. After that, the boy would be at rest. All his earthly tasks were nearly finished. Yet he had another gift to give. The gift of sight.

Somewhere in Louisiana, Chuck and Arlene were blind or nearly so. Only a corneal transplant would return to them that most valuable of the five senses. Corneal transplants aren't usually performed as emergency surgeries though they can be. Usually, the patient is slowly losing sight. They and their ophthalmologists determine a treatment plan that may determine the need for a corneal transplant. Keratoconos and Fuchs' dystrophy are two of the most common conditions that result in corneal blindness. In those cases, a penetrating keratoplasty or an endothelial keratoplasty will be performed. However, emergency trauma can also lead to the need for a corneal transplant. Say an industrial accident, or a chemical spill. Emergencies supersede everything.

When the recipient is gradually losing sight, a transplant is scheduled often weeks in advance. A request is sent to an eye bank specifying the corneal type, the date it's needed, and the age and demographic specifics of the recipient. The goal of eye banks around the United States is to maintain an appropriate number of donor corneas to meet the needs of the requests for transplants. Eye banks don't recover when there is an oversupply of recovered corneas.

Using surgical instruments, the technician carefully began to remove the corneas from Christopher's eyes. He put them in small containers of sterile solution, sealed them, placed ID stickers on the containers, and put the containers in a cooler of ice.

What would Christopher have said if he could have spoken at that moment, if by some miracle he could have been aware of the events that had brought him into that room? What would he have said if he'd known what was happening across the southeastern United States?

"Go ahead," he might say. "Take my eyes. They're of no use to me now. But know that when they gaze upon a little child, I'll be smiling in heaven. Take my heart that someone else might love. With these gifts, my love remains in this world. Take my lungs so someone else might sing. But know that when they sing, I will sing with them."

Before departing, the recovery technician covered Christopher's head with the sheet that lay over the rest of his body. Even then, respect was necessary. The technician with his cooler of sight exited the room. The whole procedure took no more than forty-five minutes. Christopher was alone. The room was silent. The funeral director needed to come to prepare what remained for his funeral. He would be sent home to Maryland, where his parents waited for him.

"Take me home," Christopher would say. "Take me home to my friends and my family I love so dearly. Let them pray over me and cry over me. Let them tell stories about me in my presence. Let them be free to embellish and exaggerate my exploits. Let them offer up toasts and celebrate our too short time together."

His final gift would be taken by the technician to the Southern Eye Bank offices in Metairie. They would be kept safe there until Chuck and Arlene needed them. They would be evaluated for their suitability for transplant. Corneas must be recovered within twenty-four hours. Much as the transplant process has an ischemic time for the organs, that time after blood flow is interrupted, so too do the eyes. Their cell count would be measured. They would still require a visual inspection just like with his thoracic and abdominal organs.

"Say good-bye for me. Good-bye to John and Colin, who I looked up to all my life. Good-bye, Matt, and Mrs. Abdo, and

Steven Hall. Good-bye, Jenn. I'm going to heaven now to be with Nanny and my two grandpops. I'll wait for you all there."

Chuck and Arlene's ophthalmologists would soon send requests for corneas. Perhaps their doctors would perform a penetrating keratoplasty (35 percent of the time) or an endo-thelial keratoplasty (54 percent of the time). Donated corneas have to be used within fourteen days of recovery. Some eye banks cooperate with each other to not let such precious gifts go to waste. In some cases, donated corneas can be sent out of the United States. Their procedures would be scheduled, and in about six weeks, they would have full visual acuity again. Some minimal antibiotics would be all they'd require post-op. Since the corneas don't have a blood supply, there's no need for antirejection drugs. In a matter of weeks, Chuck and Arlene, just like the recipients of Christopher's organs, would live sig-nificantly improved lives.

"Take my eyes," Christopher might say. "Take whatever else of me you can that might make someone else's life worth living. They need it more than I do. It doesn't matter if they're rich or poor, black or white. It doesn't matter how they vote or where they go to church. If they're near or far, take what you need. Take all my tomorrows. I ask nothing in return.

"But when you're done with me, take me home. Take me home and lay me to rest in the soil of the place where I was born. Come and visit me when you can. Say a prayer over my grave. Maybe leave a flower. Look around that place and remember me warmly. I'm sorry I didn't have more time to spend with you. I'm sorry I didn't have more hugs to give, or jokes to tell. But I did my best to make others smile. Even on this, my last day, I did my best."

saturday, march 29, 2008

※

OCHSNER MEDICAL CENTER

The nurses arrived to take Xavier to the operating room. It was after midnight, but it was time. He had already had an IV inserted, and the whole apparatus that was Xavier was wheeled from the ICU to an elevator that would take them down to the second floor OR. Pam walked alongside, the only one in the entourage not dressed in scrubs or in Xavier's case a gown. Her heels clicked as the group made its way to the elevator.

Once on the second floor, Pam gave Xavier a hug, whispered in his ear, and gave him a kiss on his cheek. She was nervous of course watching as her husband was wheeled down the hall, around a corner, and out of view. She made her way to the waiting room. By the time she arrived, Michelle Whitacre and Carl Jackson had departed and rejoined their loved ones in the ICU.

Pam tried to make herself comfortable, but the little sofa wouldn't cooperate. So she sat and studied the status board. She found Xavier's patient ID number; patients were never identified by name. She saw he was "in surgery." Despite having worked the day before, Pam wouldn't sleep until the doctors came to see her after his surgery.

Xavier was conscious when he was wheeled into the operating room. Nervous but relaxed, he was aware of his surroundings. As they entered the OR, he saw someone in surgical garb standing over a tray on a stainless steel table. Everything looked so clean and antiseptic. His gurney was maneuvered next to the operating table. As the figure over the tray came into view again, he saw the contents of the tray. It didn't gleam as did the rest of the room. It was not silver or green, nor did it shine like stainless steel. In fact, it was the only thing in the room that was reddish brown. *Wow. There it is.*

A woman whose face was concealed by a surgical mask inserted a syringe into his IV. "Okay, Mr. Major, I want you to start counting backward from one hundred. Can you do that for me please?"

"Yes ma'am. One hundred, ninety-nine, ninety-eight, ninety-seven ... ninety-six ... ninety ..."

NEW ORLEANS

There was nothing else to do in New Orleans. We'd cleaned out Christopher's room. We'd attended the memorial service. It didn't matter what time or date they occurred, events were how time would be reckoned from then on. We had to go home to plan a funeral. Chris's body would follow. Then the wake. Then the funeral. Then what? News from the transplants we hoped. But that hope lay buried. We had to get our family home.

We were outside our Holiday Inn at four in the morning waiting for a cab. The hotel had called one for us because cabs in New Orleans were scarce at that hour. From the parking garage came a man in a pickup truck. He asked if we needed assistance.

"I heard y'all talking. You folks need a lift somewhere?" he asked.

"We need to go the airport, but thank you," I replied. "They've called a cab for us."

In the predawn darkness, I saw that the man was wearing the olive-drab, camouflaged BDUs of the Louisiana National Guard. He was one of the dozens we'd seen coming in and out of the hotel at all hours. National Guardsmen were working with the New Orleans Police Department, whose ranks had been decimated by Hurricane Katrina.

"I'll be happy to give y'all a lift. I live right out by the airport. It's not out of the way at all."

"Thank you," I replied, "but we'll be okay."

"Okay, folks. Good luck to you."

It almost seemed he knew we were going through a tough time. I'd become more aware of the little acts of kindness people were willing to do when you were vulnerable. Like the time Dr. Posey approached me after delivering the news of Christopher's death. He'd told me he had lost his own son the same way. I had asked him when we still had hope what my life would be like in a year. We were never more so vulnerable than at that moment.

I was touched by Amy and Brant, Christopher's nurses. Whenever we came to Chris's room from dinner, Brant would have ESPN on. He'd change it when we'd arrive, but I think Chris would rather it had stayed on. Brant became a friend of mine when he said after Chris's apnea test, "I wanted to take a breath for him."

Amy cared not only for Chris but for the whole family. Jenn was a wreck. She wasn't sleeping or eating. I asked Amy to tell her to eat something. Amy did more than that. She went to get her something to eat. Just the way she spoke to her was so sweet. I started to notice the little things people did. Things I would have overlooked only days earlier.

OCHSNER MEDICAL CENTER WAITING ROOM

Xavier Major's kidney transplant would happen on Saturday for two reasons. First, while quite sick, he wasn't in imminent danger of death unlike Jorge Bacardi or Nic Whitacre. And second, the ischemic time for kidneys is much greater than it is for lungs or hearts as in Mac Jackson's case. So while there was still a sense of urgency in getting Xavier to the hospital, there was time.

Christopher's remaining kidney wasn't transported directly to Ochsner. After surgery, it was taken to the LOPA offices outside New Orleans and put in a sterile, secure clinical area until the next kidney recipient in line could be identified and located. In this case, Xavier Major.

Pam followed Xavier's progress through the night on the flat-screen monitor. Finally, the line with his number changed color indicating he was out of surgery. Shortly after, a nurse in surgical scrubs came out and took her to a small conference room where she was told that his surgery had gone exactly as planned and had been completely unremarkable. Another testament to the scientific achievement the procedure has become.

OCHSNER MEDICAL CENTER ICU

Mac looked around his room in the ICU and decided he wanted out of bed. He experienced no pain from his surgery, but he felt the need to get out of bed. He wasn't the sedentary type in the first place. The shortness of breath and fatigue he was feeling immediately before his surgery were gone. In their place was an impatience, a desire to get up and move around. So he started to sit up when the ICU nurse spotted him.

"Mr. Jackson, where do you think you're going?"

"I have to get up."

"Not yet, Mr. Jackson. You can get up after Dr. Parrino gets here and says you can get up."

Mac lay back and looked around. The curtain was drawn. He couldn't see out in the hallway. He wondered where Carl was. He wanted to tell him he needed to get up and move around. His mind was still foggy. He couldn't tell what time it was or even if it was day or night. But physically, he felt remarkably well.

JACKSONVILLE

Jorge Bacardi looked around his room and saw an empty chair. On the opposite side of the room was Dr. Keller.

"Don't you ever sleep?" Jorge asked.

"I can sleep later," Keller replied. "This is more important."

Jorge turned his gaze back to the empty chair. He pointed.

"I want to get up," Jorge said. "I want to get up and sit in that chair."

"You will," replied the doctor. "In a short while, you'll be sitting in that chair and then walking down the hall."

heartache

✕

LAUREL, MARYLAND

We came home and started making funeral arrangements. There seemed to be a never-ending parade of visitors. The first to arrive were the Abdo boys. Little Brian just stared at a portrait of Christopher and his brothers on the wall. Shock and disbelief were the prevalent emotions. New waves of tears were shed every time another group of visitors appeared at the door. Word spread through the neighborhood. Friends, neighbors, and relatives started arriving in numbers shortly after we got home from the airport.

The cards and flowers began showing up the next day. It wasn't long before the house smelled like a florist's. The mailbox was stuffed daily for weeks. It didn't seem right to be the center of so much attention. We received flowers and cards from people I'd never expected to hear from. It wasn't so much what they said as much as was that they'd thought to do anything at all. It was nice that people felt the need to say something or do something even if they didn't know what.

I realized that people really are decent. Schools of philosophical thought will debate whether people are inherently good or bad. But in our experience starting particularly in New Orleans, the average person on the street who spots someone in trouble will usually do the honorable thing. Even if they don't know what to do or say, they generally feel the need to respond in a kind fashion.

But at first, it was easy for my anger to cloud my ability to see the kindnesses coming our way. The cards all carried the same sentiment. "You'll Always Have Cherished Memories." "Forever Alive in Your Hearts." At first, I thought, *What crap.* But that was just the bitterness I felt. I was jealous. Jealous of everyone who still had intact families. Jealous of all the parents who'd brag about how well their kids were doing in school and what bright futures they had. I started to resent them. However, I slowly realized many folks were really missing Chris too. Guys I had worked with years before and who had known Chris as a boy called me on the phone in tears. My son obviously had had a lot of friends and had touched many people's lives.

I also came to realize just how much of his life I'd missed. Friends and visitors began sharing stories about Chris. I learned of people and events that were a part of his life I hadn't known about. While the notes gave me some comfort by letting me know how much Christopher had been loved, it made me miss him so much more. I started feeling guilty for being so selfish, guilty for having missed so much of his life.

Our church and neighbors somehow managed to coordinate a dinner schedule. Meals just showed up at the door for more than a month. Sometimes, they'd be dropped off by people we'd known for years. Other times, it would be someone we barely knew. Sometimes, the food would just be left on our doorstep. For a month, we never went to the grocery store, and our freezers were overflowing. We were the recipients of a lot of love and compassion.

And then there was Mary and Brian Abdo. It's worth repeating that Mary was a second mother to Chris. His death rocked the Abdo family. Their kids in particular were hurt. Every day after school, Mary would stop by and help us with the preparations for Christopher's funeral. Unless you've planned the funeral of your child, you can't understand just what it means to lose a son or daughter. It's a bizarre, surreal experience to plan one. In our case, we wanted every detail to be perfect. It was the last thing we'd do for Chris, and we wanted it to be right. We'd never get to help him plan a wedding. We wouldn't even be able to throw him a graduation party.

Mary and Big Brian helped pick the readings and the music. Our pastor at Saint Nicholas was wonderful. We told him we wanted Fr. Frank, a Jesuit who had been at St. Nick's forever, to celebrate the Mass. "You can do whatever you want to do" was all he said. Fr. Ted and Fr. Jim agreed to make the trip from New Orleans to help bury our boy. Fr. Ted would call it a Triple Jesuit Threat.

April 4, 2008, was cold and wet and gray. The previous night's rain had stopped. The wind was chilly as it was still early spring. The car from the funeral home came to pick us up an hour before the funeral so we could be alone with Chris at the funeral home. The chairs were all lined up just as they had been during the wake the night before. The funeral home had been packed. People from work, from the neighborhood, from our families had all jammed into the funeral home. Classmates of Christopher's who were attending college out of state flew in for his funeral. Just when we thought the fire marshal might show up and close the whole thing down due to overcrowding, two vans full of kids arrived from New Orleans.

But now we were alone with Chris. Just his brothers and Grace and I. Little was said. I picked up a chair, placed it next to Chris's casket, and sat. I looked at the mementos that had been placed inside. He was wearing a knit cap with a Baltimore Orioles logo on it. It was there largely to cover up the places on his scalp where he'd been shaved for the ICP monitor. There were photographs and letters. A classmate from Mount Saint Joe gave us his hockey jersey because Chris was such a huge Saint Joe's hockey fan. Chris's uncle Skip had placed a pack of guitar strings inside the casket. And someone had managed to sneak a cell phone in Christopher's shirt pocket.

I turned and looked at John and Colin on the couch across the room. "Nothing changes, guys," I said. "Okay? Nothing's gonna change. We're all gonna be okay." I didn't know if I believed it myself, but I felt I had to offer something as difficult as it was. And that's what was really hard. I didn't know what to say to Grace or John or Colin. I had no experience at this. I wasn't sure if my words provided comfort or if they sounded hollow, or worse, if they sounded childish and naïve. Like the cards in the mailbox, I felt I had to offer something even if I didn't know the right thing to say.

We got in the car again and started to the church. At every intersection, we saw a police car or two with emergency lights on. It dawned on me that they'd been prepositioned there to stop traffic when Christopher's funeral motored to the cemetery. When we got to the church, we were stunned. The parking lots were full. Cars lined both sides of the street up and over the hill and out of sight. We'd been members of our parish for twenty-five years but had never seen that many people making their way into the church. "They'll never fit 'em all inside," I said to Grace. There were not enough seats. People stood in the back of the church and along the sides.

Among the people arriving, I saw two young men in the uniform of the United States Military Academy. They'd been classmates of Chris at Saint Joe's. They were plebes in their first year at West Point, and getting away from the academy hadn't been easy for them. One of their mothers had gotten up, left Baltimore before sunrise, drove to West Point to get them, and drove them to the funeral. After the funeral, she'd take them back. That's what Mount Saint Joe was all about. When one of their classmates lost a parent or God forbid a sibling, the boys would take time off from school and attend the funeral. It meant something. They knew there was great value in just showing up. They knew that standing with their friend in his hour of grief was more important than whatever was supposed to happen in school that day. And so that day, the Mount showed up for Chris. They came from all over the country. They knew they didn't have to say anything. They didn't have to do anything. But in their hearts, each knew he had to show up. Their silent presence thundered.

Among those standing at the back of the church was Gerry Nolan. Every time I turned around, there he was. Like the guys from Saint Joe's, just being there. And that was plenty. God didn't make me do it alone. He sent angels to be with me. Gerry was one of those. As they started down the aisle with Chris's casket, Gerry put his hand over his mouth and began to weep. It was eating him up too.

It was a lovely service. The music was perfect. Fr. Frank, Fr. Ted, and Fr. Jim officiated over a dignified Mass, and maybe Ted's homily had some answer as to why so many people attended his funeral.

"One thing was clear," he said describing Chris at Loyola. "He was surrounded by people who loved him. And how does this happen? By loving people in return. Listening to stories of his time here at Loyola, I'm truly amazed how he touched people in ten short months at Loyola. His open heart, his trust, his arms. It doesn't matter if you live nineteen years or ninety, what's important is the *kind* of life you live."

I was so proud of John when he offered a few thoughts about his brother. He opened with a quote from *The Big Lebowski*, a movie whose lines the boys often quoted to one another. John described the relationship he'd had with Chris. He said Chris was not just a brother who was obligated to a relationship but a friend who wanted to be a part of another's life.

"In his younger years," John said, "he would often imitate my actions and attitudes, and I absolutely could not stand it … Through hearing everyone's stories over the last week, I've found how much Chris still took after me. And I can say that I'm no longer mad about it. In fact, it's just the opposite. I'm so proud to have influenced such a tremendous person as Chris in any way. I wish for only one chance to say to him what I never did in real life but I think he probably knew it anyway. That I love him and that I'm so proud to be part of his life."

Near the end, I had a chance to say something about Chris. I couldn't let the day pass without telling everyone what I remembered about their friend. I told them about hearing a little boy's voice calling me through an open bedroom window and looking outside to see him in a tree just outside. I remembered picking him up from Cub Scouts and on the ride home how proud he was of the horse he'd carved from a block of soap. How I came downstairs to find a little boy staring at the jar containing his lifeless guppy and the tears that rolled down his cheeks. I told them of waking up to Christopher serving us breakfast in bed. Toast, no butter, an apple, a bowl of cereal all served with a big smile. The world would surely be a less happy place without Chris. All our lives were going to be so as well.

And so through the gray day, we made our way to the cemetery. Had it not been for all those police cars, we wouldn't have even extricated ourselves from the church parking lot. But we did. We prayed and cried. The best man from our wedding played "Amazing Grace" on the bagpipes. It was cold, and there was little to be gained by staying. We knew we would be returning to the cemetery a lot in days to come. So we patted the casket farewell and left.

After the funeral, we gathered at our home for food and refreshments. Anyone who asked if there was anything he or she could do was told simply bring along ice and beer. It resulted in what would be known thereafter as the founding of the Polish Republican Army. In the middle of the raucous party, the UPS man showed up with the six large boxes containing Christopher's personal effects from school.

Just as the family headed for home, the neighbors showed up and it started all over. Toasts were made to Chris. And stories were told. And photographs were shared. Chris's friends wanted to visit his bedroom and in doing so "discovered" long-lost items of clothing. And through it all, I wanted to believe he could see us and was smiling his approval. I hoped we had sent him off in style.

When the last guest left, it was just us. And the memories. And then the hurt.

We tried to return to normal lives. Colin went back to New Orleans with the kids in the vans. Grace went back to school and work as did John and I. But it just wasn't the same. I found myself easily distracted. Some days were spent putting out minimal effort and spending hours staring at my computer screen or rereading old e-mails from Chris. We used to run races together, 10ks and 5ks, and I would search the race websites and those of the schools he had attended for photos of him. I actually found a few. I was searching for Chris. Where was my boy? It wasn't right. I called his number a lot just to hear his voice telling me to leave a number. Maybe he'd call me back. Maybe.

Sitting alone in my easy chair, I would reminisce about sitting there only months earlier and Chris would come up behind me and start rubbing my shoulders. It was playful and affectionate, just one of the ways he showed love to people. He wasn't afraid to be physical. And at the end of the shoulder rub, he'd pretend to mess up the hair that was no longer on my bald head. Alone with the memories. God, I missed him so.

Grace often spent time in much the same way. I'm so proud of her that she could finish nursing school. She said the ability to busy herself with school allowed her to separate herself temporarily from her grief. But when she wasn't in school, the grief would catch up with her. Often, she would just sit on the couch where Chris would sit while he watched TV. She would just sit in that same spot and stare off into nothing.

Shortly after the funeral, we received a phone call from Libbie Harrison, the Family Services Coordinator at LOPA and a donor mother as well. Her son, Justin, had died in a freak accident when he was fifteen. His organs were donated, and Libbie has become a tireless advocate for organ donation. It's her job to reach out to donor families to help them through the early months after the loss of their loved ones. When she called the first time, we had a nice, long, three-way meltdown over the phone.

Libbie told us the story of Justin and how she'd become close friends with his organ recipients. She cautioned us that that might never happen to us, and if it did, it wouldn't happen any time soon. She advised us to be prepared if one of Christopher's recipients experienced organ rejection; she'd experienced that herself. But at the same time, she remained very close to Marilyn, the grateful recipient of Justin's heart. Libbie said that as long as she had breath in her lungs, she would continue to talk about Justin and what he had achieved through his death. She told us that because of her relationship with Marilyn, she looked at Justin's passing as having a comma rather than a period at its end. An interesting concept.

We took great comfort in Libbie's call. She left us with some very valuable clues on what we should expect. Of course, what actually happened is another story altogether and my main reason for writing this book. So much of what she told us has remained relevant for so long. Like the part about not allowing Justin to disappear from her family's life. Keep his photograph out, she told us. There was no reason for his memory to have any morbidity attached. "And be certain that when you have grandchildren," she counseled us, "tell them all about their uncle Chris."

Libbie remains a friend to this day. Her kind words were sincere; they were the result of her own experience. They rang true. She told us not to expect too much but that the rawness of our pain would wear off. Slowly, but it would wear off.

However, the future looked pretty dark just then and not very hopeful.

a walk around the marina

✕✕✕

JACKSONVILLE

Jorge had to have someplace to go to recover. After his discharge as an inpatient at St. Luke's, he needed lodging in Jacksonville. The choices are pretty limited for most people. If they have family in the area, fine. Otherwise, they're checking into a hotel or an extended-stay residence. Returning to the Bahamas was out of the question. Bringing *Contigo* to Jacksonville was Jorge's idea. But before he had the hundred-foot yacht brought up from Nassau, he had to run the idea past Dr. Keller. Initially, the doc was skeptical.

"I don't know if that's such a good idea," he told the Bacardis. "You need to be close to the hospital in case something happens, but you need someplace comfortable, not cramped up like a boat."

Bu Dr. Keller had never seen *Contigo* before. He had no idea that a boat could be so comfortable and so shipshape. Her crew of three was fanatical about keeping the vessel clean inside and out. Jorge had the crew bring *Contigo* to Jacksonville for Keller to inspect. It wasn't hard for the doctor to find her when he arrived at the marina. It was the biggest boat in the marina by far.

Leslie and Jorge welcomed him aboard, and Dr. Keller instantly began to nod his approval as he looked around. The spacious *Contigo* had all the comforts of home. That was because it was home to the Bacardis. And that would be every bit as important to Jorge's recovery as his medical care.

The psychological well-being of a transplant patient cannot be overstated. A positive mental outlook goes a long way toward promoting the healing process. Onboard, Jorge could be comfortable, and Leslie, his wife-slash-caregiver could be with him. They'd be near the Mayo Clinic in case they needed to get there in a hurry. It could work.

Jorge hit the floor and was off just nineteen hours after his surgery. He walked the hall outside his room. A few steps at first, then a few more, and a few more. Eventually, he was walking with such regularity that the nurses started calling him Superman, and they posted that as his name on a sign on his room door.

Superman's progress was remarkable. It reached the point that he had to be scolded about going down forbidden corridors. His new nineteen-year-old lungs were giving him a strength he hadn't known for years. The story of Jorge's transplant and incredible recovery circulated around the Mayo community and had doctors stopping by to see with their own eyes the man whose recovery was the talk of the entire medical staff.

He could walk as often as he wished. It was necessary, and it was therapeutic. Even after he was discharged from the hospital, he was told to walk to build his strength and thus protect his gift, his second chance at life. It gave him time to ponder a future once again and to think about his donor.

A week or so after his discharge, Jorge asked Alex to go for a walk. It was a humid, overcast Sunday afternoon. A thunderstorm threatened. Alex was still in awe at his boss's transformation. The man he'd known before his transplant couldn't climb the stairs from his cabin to the salon of his ship, a mere eleven steps, without stopping and gasping; the man post-transplant was climbing them if not effortlessly at least without the difficulty everyone had come to expect. Jorge was shortly taking upward of three walks a day. That day, Jorge asked Alex to come along.

But first, Jorge wanted a quick inspection of *Contigo*, his pride and joy.

"How's the water?" *Contigo* was equipped with two reverse-osmosis devices for making fresh water.

"Full up, Chief. We're good."

"When did you change the filters?"

"Last week," Alex replied.

"When were the tender and jet ski run last?"

"Same as the filters, Chief. Last week."

Jorge is not your typical sailor. He had designed *Contigo* and overseen her construction. He knows every inch of this vessel, and he enjoys spending time aboard her. He was not above performing necessary maintenance chores and did so like a pro. Alex describes his boss as a hands-on owner. And he's as familiar as the waters he sails as he is with his yacht. He's happiest when at sea aboard his home away from home accompanied by his wife, family, and friends.

After a quick inspection, Jorge and Alex started off. Alex watched dark clouds building on the horizon and darkening the sky. It would be a short stroll, he figured. They'd be back before the rain came. They made their way along the dock toward the seawall.

"So how's your recovery progressing?" Alex asked in his thick Bahamian accent. "Progressing" came out as "progressin'" in the deep baritone and comfortable manner of the big man who quickly puts others at ease. "You havin' any issues?"

"I feel fine," Jorge said. His breathing was excellent, he said, and he was adjusting to the medications well. Alex noticed that even he had to quicken his pace to keep up with Jorge's brisk pace. Jorge told Alex about his schedule at Mayo for the coming week. What he was really looking forward to, he joked, was his naptime during the imminent lung bronchoscopy. That brought a laugh from Alex.

As they walked around the marina, Alex was concerned that perhaps Jorge was pushing it. It had only been a few weeks since his transplant. The crew was on eggshells. Transplant patients, particularly lung transplant patients, are susceptible to all kinds of infections. Mold was enemy number one aboard *Contigo*. So the crew spent hours scrubbing, wiping, cleaning, and disinfecting the living space aboard Jorge's boat. Alex must have forgotten about Superman.

"You want to turn back, Chief?" Alex asked. They had made it to the parking lot.

"No." replied Jorge. "I'm fine."

They continued to walk toward the warehouse where smaller ships were kept and repaired. It was perhaps a quarter of a mile from where *Contigo* was docked. Alex looked at the sky as it grew darker.

"You sure you don't want to turn back?"

"No. Let's keep going a little further."

The two knew boats. They liked looking at and talking about them; they liked everything about them. Alex shared Jorge's appreciation for certain types of nautical design. They liked the traditional look. The horizontal lines of a vessel ought to be parallel to the sea and not be rounded like the more contemporary design.

It started to drizzle. Alex looked back to *Contigo* and wondered if they could make it back before getting wet. "Uh-oh," Alex said as he looked west and saw the deluge already engulfing *Contigo*.

The two made a beeline for the dry-storage hangar. They entered just as the rain began pelting the massive tin roof. They looked around the building like two kids in a toy store at the vessels stored there. Ships were stacked three and four high as though in a supermarket. Two marina employees took notice of the visitors and, as southerners are known to do, sauntered over and struck up a friendly conversation.

"You fellas from that yacht at the end of the dock?" asked one motioning to Alex's shirt. *Contigo* was written on the left breast of the shirt.

"Yes we are," replied Jorge smiling at the fact that his pride and joy had been noticed. *Contigo* was likely the biggest ship by a factor of two or three that had ever been to that marina.

"What brings y'all to town?" the man asked. "How long you figure to be stayin'?"

"Well, we live in Nassau. I'm a patient over at the Mayo Clinic. I've just undergone a double lung transplant, and I suspect we'll be here until my doctors tell me I can go home." Jorge said. "Which I hope will be fairly soon but most likely not for a few more weeks."

They listened in rapt attention as Jorge described his condition and the events that led up to his transplant. They asked lots of questions about *Contigo* as well—her design and construction, her power plant and draft and handling. They were equally impressed to learn that Jorge had designed the big boat, which was the talk of the marina. The conversation alternated between bow thrusters and antirejection medicines.

When the conversation thinned out, the marina employees returned to their tasks. "Nice chattin' with ya," the last one said as he drifted away.

The rain hadn't let up. Jorge walked up to the huge double doors and looked out over the marina. Alex watched the older man simply taking in the scene, the rain, and life in general. In that quiet respite provided by rain, Alex experienced one of those moments that creep up on us when we're not in the least looking for them.

There was someone who only a few weeks before couldn't climb the eleven steps from his bedroom to the salon deck of the boat without stopping halfway and gasping for breath. Who went everywhere carrying a portable oxygen machine. Who had given up the simple pleasures of walking for a motorized Segway. Who had been dying.

Alex had been a witness to the slow-motion tragedy that seemed to be the end of Jorge's life. He'd had to bear witness to the hell that Leslie had had to endure. Watching her deal with adversity yet never allowing herself to give in to self-pity or disillusionment. But the moment meant so much more to Alex. Jorge really was a good man. Kind, decent, generous. Sure, he liked bragging about his boat, but as they say, it ain't braggin' once you do it. And besides that, he wasn't obnoxious about it.

Jorge was more than just Alex's boss. The two had grown fond of one another. A few weeks before, Jorge was dying and Leslie was facing life as a widow. The entire extended family faced uncertainty. And then there he was with a new lease on life and enjoying the simple pleasure of a spring rain shower in his element—among boats. Alex felt his throat tighten. His eyes watered. When he sniffled, Jorge turned and saw that the big man had tears rolling down his cheeks. If anyone deserved a second chance, Alex thought, it was the man standing before him.

"What's wrong with you?" Jorge asked.

"Nothing," Alex replied. "Nothing at all."

The rain let up after forty minutes or so. The two left the warehouse and walked to the end of the marina; they had made a complete semicircle of several hundred yards and were standing directly across the water from their starting point.

"You know somthin', Chief," Alex said, "do you realize how far we just walked? Do you realize you've never walked this far before and you did it without any effort at all?"

Jorge just smiled. It was a quiet, satisfied smile. They turned back, and their discussion drifted to the transplant and to his donor. The young man was never far from Jorge's mind. He had even taken to talking to the mysterious young man who was breathing with him. One day out of the blue, he and Leslie decided his donor needed a name. He had waited ten months for his donor to come along, but all he knew about him was that he'd been nineteen when a medical catastrophe had robbed him of his life and allowed him to save Jorge's. Jorge decided that Gabriel was an appropriate name. Gabriel the archangel. The angel who has a place in nearly every major religion. Gabriel sounded right. It fit.

"I wonder who Gabriel was," Jorge said. "I wonder what kind of guy he was."

"I wonder too," responded Alex.

"He was young, I know that. The way I feel right now, I suspect he took care of himself too."

"Yeah. Most likely."

"I think of him a lot. I wonder who he was. What kind of life did he live?"

Every day when he woke, one of his first thoughts was about his donor. *Who was he? How is his family doing? Are they okay?* He wanted to know. He needed to know. This was way beyond curiosity. Jorge understood that his destiny had been secured at a high cost paid for by an anonymous young man and his family. And that knowledge weighed on Jorge's conscience like a yoke. He had to know. *Who was he? Is his family okay?*

When Jorge's eyes opened with each dawn, he thought, *I'm alive.* He became aware that there was another piece to that statement. *I'm alive, but ...* And that incompleteness gnawed at him. Not because there was anything at all malicious in that incompleteness, just the opposite. It gnawed at him from a place of goodness, a place of kindness, a place of generosity. The other half of Jorge's waking every morning knocked on the door of his spirit. His nagging curiosity was his own goodness begging to be released.

The resentment was gone. The bitterness and hardness were softening. He could feel it. Resentment was being forced out of his heart by the gratitude he felt every time he looked at his beautiful wife. With every phone call from a niece or nephew, with every note from a friend, with every kiss from Leslie, he could feel his heart swell with thanksgiving. But he had to know. He had to find his donor's family.

Jorge was already mentally formulating the letter that he would write to his donor's parents. The support group at Mayo was encouraging him to do it. As were Dr. Keller and Leslie. It was another affirmation to Jorge that the transplant had been the right choice. He knew he'd take seriously the responsibility to respect and honor his donor. If that meant taking care of the physical gift, he'd certainly do that. But that wasn't enough for Jorge. Maybe that's why Alex had been moved to tears; he knew

Jorge would of course respect his gift but would also acknowledge it. That's why he was so curious about Gabriel.

But first, he had to heal physically, though he was well on his
way to that. Jorge was committed and focused and motivated to
get better and then give something back. The two returned to
Contigo and strolled down the dock.

"That," said Jorge, "was a hell of a walk."

spearfishing

Every summer, the Bacardi clan gathers in the Bahamas for a little spearfishing. Jorge and his brothers will take their ships to a secret lobstering spot and tie up together. The kids will giggle and splash, the men will tell stories and swap lies, and the women will admire the scene with satisfaction. It's a time for family and love. It is a time of relaxation and renewal. A time to reaffirm what is important in life. In 2008, this was especially important. Tio Jorge was there.

As practiced by the Bacardi clan, the art of spearfishing is still a primitive skill. The diver wears a snorkel, mask, and fins. The spear is a long rod inserted through a tube with a point at one end. A length of rubber tubing must be drawn back to launch the spear. It's like a slingshot. Divers float on the surface until they spy a likely hiding place for crustaceans. They take a deep breath and dive for the bottom. The tubing is drawn back, the spear released, and if the diver's aim is true, the lobster is skewered. It's hunting, or fishing, in its purest form.

And so it was in the summer of 2008. Jorge was alive and well on the way to a full recovery. And his family was as thankful that he could be with them. They had found a particularly promising spot. It was naptime. Jorge was in the cockpit, the aftmost part of the boat and closest to the water speaking with Alex, the boat's captain. Sonia, Joy Tobin, and Leslie were seated around the table on salon deck chatting about nieces and nephews and schools. The sun was bright, but the sun canopy provided them with shade. Jorge looked out over the water. "Hey Alex," he said.

"Yes, Chief," the big man replied.

"Get me some fins," Jorge whispered. "And a mask."

"Excuse me?" Alex replied. The hair rose on the back of his neck.

"Some fins. Get me some fins. And a mask." Jorge said it quietly so as not to be overheard by the women.

Alex felt powerless to stop what was about to happen. But he was in on the secret, and it thrilled him. He slowly retrieved a set of fins and a mask and placed them on the swimming platform next to Jorge. He put a spear and sling down too. He knew he was risking the full wrath of Mrs. Bacardi. All of the Mrs. Bacardis.

The lazy afternoon quiet was suddenly disturbed by the sound of a splash that drew everyone's attention. It's its own unique alarm. The children were all playing inside or asleep and thus accounted for. But the splash meant someone had just gone into the water. The women raced to the rail to see who had gone in fearing it might not have been on purpose. "Who was that?" they asked in unison.

Alerted by the splash, the chairs sliding on the deck, and the urgency in the voices, First Mate Dwight Miller suddenly appeared on deck. Alex stepped from the cockpit out onto the swimming platform and was staring into the water. Dwight's eyes snapped to Alex's. Tension pervaded the boat. Seconds that seemed like minutes went by.

"Alex?" called Leslie.

Alex tried to ignore her. But he knew that would be futile.

"Aaaaleeeeex!"

"Yes, boss lady?" A response calculated to put her at ease. Alex called Mrs. Bacardi boss lady under only the most private, informal circumstances.

"Aaaaaleeeex? Who was that?"

The water broke. The women gasped collectively. "Oh my God!"

Tears began to flow. Tears prompted by laughter. No tragedy at sea. Just the opposite. Just off the stern of *Contigo* emerged the cause of all the commotion. Four months after his transplant, Jorge was raising his hands out of the water. Shouts of jubilation went up. In one hand was the sling and in the other was the spear with not one but three lobsters on it. In between the raised arms was the huge grin on Jorge Bacardi's face.

gabriel's message

>✕✕⟨

"Take some time for yourselves. Get away and forget about things for a little bit." That was the advice we received after the funeral. As if getting away or forgetting anything were possible. The entire family was in school. Our scholastic commitments provided some welcome distraction but little more.

I admired Grace, John, and Colin for being able to get back into their schoolwork. I couldn't focus. I was taking one class, and I couldn't keep my head on straight. The only commitment I had was a twenty-five-page term paper, but I had to ask my professor for an incomplete on it. That was in April. It took me until September to finish it.

We eventually made it to the beach, but it was July before we did, and Kevin Abdo came with us. It was the worst time ever. As much as we welcomed Kevin's presence, we were all miserable. There's a chair in the living room of the beach house Grace's family owns. Chris had slept in it when he broke his collarbone in high school. He couldn't sleep lying down because of the discomfort. Looking at the chair was a constant reminder of him. At some times, I couldn't bear to look at it. At other times, I couldn't pull myself away from it.

One night, Grace, Kevin, and I went to play miniature golf. Despite the laughing and joking, I was miserable. Smiling on the outside but dying on the inside. Kevin tried so hard to make us feel better. And I knew losing Chris was absolutely eating him up. He was looking for us to help pick him up also. We all looked to each other clinging desperately to some connection to Chris. The grief was unbearable. It was like a car crash. Nobody's hurt at first, but then the pain starts after a day or so and just gets worse and worse.

In New Orleans, we were in shock, and during the funeral, we were numb. We couldn't quite process what was happening to us. And then weeks later, it was starting to sink in. Everything was a reminder of Chris. Songs on the radio. Television shows. The never-ending flood of sympathy cards that clogged our mailbox. All these things were constant reminders of our loss. Chris was gone from our lives. In hindsight, that night was the lowest point of my life.

It's all very raw. It's unlike anything you've ever felt before, and it gets stronger and stronger until sometimes you can't concentrate on anything else except how much it hurts. Eventually, you're left with a deep, dull ache that regardless of however else you feel never goes away. Slowly and surely, I felt myself slipping away into despair. Then on a Friday, the phone rang at the beach. It was John.

"Hey. A Sally Gentry from LOPA called. They have a letter from one of Chris's organ recipients. She wants to know if you want it."

We were stunned. We remembered what Libbie Harrison had told us. "Don't expect to hear from anyone," she'd said. "If they do contact you, it may not be for a couple of years."

It was a new chapter in our lives. The folks at LOPA had lowered our expectations about receiving any communication from Chris's organ recipients. As to the kind of contact that might happen, well, we'd been advised not to expect too much. The recipients had their own issues to sort out. Maybe some guilt to work through. They may just not be up to writing. And of course, there would be complete anonymity. No last names. No phone numbers. No addresses. Still, only three months after burying Chris, we had something to look forward to.

John gave us Sally's number, and we called her immediately. It was a Friday. I suggested a next-day service; we'd have it by noon Saturday. Grace said put it in the mail. That would give us time to prepare and extend the feeling of anticipation. Wow. Only three months. It was from Jorge. *He'd gotten Christopher's lungs, right?* He was in the Virgin Islands we were told. *I wonder if we'll get to meet him. Maybe we could visit him. Maybe we could meet his family. Wait. Did he have a family?* LOPA's first letter said he was divorced. We tried to remain cool and composed on the outside, but each of us tried to keep up with our minds running at a hundred miles per hour.

The letter was waiting for us when we got home. Grace had been right about having it snail mailed. In part, it was like not wanting to rush the anticipation before Christmas. It also allowed us to prepare emotionally. It didn't matter. We slowly opened the envelope together as if it were a long-awaited gift. We carefully unfolded the pages and read them silently together. It began,

> To _____ and his family: I am the recipient of a gift from your son that is beyond repayment.

Like the name in the salutation, the next two and half lines were obliterated by black magic marker and pasted over with whiteout.

> I cannot possibly imagine the grief caused by your loss, and certainly there are no words anyone can say or write that could extinguish that pain. Nevertheless, you have shared with me the grandest gift I will ever receive— the gift of life.

We felt an instant connection to the writer. We held each other and reached for a box of tissues. Our tears were already flowing.

> It is what will allow me to carry on a legacy in your son's memory and honor. My greatly improved health will afford me the luxury of reaching out to help others less fortunate, and I have already begun this endeavor.

The letter had clearly been penned by a mature, caring individual. And to think he had already committed to helping others is something Chris would surely have approved of.

> My health condition is genetic, so I have had problems since birth, and although at a disadvantage to most other individuals healthier than me, I never allowed myself to be less than I could be.

How so very much like Chris.

> Up until a few years ago when my condition began to deteriorate, I had always been a very active person enjoying tennis, swimming, fishing, and many other sports and activities, and I hope to excel in his honor. Indeed he has become literally a wondrous, vital part of me.

I don't know if you will ever receive this letter, but if you do, please know in your heart that your magnificent generosity is infinitely appreciated as is your compassion and high regard for human life.

In the hope that this letter may bring you some comfort, I am and remain gratefully,

One of your son's survivors.

By the time we finished reading, we were basket cases. I buried my face in Grace's lap and sobbed uncontrollably. We read and reread the letter trying to get a sense of its wonderful, compassionate author. The letter itself was handwritten in blue ink. Obviously much thought and care had gone into its crafting. It was dated June 20, 2008, less than three months after Chris had died. Someone had received his lifesaving lungs. I kept sobbing and calling Chris's name. Crushed by the loss of our dear son yet filled with pride at what he had accomplished. My son had saved this man's life, and his gift was being acknowledged by the one person who appreciated it the most. The one person whose gratitude was genuine beyond doubt. Who understood what had been at stake. Life and death. Who understood that his triumph had been born of our defeat. Who reached out with love and gratitude to the family of the boy who had made it all possible. In hindsight, the gesture and its timing can only be described as magnificent.

What made this letter immediately so special was that it represented at that time the only tangible connection we had to Christopher. The only thing that we could touch that was Chris. Not the Christopher of the past. Not the Christopher we'd buried a few months earlier. No. This letter was Christopher in the present. Still in the world. Still making people smile.

We were curious. What could have been so problematic with those first few lines that UNOS felt the need to redact them? The CIA couldn't have done a better job of obscuring those lines. Our curiosity was piqued. I held the letter up to the light. I held it under a light. I held it up to the sun … not so smart. Nothing would reveal the words some anonymous bureaucrat had felt it better to hide. Who was UNOS protecting? Were they protecting us or Jorge?

We'd learned that the transplant community had established protocols for allowing contact between recipients and donor families. But we were already way ahead in the dues-paying category. We wanted to know of Chris's organ recipients. We needed to know about them. We had earned the privilege of knowing as long as they were willing to open up to us. The redacted lines in this first letter were obviously a window into some greater understanding. But it would be months before they were revealed to us.

breaking the ice

EXUMAS, BAHAMAS

It was another perfect day in the Bahamas. Jorge was sitting at his desk in the salon aboard *Contigo*. It was months after his transplant, and he was feeling much better. They had taken a stack of mail with them, and as Jorge sorted through it, he came across an envelope from the Mayo Clinic. *Another bill.* He placed the envelope on top of a stack of bills and invoices he'd get to later. He looked outside and admired Leslie, who was seated at the table working a crossword puzzle. Life was good. He'd never felt better.

When he turned his attention to the stack of bills, he again came across the envelope from the Mayo Clinic. *Organ transplants aren't cheap*, he thought. As he started to extract the envelope's contents, a small piece of paper fell to the deck. *A business card perhaps?* He bent over to pick it up. Before his hand could reach it, his heart stopped. The face of a young man gazed at him. Short, brown hair, green eyes, and just the trace of a smile behind closed lips. Jorge knew instantly who it was. The envelope from Mayo wasn't an invoice. His throat constricted, and his face went numb. Leslie entered the salon and saw him crying.

"What's wrong, Rabs?"

Jorge handed her the photograph. She covered her mouth.

"It's him," was all Jorge could say.

Leslie took the photo from Jorge and was suddenly Leslie awash in tears. Perhaps their emotions were magnified by the fact that they'd never had children. Immediately connected to this young man they'd named Gabriel, they cherished him even for the nineteen years he had lived before they knew of him.

Maybe Jorge's doubts and hesitation about accepting a lung transplant returned. Maybe the old misgivings had returned. Maybe even a little guilt. But there was something in that face. Something in the eyes of the young man peering back from the photograph in their hands that gripped them both. In an instant they were connected. Not just to the faceless Gabriel to whom they had grown attached but to another human being. The gravity of that young man's sacrifice hit Jorge, and he was thunderstruck. He always knew, but now he *knew*.

They looked at the envelope and the letter still inside. They read it. It was from the boy's mother. His name was Christopher, she explained. He'd been a college freshman when he died suddenly and unexpectedly. She described Christopher as a warm, generous person with a big heart. He was an Eagle Scout and a lifeguard. He ran cross-country in high school and enjoyed playing guitar. Jorge looked deep into the eyes of the young man in the photograph and was overcome by the emotion and gratitude that swept over him. Gabriel had a face and a name. Christopher.

Jorge's mind was suddenly clouded with a rush of emotions and memories. All the doubts and the hopes of the past two years enveloped him. *Should I do it or not? I'm too old. It won't work. Why should I? Someone else is more deserving. Okay, I'll do it. I'm on the list. I'm waiting. I'm not getting better. I'm going to die. Wait. There's a call. Never mind. Someone else's turn. Wait. There's another call. It's my turn! God, I hope this works. I'm awake. I'm alive. Oh my God, I'm alive. Who was my donor? He was young. He had a family. What was his name? I'll call him Gabriel. I'm getting better. I'm getting stronger. The mail's here. It's just a bill. I wonder how much they want this ... Oh my God. It's him.*

LAUREL, MARYLAND

As the months went by, we continued to watch the mailbox. Any news from anyone would be as close to Chris as we could get. There was a huge hole in our hearts, and we ached for any consolation. Often, these moments came through personal contacts. Grace would get a message from one of Chris's friends through Facebook or e-mail. These little moments were like God saying, "Here, I have something for you."

Grace had responded to Chris's recipient with some details about Chris. That he liked to camp and generally be outdoors, that he was a runner and a lifeguard. She included a picture of Chris, a graduation photo from Mount Saint Joseph.

In October, we received a response this time from Leslie and without redactions.

> Oh my! What a handsome young man and what warmth his beautiful face shows. Please know that the face now wearing

Christopher's lungs is also very handsome, and carries a warm and generous heart as well.
Your generosity in writing back to us what must have been the most difficult letter of your lives told us how brave and strong Christopher must have been.

She couldn't have been more correct. Leslie wrote that Jorge had two brothers and a sister. Though he was the youngest, he took it upon himself to look after everyone. How like Christopher.

He is the happiest when he is on the water whether he is line fishing, spearfishing, water skiing or snorkeling. If he is not on the water, then put a computer in his hands, and he will make it talk to you.

We noted the striking similarities. Jorge enjoyed being outdoors as had Chris. Chris would have lived outside if Grace would have let him. Chris had spent a summer with his Venture Crew learning to sail on the Chesapeake Bay. He was also a lifeguard at Boy Scout camp during the summers. Chris and Jorge were both good with computers. Chris had been our in-house IT guy. While Jorge liked to sing, Chris enjoyed playing guitar. These two guys had more in common than what fate and modern medicine had done to bring them together.

Please know that as we rejoice in our gift, we grieve with you in your loss. Every day I put my arms around Jorge and thank Christopher for his gift. He will never be lonely or lack love.

That did it. I was a basket case again. How could she have known that what I prayed for daily was that Chris would be with God? I was his father, and I was still responsible for him. How could they know that I prayed he was okay, that he wouldn't be alone or afraid or forgotten? That he would still be loved? And here it was in black and white. Written in the words of a stranger. "He will never be lonely or lack love."

I believe that Christopher's legacy will live on in a manner that I think he would be proud of.

Warmly,

Leslie—Jorge's wife

Who were these people? What compassion they were able to express through their correspondence! We felt a link developing even at that early stage. We just knew they were genuine people. Their words conveyed a maturity and care that comes through the testing of one's self through difficulty. It was obvious that they loved our son. They'd never known him and yet they loved him. They were grateful for Chris's gift, and they had opened their lives to him. He had found a new home.

But what had been in those first lines of Jorge's letter that UNOS had felt needed censoring? Every month or so, I made another effort to read the missing passages. I would share the letter with family and friends. It became an instant heirloom. After reading it, everyone would look oddly at the letter, carefully hold it at arm's length, and hold it up to a light hoping to discern the passage. Nothing.

It took months, but the answer finally came in a most unusual turn of events.

Once you stand at the intersection of life and death—and especially if you end up on the wrong corner—it's amazing to see just how quickly and radically your priorities change. Suddenly, what was once of great significance melts into the trivial. What used to pass for newsworthy was often meaningless. At least to me. What passed for tragic in some folks' lives just didn't register in mine. I found myself really annoyed by anyone trying to achieve what I called victim status. I'd be watching TV and becoming increasingly annoyed when I sensed that was what people were trying to do. "Yeah?" I'd say. "Pick out a casket for your kid and tell me how bad you got it." It was easy to get angry or to feel sorry for myself. But at the same time, I found I could turn my tragedy into a strength.

Every day, I'd drive to work and slowly pass Christopher's grave. The wooden cross his friends had made for him still marked where he rested. And so no matter what lay ahead for the rest of the day, the worst part of it would be already behind me. If the boss was having a bad day, so what? I'd just driven past the cemetery where my son was buried. *Not making the numbers this month? Really? Not happy with one of my decisions and want to chew my ass about it? Bring a lunch, pal, 'cause it doesn't matter anymore.* I just didn't have time for that.

What did prove difficult and still does was the simple question, "So how many kids do you have?" As I was leaving a Mount Saint Joseph event one evening months after Chris had died, someone asked me, "So are you an alum or a dad?"

"A dad. My son went to school here."

"Oh, so he graduated. What year?"

"Two thousand and seven," I replied.

"Where's he now?"

I froze. I didn't know how to answer. *Not here. Not now.* I hadn't seen it coming. I couldn't respond.

It took me a while to learn to answer that question. It always started out innocently enough but inevitably led to an awkward moment. What was the right answer? He was in heaven? In the cemetery? I still get uncomfortable especially at work when introductions are being made that include family history. People ask, you start to tell them about your child who died, and you watch them turn and walk away.

It took me a while to learn how to answer. We learned to understand the situation. When we'd be asked, "How are you doing?" we had to discern whether the questioner wanted to know how we were doing emotionally with the loss of our son or asking the question with more of a rhetorical intent. At times, that was hard to figure out. And when we tried to answer the question truthfully with "Actually, not too well," it inevitably led to uncomfortable moments.

I stopped by the chaplain's office at Georgetown and met Fr. Tim Godfrey, a Jesuit and a friend of Fr. Jim Caime. I didn't know why I was there or what I was looking for. I guess I just wanted somebody new to talk to. Tim opened the door to his office and said he'd been expecting me.

"Really?" I asked.

"Jim Caime told me about you. He said you might stop by."

"Caime's a good man," I said.

I told Fr. Tim what had transpired in New Orleans. I explained that Chris was my son, and I was responsible for him, and he was dead. And I felt there was nothing I could do to save his life but maybe should have tried harder. Maybe I should have prayed harder. I needed to know he was okay. But I couldn't. And it was all too late.

I told Fr. Tim about standing at the end of my driveway and looking up and down the street. Staring at the spots where Chris would shoot baskets or practice flipping his skateboard. I'd look up and down the street hoping maybe to catch a glimpse of him. Standing in the street, I asked Chris all the time, "Are you okay, son? I'm still here. I'm still your dad, and I love you. Please let me know you're okay."

With tears in my eyes, I told the priest I no longer feared dying or my own mortality. Not that I was suicidal. I wasn't. Rather, it was as if I was trying to figure out how much time I had left on earth and what waited for me after I died. And what heaven might be like. And what forever would feel like. I'd scare myself thinking about it. But no more. Chris had taken that fear away from me.

Fr. Tim handed me a box of tissues. "Perhaps that feeling you have in heart about not fearing death. Maybe that's Chris telling you he's okay."

Christopher soon became conspicuous by his absence. Thanksgiving, a day commemorating gratitude, is traditionally spent celebrating with family and friends. For us, it meant a continuing emotional descent. Christmas lights and store decorations and 24/7 Christmas music on the radio. It had an effect opposite of what it had had in years past. It seemed the prettier the music, the sadder the mood. Chris's girlfriend, Jenn, came up from New Orleans that first year. What a special treat. Everyone was so happy to see her and to get to know her. It was so sad to know that except for Colin and Matt Nolan, nobody had known her before Chris had died.

I drove her to the airport on Saturday after Thanksgiving. As we said farewell, I gave her Chris's pledge pin I'd been carrying in my pocket ever since we cleaned out his dorm room. She held it tightly in her hands and said, "I have something for you as well." She opened her purse, dug into her wallet, and handed me Christopher's student ID. We had tears in our eyes as we looked at our newfound treasures. "My dad always told me that a gift isn't a gift unless it hurts to give it away," she said. *How true*, I thought.

That first Christmas without him was like really low key. No tree, no decorations. We put an electric candle in the window of his bedroom. John plugged it in every night. Chris's bedroom was left just as it was the last time he'd slept in it—at Christmas the year before. We hadn't picked up his clothes or changed his sheets. We dusted some and maybe vacuumed, but everything else remained right where he'd left it. Just in case.

I felt bad for John and Colin because I knew they wanted to celebrate the holidays, but Grace and I just didn't have the energy for it. We did start a tradition of celebrating his birthday. Since it was on December 13, we felt it appropriate to have a birthday party of sorts. That first year, Fr. Frank, he of the Triple Jesuit Threat who had buried Chris, came to the house and said a Mass. A lot of our friends and family attended, and it did make for a nice day. But for me, the day was overshadowed by the fact Chris wasn't there.

Grace suggested we attend Christmas Eve Mass at St. Mary's, where all the boys had gone to grade school. All of Christopher's friends would be there. Matt and Kevin Nolan were going to join all the Abdos as part of the youth choir. Grace said all the kids our boys had grown up with would likely be there, especially those who'd gone away to college.

I sat next to Mo Hasson. The music was beautiful. Too beautiful. As the choir sang "Silent Night," I sat with my face buried in my hands and cried like a baby. On Christmas Eve. A grown man crying like a baby, sitting next to Chris's friends. I didn't know if it could get any worse.

We ran into Gabe Scasino at the fall play at Mount Saint Joseph. It was October 2008, and we felt close to Chris whenever we visited the school. It was odd, but we could feel close to him by being in the same space and seeing the same sights that he had. Gabe had been Chris's Spanish teacher, and they had become good friends. Gabe stopped by where Grace and I were sitting during the intermission and reintroduced himself. He is a very likeable young man who is now a Franciscan friar, but in 2008, he had left Mount Saint Joe and was teaching in a Washington, DC public school. Gabe said he was perhaps looking for a job change, and I told him of the constant need for job counselors at a nonprofit I was involved with. I told Gabe that I thought he'd be a good fit and that I'd mention his name to the executive director when I next met with her. As it turned out, that wouldn't be for another couple of months.

Those couple of months passed quickly enough, and in February 2009, Gabe was very much on my mind as I would attend a meeting at Jubilee Jobs, the nonprofit I had mentioned to Gabe, the next day. I had made a note to myself to mention his name at that meeting. I was home alone one night and happened to be watching a movie in which the main character, a spy, sees his target scribble a note and then takes the notepad and gently shades the next page with the side of a pencil. The result is that the spy can read the impression of the bad guy's writing. *Hmmm.*

I got the letter, covered it with a piece of tracing paper, and stroked a pencil back and forth like a crayon on a coloring book. Nothing. I tried it again just as I'd seen in the movie but a little harder. Nothing. I was about to put the letter away again. But I wanted to find out what was written on that page. Who was the addressee of this priceless, sentimental document that had become so important to us?

Looking very carefully at the second piece of tracing paper, I noticed there were words there, but they were very faint. Perhaps a magnifying glass would help. Nope. I was no longer frustrated. I was now obsessed. A man on a mission. "Today's the day," I said aloud. Maybe if I turned the light up from behind the paper. I retrieved a high-powered flashlight and held it up behind the page. Nothing. I looked at it under the flashlight and through the magnifying glass. I discovered that if I moved the flashlight ever so slowly, the shadows ... of the indentations ... of the blacked-out writing began to come into view. And if I held the flashlight at just the right angle and kept the magnifying glass at just the right distance ...

It took several minutes to manipulate the light, magnifying glass, and the paper just so. But the words slowly came into focus. I wrote them down one by one. My heart started racing; I realized this was actually going to work. Blood rushed to my face. A lump was developing in my throat. I began to feel warm and tingly as the words were revealed. Once I grasped their significance, I was overwhelmed with emotion and began to weep.

To Gabriel and his family:

I am the recipient of a gift from your son that is beyond repayment. Since I do not know his real name, I have chosen to refer to him as Gabriel after the archangel known as the angel of the incarnation and of consolation.

I called out Christopher's name as I cried. I was alone in the house. There was no one with whom I could share this revelation. "My boy! My boy!" I cried over and over. The angel of the incarnation and of consolation. I was overwhelmed with emotion. Incarnation, the good news told by Gabriel to the Virgin Mary that she would bear the son of God. Birth. Incarnation. Death. Consolation. So many thoughts spun around in my head. Chris as Gabriel. Chris as an angel. It was something more than a metaphor. It was real. Gabriel told Mary, "Do not be afraid." Here was same message being delivered to us. Do not be afraid.

Months earlier as I watched my son dying in a hospital, I put all my eggs in one basket. I placed all my faith in the first lesson I'd ever learned way back in Sunday school as a kindergartner—that while the body dies, the soul lives forever. It was a concept reinforced by Fr. Jim when he suggested to me that life changes rather than ends. And here was affirmation. Someone who had never met Chris now knew him and called to him as an angel. Chris had taken on a new life in a new form.

Hearing Chris called an angel gave us validation he was in heaven. God had indeed made my son an angel and given him new life. I had held that letter in my possession for nine months. For nine months, I didn't know what it was saying. But here was its true meaning. It was telling me, "Do not be afraid." Where once there was nothing but darkness was now hope.

december 22, 2008

✕✕✕

SLIDELL, LOUISIANA

On December 22, 2008, Nic Whitacre was feeling great. He was nearly nine months post-transplant. His health had steadily improved. He was no longer diabetic thanks to the insulin his new pancreas was producing. His kidney function was normal as well. Every morning, Nic woke up, went to the bathroom, took a pee, and smiled. *It's going to be a good day,* he'd tell himself.

The gastroparesis no longer left him retching. His blood vessels were no longer brittle. And perhaps most miraculous of all was that his once-constant neuropathy, the funny bone tingling in his arms and legs was gone. The absence of neuropathy left his doctors completely baffled. Thanks to his donor and some excellent surgeons, Nic was literally a new man.

He had been pondering his circumstances and what to do with his new chance at life. He was grateful for the love of a beautiful woman. Michelle had stood by him and cared for him and nursed him and cried for him. And now, he had the chance to repay her love and kindness. His parents, family, and friends had stood by him during some very difficult years. Countless prayers had been said on his behalf, and finally, Nic could look forward to many years in the company of his loved ones.

Always an entrepreneur, Nic was forever thinking ahead. Ahead to the next opportunity, the next project. It was just part of his nature. A born salesman, he had always maintained his optimism even when he was at his sickest. He was ready to get involved in the world again. He was wrestling with ideas about advocacy. How could he be a more active participant in the miracle that had saved his life? How could he enable others in the lifesaving miracle he had experienced? He thought about the nurses who had cared for him. He had been particularly impressed with one special nurse at Ochsner who he felt set the perfect example of what a nurse should be. He had explored the nursing program at Delgado Community College. He talked to the counselors there and kicked around several ideas about how to put his gratitude into action.

He'd survived five seconds at a time as his grandmother had told him he should. But no longer. He could look beyond the next five seconds. Even beyond the next five hours. He could allow himself to think about his future with Michelle and family and friends. On December 22, 2008, Nic went to bed that night a grateful, happy man.

In a dream that night, he was visited by a young man. The details were a little difficult to discern, but it was clearly a young man. Tall and handsome with close-cropped, brown hair. "Nic," the vision told him, "you gotta work with college kids. Get them to become organ donors. You have to start a movement. Call it the HERO Movement. Help Everyone Receive Organs."

Everyone dreams. Some leave us terrified or confused. Others give us direction and motivation. When Nic woke the next morning, he realized he had never been more certain of anything.

He was uncertain what the movement would accomplish. He didn't have a clue exactly what would be involved, but he trusted his experience and instincts as a salesman. It was a beginning, and the mechanics of the advocacy initiative would be developed over time. But Nic was certain of one thing. If the H-E-R-O Movement served to register only one donor who saved only one life, it would be worth the effort.

Among the first people he discussed the H-E-R-O Movement with was the student affairs staff at Delgado. They agreed that perhaps Nic could make a presentation on campus and actually register students to be organ donors. Nic could tell his story and explain the impact that one person could have on the world by registering. The concept was simple. Every person Nic could touch would register and then tell his or her friends to do the same. The effect would be a chain of heros. As more and more people told their friends, their efforts would be fueled when real-life stories of actual donations became part of the narrative. He was on a mission. He was going to save lives and at the same time honor the unknown hero who had saved his.

Like Jorge Bacardi, Nic had been thinking a lot about his donor, but he was uncertain about what to say. *What are the right words?* Writing to a donor family involves no small degree of emotional risk. Transplant patients are often encouraged to write their donor families; that often helps donor families cope with their losses. Unsure of himself, Nic composed a letter on the first anniversary of his transplant.

To the wonderful family who saved my life:

Today is the first anniversary of my kidney and transplant surgery, and I was thinking of you. I have so much gratitude for the gift of life that has given me a second chance to live. My life and the lives of my wife, family, and friends have changed so dramatically. I hope I am able to express how thankful I am for this gift. The very special person who was my donor and you all are my Heroes. I will not waste a precious moment of my new life.

I am a forty-seven-year-old married man. I had suffered from diabetes since age thirteen. Since the onset of the disease I have had complications. I had nerve degeneration, vision problems, digestive complications, and kidney failure. After kidney failure in 2006, I began dialysis treatment three times a week for five hours per treatment. I decided to get on the transplant list. While going through the process of qualifying and waiting for a transplant, I almost died several times. On March 28, 2008, I received the gift of life from your family. During my recovery, I decided I would do something to honor this gift. I am currently attending Delgado Community College where I am majoring in Nursing. I plan to work with the transplant team at the hospital where I received my transplant. I am also an organ donor registration activist and a volunteer for the Louisiana Organ Procurement Agency.

I have started an organ donor awareness organization. It is called the H-E-R-O-Movement (Help Everyone Receive Organs). I am kicking off the movement by having an organ donor awareness event at the college I am attending. By telling our story and other transplant stories, I hope to bring awareness to organ donation and significantly increase the number of people registered to be organ donors. It is named this because everyone who is an organ donor is a Hero, and you all are my HEROES. I am so appreciative that your family chose to save my life. Your loved one lives on in me, and I will honor them by enjoying every precious moment I live. I will continue to pay forward this gift of life.

I will remember this day and your family for the rest of my life. I would be happy for any type of communication your family desires. Your family is always in my thoughts and in my heart. You will always be my Heroes.

With respect and love,

Nic Whitacre

Nic sent the letter off to LOPA and wished for the best.

He doesn't exactly do things halfway. Impressed by the care he'd received in the hospital, Nic registered for classes in the nursing program at Delgado. The study of nursing complemented his advocacy initiative. He was certain he wanted to devote his new life to the process of organ donation and transplantation. The two activities, while time consuming and not inexpensive, satisfied his desire for action.

Nic enlisted the support of LOPA, which sent a representative to assist in the registration process at school. Nic was nervous when he stood in front of a group and told his story. But it wasn't stage fright. Nic had been a salesman his whole life. This was different. This was personal. Nic was doing this not only for the cause of organ donation but also to acknowledge publicly the gift he'd received from his hero, an unknown individual who had saved his life. That young man who had visited him in his dream was on his mind when he addressed the students assembled that April afternoon in 2009.

Nic's initial reaction to the results of that first event was disappointment, but thirty-eight students had elected to register as organ donors, and the representative from LOPA was ecstatic. They assured him that thirty-eight new registered organ donors wasn't an insignificant number. He hadn't known what to expect from that first event. *What could be done to build on this humble beginning?* he wondered. Still, thirty-eight had had heard his story and had been moved to action.

Nic was drained physically and emotionally when he arrived home. He put down his backpack and went into his office to check his e-mail. He felt blood drain from his face and a chill go up his spine when he read the subject line of one: "From your donor family."

Dear Nic,

We are so happy to hear from you! It is wonderful to hear what an impact our son's organs have had on your new healthy life.

We wanted to share a few things with you about your donor, our son. His name is Christopher Gregory, and he grew up in Maryland. He was 19 years old, a freshman criminal justice major at Loyola University in New Orleans. He developed a fatal brain aneurysm. Chris is the youngest of three brothers, and the tallest. He was over 6'4" (a fact he was very proud of). He was smart, fun loving and had a heart full of compassion. He loved the outdoors: camping, sailing, running cross-country and was an Eagle Scout. Chris also loved playing the guitar and actually constructed an eight-string guitar as his senior project in high school.

Chris believed in organ donation. Coincidentally, the week before he passed away he very clearly told us that he wanted to donate all of his organs. We are overwhelmed that his choice to give life has brought so many amazing people into our lives.

We have prayed for your continued recovery and are thrilled that your health has greatly improved, and allowed you to begin your work toward a new career as a nurse, while volunteering with LOPA. Your website is wonderful! We thank you for honoring our son as your Hero.

We would like to stay in contact with you to enjoy all the success that your future holds for you. We know our son lives on in you, and we thank you for honoring him. We are attaching a photo of your hero, Chris.

All the best,

Grace and Eric Gregory and family

Tears streamed down Nic's face as he reread the e-mail. In an attachment was a photo of a young man in a high school senior portrait. He recognized the face instantly. It was the same face he'd seen in that dream four months earlier. It was the face of the young man who had told him to start the H-E-R-O Movement.

dear mrs. gregory,

I realize this is very forward of me, but I finally found the words. I need to thank you for raising such amazing sons, especially Chris. He kept me out of so much trouble and kept me from making some of the worst decisions ever. Chris, Kevin, Matt, and Brian picked on me constantly, but I wouldn't have had it any other way. They were the only ones willing to stand there and tell me how I was being a stupid girl.

But the beauty of this was that they didn't just stop at making fun, they also all got me out of countless situations. I've told very few people this story, and I normally don't share it with anyone, but I need to tell you how amazing your son is and why I loved him so much and can honestly say I owe him my life.

Toward the end of my senior year, things were going well. I decided on where I was going to college. Classes were winding down, and it was almost summer. However, no one approved of my boyfriend at the time, and Chris, Kevin, and Brian made that known constantly.

One night during senior week, my boyfriend told me he didn't like the fact that I wanted to walk along the boardwalk with my best friends. Being intoxicated and jealous, he grabbed me, pulled me to a corner, and started screaming at me and calling me names. I tried to pull away from him. I was petrified. He hit me across the face. And just as it seemed that he was about to hit me again, Chris walked right past us by the grace of God. He saw me and the condition I was in and stopped dead in his tracks. He walked over to us and asked if things were okay. My boyfriend responded it was none of Chris's business. Chris of course responded with something to the effect, "Well, you see, it is. Because that girl right there, she's my friend. And I really don't appreciate it when anyone treats her any less than perfect. And seeing how there are tears down her face, I think it might be best if you just let me walk her home." I don't know how far my boyfriend would have gone, and there is no doubt that after that night, I believed he would have left me for dead.

Since that night, Chris has always been my guardian angel. We talked less when he ventured to college. But when we did talk, the first question he would always ask was if I happened to be dating any guy he hadn't preapproved. He got me through a lot, and I have no doubt he'll continue to do so.

I'm sorry I couldn't find these words earlier. I normally don't like thinking about that one night much less talking about it. But I realized earlier today that this was a memory I needed to keep in my heart constantly because it reminded me of how beautiful and amazing Chris is. I talk to him every day now that I know he doesn't have class or "work" to keep him busy during the day. I let him have his nights.

Thank you for my guardian angel, and I can't wait until the day I see him again. God bless,

one year

×

Christopher died the week after Easter 2008. The week before Easter a year later, our spirits got a couple of serious pick-me-ups. We'd become pretty comfortable sharing our thoughts about Chris with the Bacardis after a few letters back and forth. All we knew about Jorge and Leslie were their first names, that they lived in the Bahamas, and that they really liked fishing. We didn't know their last name or anything about them, and googling Jorge-Leslie-Bahamas returned zero hits. Regardless, I was determined to find them or at least make it easy for them to find us if they wanted.

To protect the privacy of donor families and recipients, most organ procurement organizations go to great lengths to redact personal information. We had to write to Jorge through LOPA, which would pass the letter to UNOS, where it would be edited, forwarded to the Mayo Clinic, and then sent to Jorge. The process took months. But I didn't care. We were desperate. On January 24, I was alone at home when I decided to compose another letter. I was missing Chris very much that evening, and I poured my heart out onto the pages I wrote.

I told them about Grace graduating from nursing school. I told them about finishing a marathon that fall. I told them about Colin and John's upcoming graduations in the spring. I told them about Jenn visiting us for Thanksgiving. I expressed our heartfelt wish that their lives would be filled with love and joy and happiness. We wanted nothing but good things for them because that would help us heal also.

At the end, I included my e-mail address. I was determined to establish contact.

On January 25, I dropped the letter at the post office on Main Street and drove to work by way of the cemetery so I could say hi to Chris. And then I waited and checked my e-mail. I waited. And waited. And waited some more. I got in the habit of checking my personal e-mail as often as I did my work e-mail. I don't think anyone at work would care at that point, but I wasn't excited about work just then.

Professionally, I was just going through the motions. Going to the office or to meetings was simply a distraction from life. If I wasn't actively engaged in an important task at work, I was thinking about Chris. I make no apologies. That's just the way it was. Work was just a place to go to keep from dealing with the grief. I know this is true because I know other men who've buried their sons. There were days when we'd just go to the office, stare at our computers, and cry. So I checked my private e-mail religiously. Several times an hour.

At times during that first year, I'd look down the street half expecting, hoping, I'd see Chris come around the corner. Sometimes, the feeling was so strong that it was incredible. I'd look at the basketball hoop where he shot baskets for hours at a time or the spot in front of the neighbors' where he used to ride his skateboard. I could hear the rim shaking or the wood of his skateboard striking the street. I'd look down the street.

"Christopher? Are you okay? It's me. It's Dad," I'd say aloud. "I'm still here, son. I'm still here, and I still love you." In spite of my deep longing, I'd hear only the wind rustling through the trees. In the months after I'd e-mailed that January letter, I checked my e-mail, waited, and counted the days.

And then it happened. On April 8, 2009. Three hundred and seventy-nine days after we got the call. Three hundred and seventy-eight days after the apnea test. Three hundred and seventy-seven days after he was pronounced dead. Three hundred and seventy-six days since cleaning out his dorm room. Three hundred and sixty-nine days since his funeral. On Holy Thursday, it happened. I checked my e-mail that morning just like every morning. The Georgetown University e-mail server was down. I checked back. It was still down. Ten minutes later, still down. I had a meeting to attend, so I logged off and left the office for a while. And when I returned a couple hours later, I checked again. And there it was.

I had invested everything emotionally possible in that letter of January 29. And that is why I checked my e-mails so frequently. I had pinned all my hopes and dreams on trying to develop closer contact with this man and his wife who were at the time a big connection to Chris and to whom we were connected by Chris. So my heart stopped when I saw the subject line: "Chris and me" and read whom the message was from: Jorge.

Dear Eric and Grace:

Thank you so much for your letter of January 24th, which we received only a few days ago. Luckily, UNOS did not block out your e-mail address, and we can dispense with the slow mail "delivery."

Leslie and I were most concerned about your holidays with that huge part of your life missing. It was comforting to learn that you had family and friends to share your time with. Chris would have been welcomed at our refrigerator any time! Leslie is a fabulous cook (my waistline is not all due to the prednisone!), and I think Chris would have liked what she had to offer. Because of my congenital condition, Primary Ciliary Dyskinesia, we were never able to have children of our own. However, we do have 18 nieces & nephews, and they sure do love to hang out here whenever they can.

As my one-year anniversary evaluation approached a few weeks ago, I had your family on my mind a great deal and what an incredible gift you shared with me. I can assure you that Chris and I are getting along famously - the results of the evaluation, which was extensive, were delivered by my doctor with a big smile on his face. His word was "excellent": no sign of rejection, no infections, no complications and thanks to Chris's help my lung function is 113 percent of normal. I'm thoroughly enjoying boating, fishing, biking, even some tennis—not quite ready for a marathon, but I think it's com-mendable that Eric runs them!

Our heartiest congratulations to Grace on her nursing degree! What an amazing field of medicine it is that gives so much in the way of compassion and comfort—I was a prime recipi-ent—hope she loves it. Obviously, education is an important part of your family with John getting his masters at George-town and Colin graduating from Loyola—no doubt Chris would have followed in their footsteps. Education has also played an important role in our family: Leslie has a teaching degree from Chico State in California, and I graduated from Stanford way back in '66 and then went on six years later and got an engineering degree at U. of Miami, Florida.

We have always been blessed with the love, joy, and happiness that you spoke of in your letter and your Chris has given me the health I never had—for that and more we are eternally grateful, and we think of him every day.

We want to wish you and your family a blessed Easter,

Jorge & Leslie

My reaction was immediate and predictable. I started crying. And I read the e-mail over and over. My spirits had been lifted immediately upon receipt of such a gift. And lifted a little higher when I read that second line, "and we can dispense with the slow mail delivery." They were open to the idea of continued communication. The long waits between letters were over. Contact would be more frequent, and we would get to know just how Chris was making a difference in their lives. The letter I'd written on January 24 had taken over two months to reach them. I dare say that remains something the national organ procurement community needs to work on.

I decided to stop by the cemetery on my lunch break to tell Chris the good news and offer a prayer of thanks for whatever role he'd played. The children from the school were out for recess as I plucked a few weeds from around his headstone. Normally, that combination would only make me feel down in the dumps. But that day, things weren't so bad. That day, I received another hint that maybe Chris was okay wherever he was. I began to realize that perhaps God had his way of sending me clues. I began to look at these little moments as God's way of saying, "Here, man. Got something for you."

I got in the car and drove home for lunch. Green Day's "Good Riddance" came on the radio. It was a song Chris had learned to play on the guitar in school. He practiced the opening riffs for hours on end. It was automatic whenever he picked up a guitar. He played it until he developed complete muscle memory and could do it without thinking. It was the unofficial anthem of his senior class. His friends sang it for him at his funeral. Coincidence? Maybe. But my reaction was more tears. I mean I was crying so hard I nearly had to pull over and stop the car. That ... that was a moment.

The next day, we were on our way to New Orleans and then to Lafayette for a 5k race to benefit LOPA. There, we met Libbie Harrison for the first time. Libbie's son, Justin, had died in a freak accident when he was only fifteen. She became such a friend and role model over the years teaching us how to carry the grief of losing a child with tremendous grace and dignity. It was her job as a family services representative to reach out to us as and offer guidance on support services. It wasn't her job to become friends. That happened because she's a very special person. Over the years, we'd share tears over our sons. Libbie always let us know she was thinking about us on the anniversary of Christopher's death or birthday, and we were doing the same remembering Justin.

In Lafayette, Libbie had an important document for us. It was a letter from Nic Whitacre. Like Jorge's letter, we first received a phone call from LOPA asking if we wanted it mailed to us or not. Knowing we were traveling to Louisiana that weekend, we originally told them to hang on to it and we'd collect it in person. But as had become our habit with letters from Jorge, we told them to put it in the mail. That gave us something to look forward to while preparing ourselves emotionally for whatever its contents might reveal.

And so another of Christopher's organ recipients was about to enter our lives.

july 9–10, 2009:

THE MEETING (CONT'D)

After meeting the Bacardis in the lobby of their hotel, we spent some time getting to know each other. We told them about Chris's brothers and what they were doing in the aftermath of their brother's death. It was difficult for John and Colin. Even fifteen months later, they weren't at all interested in meeting any of Chris's organ recipients.

This caused more than a little frustration for Grace and me. For us, the transplants were all we had physically left of Christopher. Since these were real people—living, breathing, functioning human beings—encounters with them would be as close as we could ever again be physically connected to Chris. So it hurt when John and Colin wouldn't engage us in discussions about Chris. But it wasn't their fault. Life doesn't prepare you to lose your little brother at such a young age.

It's hard to understand, but there's really no such thing as closure. Even though the rest of the world seems to want to believe in such a thing for you, it simply doesn't exist. How can you be expected to close a relationship with your son?

We adjourned to Jorge and Leslie's room for some get-to-know-you talk. John had just graduated and was pursuing a career in journalism. Grace had just graduated from nursing school. We told them that Colin had graduated and was working in New Orleans as a bartender. Jorge and Leslie told us Colin was likely serving some of their products. "And what might those be?" asked Grace.

"You know, rum."

Oh. They were *those* Bacardis.

Jorge and Leslie proved to be remarkably normal, down-to-earth, regular people. A little more fortunate than some but not pretentious at all about it. In fact, they were the kind of people who recognized something Grace had taught me—that the best things in life aren't things. The Bacardis are dedicated to family. They're loyal to their friends. They have the same values Grace and I have. We hit it off immediately.

That the meeting ever happened in the first place was testament to no small amount of coaxing on our part. In our earliest letters, we dropped hints about possibly meeting. I was curious about all Christopher's organ recipients, and I had a desire to connect with them. Sometimes, it seemed a fantasy, but other times, it was very real. In every case, the first letter, e-mail, or phone call evoked the same tearful reaction in Grace and me. But every encounter left us wanting to know more about these wonderful people and the lives they were living. Not just Jorge and Leslie but also Mac, Nic, Xavier, and Carolyn. We had at least learned their first names. Even Chuck and Arlene, the two who received his corneas, were exciting to hear from.

But Jorge and Leslie had reached out to us first. Jorge had joined a support group for lung transplant patients at Mayo.

Their meetings allowed them to learn from one another and support one another in the new lifestyles they had to lead. Physical fitness and dietary needs required a discipline that most people take for granted, but not transplant patients. Especially lung transplant patients because, as I've mentioned, the lungs are our only organs directly exposed to the environment.

In addition to helping others grapple with the physical and medical aspects of post-transplant life, support groups help patients deal with the emotional and spiritual complications of their new lives. It's never lost on organ recipients that their second chances at life came at the cost of others' deaths. Those are serious considerations, and that's why the pretransplant screening process is so thorough; it's out of respect for the deceased donor as much as it is for the future well-being of the recipient.

Jorge told us that in one such support group meeting, the subject came up of writing to donor families. At that point, Jorge had already mailed his letter to us. But another recipient in the group refused to acknowledge the importance of the gesture. In fact, that person said he saw no need to write to his donor's family. Jorge was more than indignant at that. He was incensed.

As contact between us increased, we had a sense that perhaps a meeting could be possible. Jorge in particular hadn't completely unburdened himself of the emotional weight he'd taken on by accepting the lungs of a donor as young as our son. Fortunately, the social workers and support group at the Mayo Clinic offered opinions favorably disposed to getting the two families together. "Look," they'd been told. "You didn't have a choice, and they didn't have a choice."

But doubts lingered in Jorge about how we would feel once we learned of the difference in ages between him and Chris. He had no way of knowing we already knew about that. The first letter we'd received from LOPA described Chris's organ recipients with little more than gender information of the recipients, but it had included their ages. His age had never bothered us, but it seemed to be a big deal for him. I had written to him, "It seems you've presented us with a dilemma. I don't know whether to call you Son or Dad. Either way, we know you're more than just a friend." That had done it. Once they'd read that, Jorge and Leslie looked at each other and said, "We're going."

So there we were. Together. The answer to my prayers. We were joined at dinner by Leslie's niece, also named Leslie, and Brad, her husband. Brad and Leslie Schoener also live in Maryland, so it was an easy invitation for them to accept. We sat at our table, and after ordering drinks and dinner, we engaged in the usual talk about families, etc.

That's when Brad took me by surprise. Pointing to Jorge at the end of the table, he said, "You see that man right there? He's the central figure of his wing of the family. Even though he's the youngest, he's the patriarch. He's the one everyone in his family looks up to. He's the one everyone turns to, and he takes care of everyone. He's done so much for all nieces and nephews that they could never begin to repay him. And if you could have only seen him a year ago."

Everyone fell silent. Brad's eyes were moist with emotion. Jorge was looking at him with a gentle smile.

"And to see him now. This is not the same man he was little more than a year ago. We almost lost him."

I looked down in fear of losing my own composure.

"We don't know how to thank you. We don't know what to say."

Nor did I. It was a rare moment in history. I was actually speechless for a while.

"I don't know how to respond," I said. "No one has ever said anything like that to me before. Ever. I can only say thank you."

The next morning, Jorge and Leslie met us at our house early. The plan was that we would go to Mass at 8:00 a.m., get some Starbucks, and visit Christopher's grave. After that, Grace and I were hosting a luncheon at our house so family and neighbors could meet Jorge. We thought it would be nice if Chris's friends and relatives could see some tangible benefit to all the tears that had been shed.

Christopher is buried next to the playground of his grade school. It's a perfect spot. In the spring, the air is alive with the sound of laughing children. A fitting if bittersweet spot. His grave is in the row closest to the street. That makes it easy to spot on the way to work or home. It was July, so no kids in the playground. The only sounds were passing cars. I was touched by how quickly Leslie joined Grace in tending to Chris's grave. A few stray weeds needed to be pulled, the old flowers removed, and new roses put in their place. Their reverence for this place was touching to say the least.

Jorge had written a letter he wanted to read at the grave. In it, he described the life he was living in the Bahamas. He was boating and swimming and snorkeling and fishing, activities his disease had robbed him of for a long time. And Chris had returned them to him. Chris had also returned Jorge to his wife and his extended family. And for that, he would be eternally grateful. Grace, Leslie, and I were sniffling.

"I will never forget you, Chris," he said. "I will honor and respect this gift you have given me for the rest of my life."

The four of us had our arms around one another as we gazed at his headstone and wondered what Chris would have thought about what Jorge had just said to him. I knew he was smiling.

We returned to our house and awaited our friends and family. Jorge continued to tell us about a project he'd mentioned in an e-mail in April. He explained that when they left Maryland the next morning, they were going to Jacksonville and the Mayo Clinic. They were on a mission to honor Chris. They were meeting with the CEO of the Mayo Clinic to discuss a gift that would allow for the building of a fitness center or a hospitality house. He explained that during his recovery, he'd learned that Mayo had neither. A fitness center would greatly aid in the recovery of transplant patients. On the other hand, the lack of affordable, clean lodging for transplant patients before and after their transplants was a challenge in the Jacksonville area. As a way of paying back the Mayo Clinic, the Bacardis wanted to make a sizeable gift for something like that. That was just the beginning. They floored us when they said they wanted to name it for Christopher.

Leslie and Grace were in the kitchen preparing vegetables and snacks. Jorge and I went to pick up food and beer. Like I said, regular folks. My mother was among the first to arrive. Like all grandparents, my mother adores every one of her grandkids. Losing Chris had been as catastrophic for her as it had been for everyone else. She was a little tentative with Jorge when I introduced them. Jorge was a little nervous as well.

"It's okay, Mom. You can hug him."

She reached out and touched his chest. Jorge smiled patiently and gave her a big hug. Mom had it doubly tough. "They're special," she had always told me referring to her grandchildren. As much as she loved my brothers and me, she absolutely doted on her grandchildren. She'd had to suffer the loss of Chris and watch Grace and me suffer as well. Throughout the afternoon, Mom would stand next to Jorge and gently pat his chest knowing Chris's lungs were alive and well.

Mary Abdo was a bit different. She was quite unprepared for her own reaction. Mary had been so close to Chris. She had fed him, and housed him, and taken him to school. Her boys were like brothers to Chris, and her daughter, Meghan, had decided she wanted to marry him. At age nine.

When Mary met Jorge, she hugged him, felt Chris's lungs expand, and burst into tears. And that's kind of how the whole afternoon went. All of Chris's friends who were there experienced something unique. How do you explain to a twenty-year-old that yes, your best friend has died, but look, look at what he did. Look at the face of the man standing in your friend's living room and finally breathing freely. Look at the smile on his face and the gratitude in his eyes. Hear the comfort in is voice and tell me he hasn't somehow brought Christopher home. Those same lungs that had breathed the air in that living room for years were there again. For all of them, especially when they recalled all the pain they'd felt for the past year, the experience was very close to incomprehensible.

The emotion of the weekend built throughout that Sunday at our house. Stories were told. The Bacardis learned about Chris from the people who knew him best. We in turn learned about Jorge and Leslie and their family. The afternoon turned out to be a bigger success than I could have imagined.

I'd hoped everyone else would leave before the Bacardis did. Perhaps we could have gotten around to looking at some old pictures of Chris and maybe peek into his room. I was sad when Jorge and Leslie announced that they had made plans to meet up with some of the Schoeners' family they hadn't seen in some time. They slowly said good-bye to Christopher's family and friends. We stepped out onto the porch, just the four of us. By then, I had had enough. I threw my arms around Jorge and began sobbing uncontrollably. Jorge was crying as well, and then, with our wives watching, he whispered, "This is Jorge. Chris is with me. I'm taking care of him. Chris is with me. He's okay, and I'm going to take care of him."

They walked to their car. We waved, and they were off. But not gone.

meeting nic

XXX

NEW ORLEANS

I swore I wouldn't cry when we met Nic. I figured I had this whole thing about getting along with Chris's organ recipients figured out. LOPA, unlike UNOS, doesn't censor communications between donor families and recipients. And since Nic was in Louisiana, LOPA was the only agency to receive his first letter to us. It arrived just as he had composed it. That enhanced our ability to establish communication by e-mail and then phone.

Before reaching out to Nic over the phone, we were contacted by Sally-Ann Roberts, a New Orleans television news broadcaster at WWL. It was May 2009, and Sally-Ann regularly did features for the afternoon news program profiling "Quiet Heroes" in the New Orleans community. We had no idea how she'd chosen Nic and Chris to profile, but she called and asked if we'd be willing to provide some background on Christopher.

We were more than a little flattered and very proud of Chris. The one-year anniversary of his passing was just behind us, and LOPA had sent us a letter informing us that all his organ recipients were doing well. We already knew that about Jorge and Nic, and we took every chance to brag about Chris and his lifesaving sacrifice. Right after people would ask, "How are you guys doing?" they'd ask, "And how are Chris's organ recipients? Do you hear from them?" I told Sally-Ann that we considered them all extensions of the family. We were proud to tell the story of our son, the life he had lived, and the impact he had made in the short time he was with us.

The episode was scheduled to run May 19, 2009. We of course were in Maryland and had no way of knowing if the story would air or be bumped by late-breaking news. We weren't worried for ourselves, but we knew Nic would be disappointed. So we waited until the following evening to call Nic and ask how it went. Of course the story turned out to be a smash. Only Nic wasn't the Quiet Hero we'd expected. Chris was.

Shortly after, Nic e-mailed me a copy of the video. The opening moments featured photos of Chris and described him as an Eagle Scout, altar boy, athlete, and musician. Wow! Chris and Nic were the Quiet Heroes profiled. They shared the spotlight. It was an emotional thing to watch only months after losing him. The emotions were still so raw.

We called Nic and congratulated him on the story. Nic turned out to be gracious and sincere. Wherever we wanted the relationship to go, he was willing. He wanted to save lives by championing Christopher's life and the cause of organ dona-tion. He told us all about his plans for the H-E-R-O Movement and about his dedication to preserving Christopher's memory. If there was one sentiment that came through the phone that evening, it was gratitude. Nic was grateful just to be alive. During that first tear-filled phone call, we knew we had to meet. It wasn't long before we made arrangements to go to New Orleans.

Three months later, in late August, we again nervously walked into the lobby of a hotel. Colin was working, and he and Matt Nolan were roommates. They were excited to meet Nic, and we were pleasantly surprised they felt this way. I thought it was a big step in the healing process for them both.

Nic and his wife, Michelle, drove from Slidell to our hotel on Saint Charles Avenue. I knew it was them the minute they hit the front door. I watched them ascended the elevator to the lobby bar. I smiled at Grace and nodded in the direction of the Whitacres as they stepped off the escalator. "I swore I wasn't going to cry," I told Nic as I wrapped him in up in a big bear hug.

The reunion with Nic and Michelle was every bit as emotional as that first meeting with Jorge and Leslie had been. There were lots of tears and awkward introductions. I was pleased to introduce Colin and Matt. They had been through so many dark moments after losing Chris. But here, in the flesh, they could see what had come of those awful nights only a little more than a year earlier. It was a special moment, a special experience.

Each of our meetings with the recipients was special because each recipient was special. That started me thinking more about the value of each human life and appreciating all the more what Christopher had accomplished during that week in the Tulane University Medical Center.

I saw it first with Nic. He's different from Jorge in many ways. But in other ways, they could be twins. So each experience was different. Not better. Not worse. Just different. That was something we always treasured in our sons. John, Colin, and Chris had different talents and skills growing up. One wasn't ever better or smarter than the others; each had been gifted with his own character. And that's what makes them special.

The same goes for Chris's organ recipients. When we committed to try to bring them into our lives, we did so willing to accept them for who they were. We took that first step in the lobby of the Intercontinental on Saint Charles Avenue when Nic and Michelle Whitacre arrived.

We decided to stroll down the street and find a place for dinner. We found a quiet enough place and began learning about each other. The biggest thing I learned that night was that if it was possible to live on love alone, Nic did it. The stories Michelle told us about Nic's illness and the trips to the hospital were heartbreaking. She told us about Katrina and having to pack up all their belongings except their wedding pictures. And checking into an El Paso emergency room and finally convincing a nurse to get a doctor to write the prescriptions they knew would stabilize Nic. And living in a toxic FEMA trailer. And the constant worrying. I decided then and there that there must be a special place in heaven for caretakers like Michelle. Nic got by on his Granny's advice and his wife's love. And for much of the time, that was enough.

It was a wonderful weekend. Getting to know this new addition to our family made us only prouder of what Chris had done. Nic had been sick, really sick, before the transplant. But he was okay. Nic had lived through some very dark times, and despite all he'd been through, he wasn't bitter. He had stood at the intersection of life and death and had ended up on the right corner.

But he wasn't going to forget about the kid who ended up on the other side of the street, the kid who had put him on the corner where he was standing.

the gabriel house of care

XXX

JACKSONVILLE

The letter Jorge read at Christopher's grave was not the first or only letter he wrote after his transplant. He also wrote a letter that had repercussions far beyond our families. A third letter resulted in a project that would blossom into a gift that has touched the lives of people whose names Jorge and Leslie will never know.

> I have just undergone one of the most critical surgeries on this planet. I have come through this ordeal in astonishing fashion, thanks to Mayo Clinic, Cesar Keller and his magnificent lung transplant team and, most of all to the grand generosity of one young man—an unknown entity I have named "Gabriel"—and his selfless act of organ donation.
>
> I have a debt that is impossible to repay. Nevertheless, I am determined to honor and give thanks to Gabriel, as well as the many other "Gabriels," both alive and dead, and to the medical staff at Mayo Clinic who help people like me achieve this miraculous rebirth.

After leaving us in Maryland, the Bacardis returned home via the Mayo Clinic in Jacksonville. Jorge had to have a checkup and some lab work done. They were also meeting with the leadership team of the Mayo Clinic, including its national CEO, Dr. John Cortese, and the CEO of the Jacksonville Campus, Dr. Bill Rupp. Mayo is an interesting organization in that all its physicians, including its CEOs, continue treating patients. So though Dr. Cortese and Dr. Rupp were running what is considered the premier medical system on the planet, they were also expected to continue practicing their craft.

During his evaluation, Jorge's lung function was measured at 130 percent over baseline, thank you very much Christopher, and he continued to be the poster boy of the lung transplant section; Superman was alive and well and showing no signs of rejection. He was caring for his new lungs with great discipline and commitment.

Leslie and Jorge wanted to honor the second chance they had been given. They'd already made a sizeable gift to Mayo that was in escrow as a sign of their desire to return the favor so to speak. Jorge in particular wanted Mayo to move on it, but he and Leslie had different ideas about how the money should be spent. Jorge wanted a fitness center. Despite its cutting-edge technology and state-of-the-art facilities, Mayo Clinic in Jacksonville didn't have one on-site.

Leslie felt differently. The Bacardis had been introduced to the Saint Andrews Lighthouse organization during Jorge's recovery. After visiting the Lighthouse for lunch one day, they committed themselves to its support. Saint Andrew's Lighthouse was a project of Saint Andrew's Lutheran Church in Jacksonville. It had opened the doors of a four-bedroom house in 1996, and it had an ongoing relationship with the Mayo Clinic.

Ed Asher was its original executive director. On the first night of the Lighthouse's operation, Ed and his wife, Sandi, were visiting with their first guest. They sensed some nervousness in her voice. The Ashers had said goodnight to her and were preparing to leave. Suddenly, the young woman explained that she was afraid to spend the night alone. Ed and Sandi were surprised. They thought they'd best give their guest some privacy, but privacy wasn't what she wanted. She was in a strange city. Facing very serious health issues and a very uncertain future. And she was completely alone. The Ashers returned to their home, gathered sheets, blankets, and pajamas, and returned to the Lighthouse.

They learned a very valuable lesson that night, one that became central to the mission of their organization. People need community; caregivers of course, but also the friendship and support of others who are also facing difficult situations.

In March 2007, Saint Andrew's Lighthouse had proposed to Mayo the idea of a twenty-bedroom House of Care similar to the Lighthouse where patients waiting for or recovering from transplants could stay near the hospital. "Come back with a million dollars and a plan," was what they'd been told.

So they did. In June 2008, the organization returned to Mayo with plans for a building drawn up by Saint Andrew's board member Trevor Lee and pledges of more than $1 million. But just as things were looking promising, September arrived. Lehman Brothers failed. The financial crisis of 2008 seized up credit markets and put plans for expansion around the world on hold, including those of the Mayo Clinic.

Fortunately, just as the financial crisis ground the global economy to a halt, Dr. Bill Rupp arrived as CEO of the Mayo Clinic's Jacksonville campus. He's a graduate of Dartmouth and the University of Minnesota Medical School. With an undergraduate degree in economics, Rupp understood the implications of the financial crisis for Mayo, and he recognized the importance of benefactors such as the Bacardis and what their generosity would mean at such a time. When Dr. Rupp met Ed Asher and learned of the plans for the House of Care, he told Ed, "I'll see if I can stir the pot for you."

And so it was the House of Care that Leslie Bacardi favored when she and Jorge, their heads still swimming from our reunion in Maryland, met with Drs. Rupp and Cortese and the development team at Mayo. At first, the meeting didn't seem very promising. The financial crisis was rapidly approaching its nadir—but no one was sure where that would be—and had everyone nervous. And the idea of a fitness center just couldn't be realized for at least five years. Maybe ten. Dr. Cortese laid out a list of reasons why such a project was simply not feasible. Not just then.

The Bacardis' trip to Maryland hadn't turned out exactly as they had expected. They'd come with the goal of giving us as much thanks and hope as possible. They'd come wanting to lift us up but left feeling we had lifted them up. They were on a mission of giving, and up to that point, they felt they'd done most of the receiving.

And the meeting at Mayo might not turn out the way they had dreamed either. The tension in the room was palpable when Leslie took command of the meeting. "Well then, Dr. Cortese," she asked in her calm, measured voice. "Would you consider allowing us to take the money in escrow and funding the House of Care?"

Cortese and Rupp shared a long sideways glance. Cortese was technically Rupp's boss. A slight smile appeared to form on Rupp's face, and his eyes seemed to brighten. The senior of the two responded. "Yes," Cortese said. "Yes, we can."

Leslie turned to her husband. "Well, Rabs, can we fund the House of Care?"

Jorge paused. He thought about the conversation he'd had with Dr. Keller before his transplant. When Keller tried to convince him to wait it out in Jacksonville. It would be easy for Jorge. He could live on *Contigo*. But most others waiting for transplants or recovering from transplants didn't have such an option. They had Saint Andrews Lighthouse or hotels. He agreed with Leslie that nobody should have to worry about a place to stay. It didn't seem fair. The House of Care made sense.

"Yes." That was all Jorge needed to say. The goal of their trip was realized. Leslie burst into tears of joy. "Thank you." She wiped tears from her eyes. Her husband was alive and well, and they had the chance to pay their gift forward. Really pay it forward. Their journey was a smashing success. Leslie's enthusiasm infected the entire room. Almost immediately, tears were on the cheeks of all. That started with Jorge and then the doctors and the folks from the development office. The room was filled with laughter and tears. Everyone had been infected with the Bacardis' joy and gratitude.

Somewhere at the center of all this emotion was that nineteen-year-old college freshman with the wry smile and quick sense of humor. Two phone calls in the same night after ten months of waiting. And here they were. Thanks to the six four kid who took such care of himself and had his whole life before him. The kid with the big feet and even bigger heart. The gift was being made to Mayo, but the thanks were all to Chris.

Gratitude can be an elusive emotion. Feeling gratitude and expressing gratitude are different. Many of us feel grateful but neglect to say thank you. Some of us say thank you but wish we could do more. Jorge and Leslie, however, had the gift of being able to say thank you to the Mayo Clinic, to Dr. Keller, to Chris, and to organ donors everywhere. And when their commitment to the Gabriel House of Care was accepted, they wept tears of joy yet again.

The final blessing for the Gabriel House of Care came in the form of an e-mail from Dr. John Noseworthy on November 16, 2009. Noseworthy had replaced Dr. Cortese as CEO of the Mayo Clinic system. He said that the entire Mayo board of trustees had approved the project at their November meeting.

Jorge's determination to pay Chris's gift forward and honor his memory would be another big step for the Bacardis and our family. The Gabriel House of Care would memorialize someone who had died way before his time and honor the dedication of those compassionate medical professionals who'd given Jorge another chance at life.

It would also be such a gift to organ donors whose families often had to struggle with unbearable grief. It would serve as a monument to life, and hope, and all that could be good about people. It was time to plan a groundbreaking.

dear mr. and mrs. gregory,

✕✕

I want to offer my deepest condolences at the loss of Chris. He was a beautiful person, and I've never known anyone quite like him.

From the time I first met him, summer of 2006 at Goshen, I knew I would never be able to get him out of my head. He was the sweetest and funniest boy I'd ever met. But more than anything, I will remember all the memories he gave me.

We would go on the most ridiculous adventures that would result in nothing more than a sandwich and him on my last nerve. He loved to argue about everything, and he knew just how to get under your skin. Yet I still couldn't help but love him.

The memory that I will treasure the most was one afternoon at camp. I had been bothering him for most of the summer to take me out on a sailboat, and he finally did. It was just a simple Saturday afternoon on the lake, but I will never forget it. Many of my other memories of him are of just sitting around, talking, and laughing. He had a way with people and loved to make them laugh.

I find great comfort in knowing how well loved Chris was by everyone and how many lives he touched. No one that young should have to leave this world, but maybe it was just his time to go on. He made his mark on this world and will never be forgotten.

The loss of a deeply loved friend is not the same as the loss of a son, but we are here and will make it through this tragedy together. The heart is mendable.

Chris was a true sailor and will forever be sailing on in our hearts.

My deepest sympathy,
Michelle Dellapenna

groundbreaking

✕✕✕

JACKSONVILLE

There had to be a groundbreaking ceremony to mark the beginning of construction. That would be our first hint as to the magnitude of what Jorge and Chris had set out to accomplish and just what we were in for. I'd never been much for celebrity. I like to mind my own business and live a nice, quiet life. And we made sure the people at Mayo Clinic and Jorge and Leslie knew we weren't interested in being the center of attention. But if it would recognize Chris and help the cause, they could count us in.

The groundbreaking was on March 25, 2010, two years to the day after we received that first dreadful phone call. It was only the second time we'd been together with Jorge and Leslie. It was special. We spent time with them getting to know them even more and learning about their lives. Beth Knowles from the Mayo Clinic Development Office served as our unofficial host. Beth works with many Mayo benefactors. She repeatedly told us how the Bacardis weren't interested in garnering any lasting recognition for themselves; their gift was a gesture of their appreciation for what Dr. Keller and his team in the lung transplantation department had done for Jorge. But mostly it was about Chris. It was about the generosity of our son. We met a few of Jorge and Leslie's friends and relatives. It was clear from the beginning that Jorge was a rock star in the Mayo Clinic community. And so was Chris for that matter.

My brother David and his wife, Jane, attended the dinner the night before the groundbreaking. Jane is a native of Jacksonville. Colin came down. So did my mother. Grace's sister, Kathleen, and her husband, Skip, attended. And their son, Rob, came up from Fort Lauderdale. There were also some prominent figures from the Jacksonville business community. The Mayo Clinic enjoys an excellent reputation in Jacksonville. The land for the medical campus had been donated by the Davis family. Of course, Dr. Noseworthy and Dr. Rupp were there. Dr. Rupp had reason to be proud. The country was still in the grips of a severe economic recession, and here we were about to launch a multimillion-dollar building project. It was a big deal.

Grace and I were asked to be interviewed by a writer from Mayo Clinic's communications staff. Mayo wanted to commemorate the event and publicize the Gabriel House of Care. I guess as Christopher's parents we were, like it or not, part of the story. Under bright lights we were miked up and photographed. The camera guys did light and sound checks. Matt Derechin, our interviewer, started off with some pretty basic, open-ended questions to get the ball rolling. Innocent enough, you know?

Eventually, the interview turned to the week of Christopher's death. We described the events of that week. Grace was moist-eyed pretty much during the whole thing, and I choked up a few times too. Then the sound technician, and the cameraman, and Beth Knowles took turns grabbing some Kleenex.

Her shoulders were shuddering. Any narration of that week's events had that kind of effect on people even if they'd been on the periphery of those events or were just listening to them. I remembered the nurses in the SICU that night we said good-bye and the families and friends of Chris and his recipients. Chris had done something powerful.

A few hundred people assembled under a huge tent on the site of what would become the Gabriel House of Care. The site work had begun, the ground cleared, and some silt fencing and grade stakes were in the ground. Off in a corner of the site, earthmoving equipment sat ready to go to work. In his remarks, Jorge spoke of an alignment of stars—Chris, Dr. Cesar Keller and his team at Mayo, and of course Leslie. Not near enough credit goes to the caretakers of transplant patients or any other seriously ill people. Leslie had had to watch her husband's health slowly deteriorate. She'd stood by him since the moment they said "I do" in a garden in Nassau all the way to the time she'd seen him wheeled off to surgery not knowing if she'd ever see him alive again. For better or worse. She wasn't allowed to break down or exhibit any kind of discouragement. Caretakers can't show their human weaknesses. They're expected to always keep a positive attitude. They're supposed to keep that stiff upper lip lest their loved ones feed off their doubts. There's a special place in heaven for caretakers. But who cares for them while they care for others?

The mission of the Gabriel House of Care, its core purpose in fact, was to support caregivers and patients alike with spacious, clean housing on the Mayo campus. The caretakers wouldn't be burdened with many of the logistical nightmares they usually face. A cadre of staff and volunteers would see to that. And its location would assure its guests that they were as near to the best medical attention as possible. No frantic, late-night phone calls to arrange transportation. It would already be there. They could rest a bit more easily and concentrate on their loved ones.

The construction on that beautiful building was completed in a year. We monitored its progress through e-mails and photos the Bacardis sent us. Upon completion of the basic structure, the house received a Bahamian tradition known as a roof wetting. On October 10, 2010, executives from Mayo Clinic arrived for what the workers on the project guessed was for some kind of tour and ceremony. Such events are common in the construction industry. When skyscrapers are topped out—the final steel girder or beam is put in place—a flag is placed at the top of the structure and work stops while the workers enjoy a barbeque. In underground tunnel construction, the event is known as a holing through, and it too is sometimes marked by a lavish party. Well, in the Bahamas, once a new building has a roof, it gets a roof wetting.

The workers didn't quite know what to make of the scene when Jorge and Leslie arrived at the house in the company of Dr. Rupp, Dr. Keller, Beth Knowles, and several other suits. More surprising was what they brought with them. Two bottles of expensive Bacardi rum. In some shock and more than a little amusement, the construction crew watched as Jorge and Leslie offered a toast to the success of the Gabriel House of Care and then christened the roof with two bottles of rum. Something you don't see every day.

The site would soon be a house. A big, fine house, the next step in the realization of the commitment Jorge was making to honor his gift and pay it forward. Its bricks and mortar would offer emotional as well as physical shelter to people facing difficult challenges.

Even more incredible than the groundbreaking was the trip we made to the Bacardis' home in the Bahamas immediately after. We'd been told not to expect contact from the organ recipients, but there Grace and I were with the Bacardis on a jet headed to the Bahamas. Two years after Chris's passing, the friendship we and the Bacardis were nurturing was helping Grace and me out of the darkness that had enveloped us. An ease and comfortableness grew between us. Very natural, as if we'd known one another for years.

We were accompanied by Dr. Keller, his wife, Ingrid, and their daughter, Lorraine, who was an ICU nurse at Mayo and had tended to Jorge several times. When Lorraine and I had spotted the private jet waiting to whisk us away to the tropics, we shared a brief chuckle. "Oh yeah," we agreed sarcastically. "This happens to us every day."

We landed in Nassau and traveled to the Bacardis' house. In the front door and almost immediately out the back door to the dock and then aboard *Contigo*, which would take us to the Exumas.

Jorge and Leslie welcomed us to their home in the Bahamas, but it was more like they were welcoming us into their lives. Before long, we stood on those same enchanting beaches Jorge and Leslie had told us about in e-mails. The water. I'd never seen bluer blues or greener greens. Beaches so pristine and with sand so white beneath our bare feet. This was where they lived. This was the life that Christopher allowed them to continue living. And they never let us forget that they loved our son as though he were their own. Nothing had to be hidden from each other.

At the end of our first day, we found ourselves docked at Highbourne Cay. Almost immediately after we docked, Jorge announced, "C'mon. It's time to take Chris for a walk." We took off at a brisk pace. It was a regular ritual for Jorge, a necessary part of his rehabilitation. And he continues to take it seriously. As we strolled, Jorge pointed out flowers, shrubs, and lizards. He told us all about the Exumas, the archipelago where he and Leslie loved to spend time. This was their home. Their house was in Nassau, but their home was in the Exumas. Of all the places they'd been in the world, this was where they genuinely wanted to be. At one point, Jorge and I were out of earshot of the others. I got up the courage to ask him something I desperately wanted to know.

"Are you guys doing okay?" I asked. Meaning Jorge and Chris.

Jorge looked at me and smiled. "We're doing fine."

Our time in the Bahamas was magical. The islands of the Exumas are quite unlike anything I'd ever seen before. Many are unspoiled. I imagined I was looking at what Columbus saw when he first discovered the New World. I marveled at its beauty, but I was thinking, *Why did Chris have to die for me to be here?* I tried not to think too hard about it; I just wanted to take in the moment. What was important was that I could literally wrap my arms around Christopher's lungs though they had a new home. But they were still Christopher.

After dinner, we learned to play a Cuban dice game called *coroto*, which is played with five dice that instead of "pips" on each face have either an ace, king, queen, jack, eight, or seven. Players take turns rolling the best hands they can. Simple enough. But people can exclaim, "Por abajo!" That allows them to turn the tossed dice over and use what's there rather than what's face-up to calculate their roll. The game quickly becomes rather raucous and loud.

Maybe it was the rum. Maybe it was the company and the fellowship. Maybe it was the scenery, the exotic locale. Probably a combination of all of the above. But as we played, I heard something I hadn't heard for a long time. Grace's laughter. Hers is a special, infectious laugh that brightens any room.

"Por abajo!"

The dice would be turned over. The "hand" would turn out to be worse that way.

"Ay! You shouldn't have called 'Por abajo!'"

It wasn't long before I too was laughing. And smiling. Something I hadn't done since March 2008. For two years, nothing had made me laugh. I mean really laugh. Nothing had brought me joy. I hadn't found the depths of my disappointment, but I had found that my heights of happiness had a ceiling. I just couldn't bring myself to laugh. Until then. In spite of the circumstances that had drawn us to that place, I was grateful to be in the company of these special people surrounded by such stunning beauty.

Still, the experience was bittersweet. Walking alone along the most beautiful beach I had ever seen, I thanked God for allowing me to be walking in paradise. Finding God in all things, including tragedy, is part of Ignatian spirituality. Remarkable people had become a part of our lives. We were walking on air with all the attention we'd received over the past days. But I knew John and Colin still missed their brother desperately. They were still trying to come to grips with their grief. Grace and I still held each other while we cried ourselves to sleep at night.

I was thankful to be walking that glorious stretch of beach, but I still had to look up to the sky and ask, "Why?"

dear chris,

✕✕✕

Today marks the day that you have been gone from this earth as long as I carried you inside me. I miss you so much, boy! Sometimes, I can still hear your goofy laugh, and I hope so desperately that I will always be able to hear that.

We made it through the holidays with your help, but it just did not seem joyous at all. I can't believe how hard it feels to smile some days, when I realize that I will never get to hug you again.

Today is Dad's birthday, the big five-o. I can hear you teasing him about how old he is today, but your brothers are trying to keep the teasing going for all of you.

I know you don't want me to go around crying about missing you, but some days, it really hurts that you're gone, and I can't help it. As big and strong as you were, you were still a part of me, and now, that part has left this earth. I am missing a part of me.

Thank you for being my son and teaching me so much about patience, love, and understanding. I know you are with me, and I am happy that three of your grandparents are with you, so I don't have to worry about you anymore.

I try to remember your enthusiasm and spirit for life in all that I do. Please help me.

I love you ... more.
Mom

dedication

JACKSONVILLE

Jorge Bacardi is an articulate gentleman. His command of the English language is impressive, and he can express deep emotion and a keen intellect writing or speaking. He can also capture a moment with perfect timing or a flair for the dramatic when appropriate. It was eleven days shy of the third anniversary of his transplant when he took the podium before about 300 invited guests in front of a completed and fully furnished Gabriel House of Care.

"First of all, I'd like to start with having you all take a nice, deep, big breath." After a dramatic pause to appreciate the moment, he continued. "Wait, wait, this is my favorite part … Ready, Chris?" And with that, he led the audience in a large, collective inhale.

As he looked out at the audience, he was especially gratified to see so many of his nieces and nephews. After all, it was they he'd especially considered when he finally decided to proceed with the lung transplant. Brad and Leslie and Henderson were there from Leslie's side of the family, and there were Paul and Juan and Jose and Victoria and JJ from Alberto's and Carmen's families. And there in back sat Joaquincito and Sonia, whose relationship with Jorge and Leslie was part best friend, part parent. Joaquincito had thought for sure his tio "wasn't going to make it." It was gratifying to see them that day. Looking into their eyes and especially into Leslie's eyes, Jorge knew he had made the right choice. That they were gathered in front of this house, on this day, only made the event so much sweeter.

It was a brilliant opening to a touching speech. As Jorge took that long, deep breath, many in the audience, myself included, choked up. He said that a breath is something that most of us take for granted. But for himself, a man who had felt as if he had breathed through a straw for most of his life, a proper breath was exhilarating.

He expressed his gratitude to the generosity of one "fabulous young man," Chris Gregory, to our family, and to the unwavering dedication and care of the Mayo lung transplant team. He paid special thanks to his lead physician, Cesar Keller. Beyond those, however, Jorge explained that the Gabriel House of Care was meant to pay tribute to all organ donors living and deceased.

After welcoming everyone to "Chris's place," Leslie assured us all that Chris would never stop giving or ever be forgotten. She read their first letter to us, to Gabriel, and explained how that moment in time culminated in the house where we were gathered. In a moment of praise for our son, Leslie declared, "Chris has lifted Jorge to new heights we never thought attainable." As she gushed about our son, our hearts swelled with pride. Especially in light of the fact that Jorge's entire family was present. Their appreciation for Chris and his family was felt throughout the day.

It was a perfect spring day. Saint Patrick's Day in fact. The assembled audience, in addition to so many of the Bacardis' family and friends, included many doctors and nurses from the Mayo Clinic, longtime volunteers from Saint Andrew's Lighthouse, and many leaders from the Jacksonville business and civic community. The building would technically be owned by Mayo, but the day-to-day operations of the Gabriel House of Care would be handled by the folks at Saint Andrew's Lighthouse. Ed Asher would be its first executive director.

When Grace took the podium, it marked the first time she'd spoken publicly about Christopher's death. She was so poised and dignified that I just knew Chris was as proud of her as we were. Grace opened her remarks by quoting the author Elizabeth Stone. "To be a mother is to forever have your heart go walking around outside your body." Words that rang true to Grace ever since our sons were little boys. "Our hearts are always with our children," she said. She acknowledged that as parents we are only lent our children, that their fates are really not in our hands. "Imagine the joy in this mother's heart to know that my youngest son was able to change the lives of so many," she said. "Every day you take a breath," she said to Jorge, "and every day you hug your wife is an honor to our son.

"As we stand here in front of this beautiful, healing place, the Gabriel House of Care, to know that everyone who walks into this building will find a warm, caring home and a place to heal as a tribute to my son makes my wounded heart soar." I was a very proud husband.

Dr. Tom Ganwa, chair of Mayo's transplant department, and Dr. Steve Buskirk, chair of Mayo's radiation oncology department, Dr. Rupp, Jorge and Leslie, and Grace and I cut the ribbon and officially opened the Gabriel House of Care. What a day. What a magnificent day. A day of achievement and victory.

Even in our loss, our hearts swelled with pride. *Look at my boy now*, I thought. *Look at what my boy has done.*

The day before the dedication, we'd gotten a chance to tour the completed and furnished Gabriel House of Care. Most of Jorge's family had finally arrived, and many of them were already touring the house when we got there. The Gregory contingent was arriving en masse at the Jacksonville airport, so it was easy enough to divert everyone to the Mayo campus to see the house they had only heard about. It was also a chance for many of the Bacardis and Gregorys to meet for the first time, including Chris's big brother, John.

The house was stunning. Entering the lobby was like walking into a hotel. Spacious, clean and well lit. The contractors and decorators had done an admirable job. There was a business center, a library, a meditation room, and a fitness center. The guest rooms were more spacious than I'd imagined. Where the old Saint Andrew's Lighthouse had four small bedrooms, the Gabriel House of Care had thirty spacious guestrooms each with a large, walk-in shower. And then there was the kitchen. Modern stainless-steel appliances lined the walls of the massive room. Granite counters glistened. Everything was state of the art, well lit, and clean. And did I mention spacious?

The benefactors' names could be found throughout the house. There was a special plaque dedicated to Dr. Keller, the only one of its kind on the Mayo campus dedicated to an employee. Mayo's funny about things like that, and it required special permission to have it placed. There was the John and Corrie J. Grado, Jr. Kitchen. The Carmen Bacardi Dining Room, funded by Jorge's sister. The Berg Family suite, the Charles and Peggy Stephenson Suite, and a large game room upstairs donated by Pat and Patricia Wilson. A plaque on the wall listed all the major benefactors who had contributed to making the house a reality. The Andersons, the Garys, the Cahills, the Stephensons, the Hutchinsons. A who's who of the Jacksonville business and philanthropic community.

But the most special dedication as far as I was concerned was the plaque that caught our eyes in the lobby. Hanging in a silver frame were two photographs side by side. One was of Jorge and Leslie and the other was Christopher's high school senior portrait. Below the photographs was an explanation of how and why the Gabriel House of Care had come to be dedicated to Chris and to organ donors everywhere. It serves to remind everyone about Chris and the special relationship between him and Jorge.

Here's some of the text on the plaque.

I have just undergone one of the most critical surgeries on this planet. I have come through this ordeal in astonishing fashion, thanks to Mayo Clinic, Cesar Keller and his magnificent lung transplant team and most of all, to the grand generosity of one young man—an unknown entity I have named "Gabriel"—and his selfless act of organ donation.

It was an excerpt from the letter Jorge had written to the Mayo Clinic about the same time he wrote his first letter to us. As sincere as his feelings of gratitude were immediately after his transplant, here, some two years later, they had not diminished one bit. If anything, his feelings, like those of his family, had grown.

I had arrived in Jacksonville with something on my mind, and I couldn't let the moment pass without getting it off my chest. So while my brothers and Grace's sisters spent time chatting with Jorge's nieces and nephews, I took Grace, Jorge, and Leslie into the library and closed the door. I told them a story.

"Some years ago, Grace's father bought us a gas grill," I said. "I think Chris might have been in the eighth grade. I came home from work one day, and he'd put it all together. And I guess I was in a bad mood or something because instead of praising him for what he'd done, I gave him crap because he hadn't done it right." At that point, I had tears in my eyes. "And I'm so sorry, but now it's too late to ever take that back. But I couldn't let this day pass without telling you how proud of you we are for what you've done. And I know that Christopher deserves as much credit for building this house as you do. I'm just so proud of all three of you."

By then, all four of us were crying. When you lose someone suddenly, you never get to atone for all the mistakes you made in your relationship with that person. My failure to praise my boy for putting that grill together weighs on my heart every day. And I knew that if I didn't tell Jorge, and I mean really tell him, just how proud I was of the house that he built, I would regret that as well. And I thought there was a prayer that Christopher would hear me, and understand, and forgive me.

Leslie took the time in her remarks to recognize so many of their friends who had traveled to the dedication from as far away as California and Canada. It seemed a reunion of those who had assembled in the waiting room at Mayo just as Jorge emerged from surgery three years earlier. Her sister, Joy, and Joy's husband, Tom, were there. And Dex and Ann Crotts. And Alberto and Mari. And Brad and Leslie, who had accompanied Jorge and Leslie to our home. All of their friends and family who had watched Jorge struggling to simply breathe. Pam and Nick, who were instrumental in getting Jorge to the airport in the middle of that fateful night when he got that call. Everyone who witnessed his slow decline and then experienced the miracle that saved his life and resulted in this joyful day.

Everybody handles grief differently. Nobody's way of dealing with death is any more right or wrong than anyone else's. I didn't really understand that until one day I tried to engage John in discussion about Jorge. Grace and I were excited to be communicating with Jorge and Leslie, and we shared those early letters and e-mails and the subsequent photos with our family and friends. But I didn't realize John and Colin weren't interested. With each new communication, I asked John, "Do you want to read the e-mail I got from the Bacardis?" No thank you. I didn't understand his reaction. Maybe to me, those letters meant Chris wasn't really gone. Maybe to John, they were a reminder he wasn't coming back.

John finally said, "It isn't that I hold a grudge against them. I'm sure they're all nice, decent people. And I don't have any animosity or resentment against them. They're alive, and I'm really happy for them. But look, I'm the one who can't sleep at night." That was a difficult moment for me.

I realized that I was being too overbearing on the subject with the boys. And that I had to back off. Perhaps in time they would soften up. I prayed every day God would ease their pain, give them courage, and soften their hearts. And in the meanwhile, if they didn't want to talk about it, we wouldn't talk about it.

In any event, there we were. The Gregorys and the Bacardis. We had begun our journeys to this moment starting from very different circumstances and yet found ourselves at the same place. This day was a celebration of life. It wouldn't be about winners and losers. This was not a zero-sum game. The respect and love for Chris and our family displayed by so many of Jorge's family was almost overwhelming at times. Alan

Dolinsky, a friend of Jorge's and Leslie's, introduced himself but couldn't say anything more than "Hello, I'm ..." before he wrapped me in his arms and was crying on my shoulder. All of Jorge's family was so gracious. I don't think before that day that very many of them understood the cost our family had paid for Jorge's life. I mean they knew, but they didn't *know*. All they'd known was that their tio had been very near death. But an anonymous young man had died. And his lungs had saved their tio's life. Their friend and uncle was alive and well. But then they were seeing that the boy who had saved him had a name and a family. And they could see the faces of this boy's family. There were brothers and cousins and aunts and uncles and yes, parents. And we knew Chris, and we loved him. We'd watched him grow up, and we could tell stories about him. Then we'd had to bury him. And suddenly Christopher wasn't just an anonymous young man who had suffered a medical catastrophe; he was somebody's son, brother, nephew, and it was all just so real.

All our family had met Jorge and Leslie and had heard of this project at the Mayo Clinic and what a big deal it was going to be. But there we were at this beautiful building. And there were all these folks from the Bacardi family and the Bacardi Company and the Mayo Clinic. And it was a really a big deal! They were all so gracious and grateful, and they were speaking about Christopher with such respect and even reverence.

This magnificent project would help so many people, and it was all thanks to Chris. Our Chris. It was an emotional, eye-opening experience for our families as they witnessed what Jorge and Chris had accomplished together.

As the families met, stories started circulating about the two men who at first glance seemed to have so little in common. But it soon became apparent that in their own circles, Chris and Jorge were very popular. They shared the same love of life and adventure. They were both deeply committed to family and lasting friendships. Both had a sense of humor that sometimes took time to appreciate. Christopher Gregory was missed very much. And without Chris's sacrifice, Jorge would have been sorely missed as well.

The day was a huge success. And of course my old friend, Ken Rittman, was there. After driving six hours to sit with us in a New Orleans hospital, he got to see firsthand just what that terrible day in New Orleans had led to. Those awful hours in the hospital, and people crying, and the feeling that the world was suddenly a dark place where terrible things could happen to innocent people. And now look. Look at what has come from that disaster, and what it means to people, as Jorge's niece Brianna would later say, "whose names you'll never know."

Afterward, a photographer wanted to take some photos of us. Leslie was very excited that we could convince John to come to the dedication. "Be gentle with our son," we asked. I was afraid he'd be turned off if anyone made too big a fuss about his being there. It took a little work on the part of Grace and me to get him to attend. "Look," I said. "You don't have to do this for me. But this is a big deal. And it's all about your brother. You need to post up for him." And so John came. In the conversation about plane tickets, I sensed that he might have been a little more excited about the idea than he wanted us to know. But he did come, and that's what mattered. While the photographer scouted a suitable place for photographs outside, I noticed John and Jorge in a quiet, private conversation. Both guys had their hands in their pockets and were sort of looking down at their shoes, kicking the odd rock. Lost in their own conversation. I felt my heart warm. Maybe God answered at least this prayer, and John's heart was softening. I nudged Grace and silently nodded in the direction of the two men. She smiled and squeezed my hand.

SOMEWHERE IN THE BAHAMAS

After the dedication, we were emotionally and physically drained. Overwhelmed is the word that comes closest to what we had been through. It seemed a battle had been fought and won. We had been dealt the loss of Chris and everything that went along with that. But months and months later, somehow, some kind of victory had been handed to us. No, it would never replace Chris. No experience could ever replace Chris. But this was still something good and decent. And it wasn't over. There would be a Gabriel House of Care tomorrow and the day after that. And people would come and go, and be helped in their hour of need next year and the year after that. Every day the Gabriel House of Care housed someone waiting on or recovering from a transplant, that would be Chris in the world. In the present. Still here.

And of course we still had Jorge and Leslie. Our new family. They still talk about Chris as if he were their own, which of course he is. Everyone was beat but in a very upbeat way. We headed off again to the clear blue waters and white sandy beaches of the Exumas.

On that trip, I took a little homework. I took my master's thesis. It was nearly complete, and I wanted Jorge's opinion. The title was "US-Cuba Relations in the Twentieth Century." Jorge being a Cuban exile, I very much valued his opinion.

It was a beautiful afternoon aboard *Contigo*. We were anchored off an island and had a pretty busy and successful day fishing. After the crew had set the anchor, Jorge grabbed the binder containing the thesis and exited the wheelhouse aft of the sundeck. He sat down on a lounge chair next to Grace, who was sunning herself. Grace smiled as Jorge took his seat beside her, and then she closed her eyes.

Jorge turned the pages reading the text very carefully. Every now and then he took a pencil from his pocket and made a minor correction or a brief note. Grace just soaked up the sun now and then glancing at another boat that came into view or just admiring the magnificent water. Then Grace heard Jorge's pencil drop to the deck. She turned her head and saw that he had fallen asleep. My thesis had literally put him to sleep.

The two of them sat there silently. Grace wasn't looking at Jorge but was keenly aware of his presence only a couple feet away. And as they sat there, she began to notice the sound of Jorge's breathing. Deep, rhythmic, life sustaining. A feeling akin to gratitude came over her. She enjoyed the sunshine and the gentle rocking listening to her son's lungs. For the longest time she wasn't sure what to think. Satisfied. And at peace. She was content with just listening to Jorge breathe. Then she realized, *This is what I came here for. This is why I am here.*

dear chris,

$\cdot \times\!\!\times \cdot$

So I feel that I need to write you this e-mail. I didn't know you all that well, but I knew you. I feel cheated that I never got to know you better. I was so psyched when I found out that Little Gregory was coming to Loyola. I love your brother to death, and I gave him so much shit about you being kooler than him. Every time I was around you, I had nothing but a good time. If only I'd hung out in the library a little more last semester, I'm sure I would have gotten to know you a little better.

I remember meeting you for the first time. I made Ian find out where you and Colin were hanging out so we could come see you. I remember hanging out with you, Colin, and Ian in the library bullshitting. Talking about how you used to hide for hours just to jump out and scare Colin, and how you hid dip cans everywhere in the house. I remember that day at the gazebo like it was yesterday. I remember driving to Charles' house and later to Tuck's blaring "Young Jeezy" in my car while you sang every word to every song. Then you ate all our cheese fries as we drank and played pool.

To tell you the truth, I think I laughed the most in a very long time at your memorial service. It was extremely sad, but at the same time it was incredible. You touched so many people and made so many people laugh even after leaving earth. That's a gift!

You are truly a wonderful person. I am so sad that I didn't know you better, but I thank God that I got to meet you and spend a little time getting to know you. I know how sad I am right now, but I cannot imagine how those closer to you feel. Poor Jenn misses you like crazy! I can see it in her eyes, but you already know that.

Colin is going to try to enjoy a birthday today, so try to help him. Please watch over all those who love you. Keep them strong. I honestly cannot understand why you had to be taken from us so early, but I have to believe that there is a damn good reason. Thank you so much for the memories and laughter you have given me. You will never be forgotten. I hope this e-mail reaches you well. I love you, Chris.

Love always,
Erica Backes

chris and the jesuits

>⋈<

There are more than a few references to connections between our family and the Jesuits in these pages. Ted Dziak and Jim Caime are the two Jesuit priests who went to Tulane Medical Center when Chris was first hospitalized. They stayed there day and night ministering to Chris, to his friends and classmates, and to our family. They stayed even up to the moment he was taken to the OR to donate his organs.

And they traveled to Maryland to assist in Chris's funeral. They concelebrated with our old friend Fr. Frank Gignac, another Jesuit whom we had known for thirty years. On Christopher's birthday in 2008, Frank came to our house and celebrated a Mass for Chris right there in our living room. Fr. Tim Godfrey, SJ, was the chaplain at Georgetown University in 2008. Tim provided me a well-needed shoulder to cry on at just the right moment. Those were difficult days, but the presence of these men in our lives helped us greatly.

If Chris had chosen to go to school anywhere but Loyola, would we have received the 24/7 attention we got from the Jesuits? What kind of support would a state university have been in a position to offer? What if Chris hadn't been in school at all? I am sure there would have been something. The death of a student is every college administration's worst nightmare. But we had the Jesuits on our side. Fr. Kevin Wildes, SJ, the president of the university, was there. How often does that happen? At any college? And they touched everyone with whom they interacted. They touched Chris and his brothers and Grace and me. They were there for Chris's and Colin's friends and classmates. They made an impression on the nurses and even on Joe Guillory, the organ recovery coordinator. The presence of Fr. Ted, Fr. Jim, and Kurt Bindewald made a huge difference to everyone who was there. Everyone. Even the nurses.

Many of the physicians and nurses who cared for Chris or were involved in the subsequent transplants had attended Jesuit universities. Amy Schulingkamp, Christopher's nurse during the day, was working on a master's at Loyola University New Orleans when Chris was in her care. Dr. Cesar Keller, Jorge Bacardi's physician, attended Jesuit schools as a child in Guatemala and Saint Louis University in the United States. Arthur Jackson's physician, Dr. Hector Ventura, completed a fellowship in heart failure and transplantation at Loyola University Chicago. Dr. Umberto Bohorquez is a product of the Pontifical Xavierian University in Bogota, Colombia. He and George Loss worked to save Nic Whitacre. Jorge Bacardi attended the Colegio de Dolores in Santiago de Cuba as a child.

Chris's older brothers attended Gonzaga College High in Washington, DC. I started going to Georgetown at night largely because I wanted to share the experience of a Jesuit education with my sons. If they hadn't gone to Gonzaga, maybe I would have had no interest in Georgetown. But that's not what happened. I wanted the Jesuit connection for all of us, including Chris. It would be another denominator the Gregory men could have in common.

Years in the future, we would hopefully make a big deal of it maybe on July 31, the feast day of Saint Ignatius of Loyola, the founder of the Society of Jesus. Maybe it would mean little more than rooting for the same teams during the NCAA basketball tournament. But it would be something. It would always be there. Ask anyone who has graduated from a Jesuit school and they'll likely agree. The connection is real. There is an identification among the graduates of Jesuit schools that is seldom ignored once discovered. It is often an icebreaker, something in common with other Jesuit alumni. It's as close as it gets to attending the very same school. That's what I wanted for my sons.

Chris loved his family. He loved his brothers, and he looked up to them, and he wanted to be like them. He wanted to attend Gonzaga even though we never pushed it on him, but he ended up happy at St. Joe. Then he applied to Loyola University New Orleans. Partly because Colin was there and partly for me. The smile on his face when the acceptance packet from Loyola arrived said it all. He didn't jump up and down—no shouts, no high fives. Just a wry smile at the corner of his mouth.

So what? you might ask. All of this hardly seems important unless you consider the following. Jorge Bacardi called the success of his lung transplant "an alignment of stars." And that's entirely appropriate. Things could have turned out very differently. Chris applied to three colleges—Loyola New Orleans, West Virginia, and Northern Arizona. Once he was accepted at Loyola, his mind was made up. It didn't hurt that Colin was already there and his childhood friend Matt Nolan was also headed to Loyola. So it was off to New Orleans and the Jesuits for Chris.

We now understand that Chris was going to suffer a brain aneurysm and wouldn't survive. It was going to happen. There's no changing that fact. Science says it was something he carried around with him for years. In a cruel twist of fate, it struck without warning. There was nothing we could ever have done to prevent it from happening. But what if Chris is in West Virginia or Arizona when he suffers that event? Guess what? Jorge Bacardi doesn't get that second phone call on March 27, 2008. Instead, someone else gets the call. Maybe someone in Maryland or Pennsylvania. Maybe Jorge calls Dr. Keller and says, "I'll be fishing with Joaquin and Sonia, and I'll be out of range." For what it's worth, Nic Whitacre, Xavier Major, Arthur Jackson, and Carolyn Harrell don't get called either. Maybe they do. Maybe later. Maybe there's a tragic automobile accident that happens that same day. But I'm not aware that anything like that ever happened. At least not on March 27, 2008.

We do know that Chris suffered a ruptured brain aneurysm. And that he was in New Orleans. And so Jorge got the call. And so did Nic. And so did Carolyn and Arthur and Xavier. The stars lined up. And these five people got called for transplants. And Chuck and Arlene got called as well about corneal transplants. But if Chris doesn't care about going to a Jesuit school if only to be like his brothers and his dad, then he doesn't go to Loyola. And then he isn't in New Orleans when it happens. And UNOS isn't looking on the list for recipients in the southeastern United States. And Jorge Bacardi doesn't get the second call, and he never flies to Jacksonville. And then he never writes the letter to Gabriel and his family. We never meet. The Gabriel House of Care is never built. And maybe our ability to laugh is never restored. God only knows how all our lives turn out. One of the pillars of Ignatian spirituality is to find God in all things. For us, that means even in tragedy.

A second pillar of Ignatian spirituality critical to this story is that those influenced by the Jesuits are asked to become men and women for others. Chris didn't need to attend a Jesuit school to learn that. He got plenty of it at Mount Saint Joe, and he got plenty of it by being an Eagle Scout and by going to our church in Laurel.

Chris cared deeply about his family and friends. He drove across town after school to visit his sick grandfather when he was in home hospice. It was nothing unusual for the phone to ring and it would be Chris calling from his grandpop's house. "Hey, ahh, this caregiver that the agency sent over to sit with Grandpop? I don't think he's gonna work out."

Chris was loyal. He cared very much for the rest of humanity. He was a man for others before he ever got to Loyola. His decision to register as an organ donor hadn't been a random act. It was a conscious, thoughtful decision. It was not a matter of "Whatever." Most important, it was a decision he shared with his family.

Once he got to Loyola, he settled into the culture of the place. The Jesuit influence would take its time absorbing Chris. It would take years of interactions with people and witnessing events. If he just opened himself to the possibilities, the culture would envelop him and mold him even more.

Fr. Ted remarked that he knew Chris only in passing usually sitting in front of the freshman dorm hanging out. He didn't recognize him from daily Mass or from the many service projects Loyola makes available to students. That's because Chris didn't go to daily Mass. That would have come later perhaps. Chris was there, at Loyola, and that was enough for the time being. He was comfortable in his own skin. In time, he would have made his mark on the school anyway. Just as he was already doing among a close circle of friends. He had become incredibly popular his freshman year. Those who knew him thought highly of him. They remarked in the days after his passing how sincere and caring he was. How he always had time for a friend. It came as no surprise to those who did know him or learned about his character after he died that he was an organ donor. It was just so like him. Sadly, we don't see the best in people except in hindsight. We don't appreciate them for who they are while they're walking among us. But in his final act in life, Christopher lived up to that ultimate Jesuit ideal and was truly a man for others.

Somewhere amid the eternities, Saint Ignatius himself has to be smiling.

I wish I could say that this story has a happy ending. It doesn't. In truth, it does not have an ending at all. At some point, though, I have to face the reality that I've written all I can. But that doesn't mean Christopher's story has an ending. As of this writing, it has been seven-plus years since he died. And yet his heart still beats, his eyes still see, and his lungs still draw breath. Most of all, the love he had for humanity wasn't buried that cold April morning when we carried him to his spot in the cemetery. That beautiful spot next to the playground where he laughed and played as a boy. Where the laughter of children can still be heard. And where the morning sun warms the soft ground.

subject: hey pop

᙭᙭

Hey dad,

... sorry for not responding to your e-mails, hectic week last week. but in other news. you should see the clouds out today. there is some kind of storm, the cumulonimbus clouds are gigantic. and they are not the only clouds. i can see, no joke, every kind of cloud out right now. and the thunder is just ridiculous. I don't know if mom told you but I got an A on that math test I took before break. And I took another bio test yesterday and got a B on that. Sometimes I feel like even when I study my brains out I can only ever get a B on the tests in that class; it is extremely frustrating. I got the flight stuff, I am really excited to be going to AZ again. It seems like it has been forever since we have been there. It is raining so hard right now I can barely see across the quad through my window, I guess that is the subtropics for you. I am going to send you the rough draft of my paper on the public schooling system, tell me what you think. What nights do you have class? I just need to know when the best time to call. I really want to thank you

and mom for giving me the opportunity to come back here and give it another shot. I feel like I am really getting this college thing right finally. The way I am looking at it is like this: work needs to be done, whether you want to do it or not, the work needs to be done. So all I can do is man up and get through it. I could not be more thankful for how patient you and mom have been over the years, but I feel blessed that I had parents who believed in me even when I didn't believe in myself. Thank you so much for all of this, again. I will talk to you soon.

Chris

epilogue

Jorge Bacardi spent the first twenty days of his life in an oxygen tent. He was baptized in a hospital in Cuba because Caridad, his mother, didn't think she would ever take him home.

In April 2015, he celebrated his seventy-first birthday. Grace and Colin and I were there along with Leslie and another long-time friend of theirs, Karen. We were anchored off an island in the Exumas and would have dinner that night out doors on the aft deck of *Contigo*. It was a beautiful evening, and the sky turned from a deep blue to tangerine. When Jorge raised his glass to offer a toast before dinner, he didn't toast his good health. He didn't toast his good fortune. He toasted his donor. Christopher. It was a special moment, one we felt truly blessed to share.

Jorge and Leslie have been married for more than forty years, and when they aren't traveling the world, they're bouncing around the islands of the Exumas. With the exception of the transplant itself, it's nearly impossible to discuss Jorge without including Leslie in the same sentence. They are that close as a couple.

We are blessed by the friendship that has developed between us. It is especially nice for Grace. How difficult it is for a mother to lose her child. But anyone who knows Jorge and Leslie wouldn't be surprised. They're a very open and sharing couple. Once you are welcomed into their lives, you are their friend forever.

The years since his transplant have given the Bacardis opportunities to expand their circle of friends, and they have taken full advantage by doing just that. They have also expanded their philanthropic efforts to include funding medical research.

I asked Jorge and Leslie what it all means to them seven years after Jorge's transplant. Of what are they the proudest and most grateful? Of course, the Gabriel House of Care tops the list. The house is still filled to capacity nearly every night. It has far exceeded its expectations from the day it was officially approved in that tearful meeting in July 2009. Hundreds of patients have found support and friendship there as they faced great challenges. It's become so much more than simply a house for sick people. While Mayo treats the disease with science, the Gabriel House of Care treats the soul with love.

Nic Whitacre is an insurance broker in New Orleans. The H-E-R-O Movement has inspired many people to register as organ donors. In part thanks to Nic's efforts, Louisiana boasts one of the highest registration rates in the United States. Nic is healthy and staying very active.

Nic and Jorge met in 2013. Mount Saint Joseph asked if somehow we could get them to visit Christopher's alma mater and speak to a group of upperclassmen. It was a powerful experience. Some of Christopher's classmates came also. The two men shared their experiences in front of a packed auditorium. The school administration was originally a bit hesitant to schedule such an event on a Friday. And during the last period of the day no less. It was expected that the boys would be distracted with the weekend imminently upon them. But you could have heard a pin drop as Nic and Jorge spoke. At Saint Joe's, the boys are taught a deep respect for those Mount men who came before them. They have learned that they stand on the shoulders of giants. That day, Chris was a giant.

Nic has traveled the state of Louisiana telling his story and promoting the cause of organ donation. He was even honored by the New Orleans Saints for his efforts. There is no doubt that Nic has inspired at least one person to register who has made the ultimate gift of life to someone else. Nic's intent when he started the H-E-R-O Movement was to create a veritable chain of heroes who would each pay forward the gift Nic was paying forward himself. That chain is gaining links today.

We finally met "Mac" Jackson. Grace, Colin, and I were in Louisiana for Ellie Trant's wedding, and so we arranged a long-overdue, in-person meeting. He snuck in the side door of the hotel where we'd arranged to meet. Mac was moved to tears when we gave him some photographs of Christopher as mementos.

Mac passed away about a year after we met. He continued working well past the age most people retire. He would have liked to quit working, he said, but the job offers kept coming in.

We had a nice lunch together and our visit was much too brief. But in the short time we spent together, Mac shared with us what the years since his transplant had meant to him. It all boiled down to family. Despite his failed marriage, he was grateful for the love of his siblings, nieces, and nephews. Above all, he was grateful for the time he got to spend with his children just being a father.

I was very sad when I learned of Mac's death. It is something that donor families have to prepare for if they intend to keep up a relationship with the recipient of a loved one's organs. We wake up every morning with the same gratitude that Chris's recipients do. Thankful for their second chance. At the same time, we worry about their future. We don't want to say good-bye again. But that's the way it is.

Mac's passing left me with a feeling of deep gratitude rather than sadness. I was thankful Mac chose to stay in touch with us over the years. He was a good man. His was a life worth saving. And besides that, if the heart of a nineteen-year-old white boy beating in the chest of a sixty-five-year-old black man doesn't give you hope, I don't know what hope is.

Xavier Major is happy that his transplant has allowed him to be active in his church ministry. He still lives in southwestern Louisiana. He remains close to his children and his family. We became friends on Facebook. It always brings me a smile when I witness the love he shares with friends and family. He's a sharp dresser, and he offers the whole world a magnificent smile. As with all of Christopher's recipients, that they can live filled with love and peace and happiness leaves Grace and me as grateful as we can be.

Jenn still lives in New Orleans. In the years that followed Chris's death, we have remained close to Jenn. It was always there just below the surface, our feelings about that week in 2008 when we met. Finally, after six years, I got around to asking Jenn if she would agree to talk about those events for this book. It just so happened that she was taking a class in thanatology, the study of death and dying, for a master's program at Loyola. My timing was serendipitous in her opinion; she told us that the events of that week had managed to bubble to the surface. Yes, she would be willing to share them with us.

During an emotional, tear-filled dinner at Joey K's on Magazine Street, we learned for the first time that the Beggars wouldn't allow her to date for months after Chris's death. It seemed for the longest while that time stood still for her and for many of Christopher's friends. As the writing of this book concluded, she married Andy, a close friend and fraternity brother of Colin's. Andy was the first to befriend us in 2005 when Colin started at Loyola. Regardless of the fact that she's married, she still refers to Chris as her boyfriend, not her ex-boyfriend. That sometimes leads to awkward explanations.

We learned that March 27, the day Chris died, was the day her little brother had nearly died two years before. The coincidence made that date in 2008 especially difficult. Since her brother survived, she fully expected Chris to do the same. She began second-guessing relationships with new people in her life. In her mind, she had to protect herself. She was afraid to get too close to people fearing they too might die.

Dr. Cesar Keller has left his post as head of lung transplantation at the Mayo Clinic. He is directing his efforts toward two initiatives that will improve outcomes for lung transplant recipients. Some of his research has focused on regenerative medicine, and the results have been incredible. They involve the use of stem cell therapy. Transplanted lungs are usually inflamed. Because the donor is brain dead, the organs are manipulated to keep them viable for transplant. The use of hormones and medications often leaves them swollen. Dr. Keller plans to isolate and grow the recipient's own stem cells prior to the transplant. After receiving their new organs, the doctors will reintroduce a few million stem cells to fight the inflammation in the donor organ. The goal of this research is to see if the body can't be trained to recognize the donor lung as its own. If successful, stem-cell therapy will replace immune-suppressive therapy to ward off inflammation and rejection.

The second project Dr. Keller is working on will address the chronic shortage of donor lungs. In 80 percent of all organ donors—people like Chris who die suddenly—the lungs aren't transplantable. In 2014, for example, over 8,600 people died and became organ donors, but only 1,925 of them had lungs acceptable for transplant. The answer will hopefully be found in ex-vivo lung perfusion (EVLP). EVLP involves removing the lungs of a deceased donor and treating the organs with necessary steroids, anticoagulants, etc. that combat infections and extend the useful life of the lungs. The goal of EVLP is to make available a greater number of lungs for transplant. At the time of this writing, 20 to 30 percent of all people waiting for lung transplants will die before a donor can be found.

Dr. Keller remains convinced that he has the best job in the world. It's a miracle, he believes, to see people so close to death suddenly have a second chance to live. And to see people like Jorge Bacardi give back in so many different ways drives Dr. Keller to keep giving people those second chances.

Ted Dziak, SJ is still at Loyola University New Orleans. Along with the tears and sorrow, Fr. Ted remembers a sense of community forming among those in the waiting room at Tulane. He describes the week Chris was in the hospital as a moment of grace. In thirty years of being a priest, he said he has found that people with faith have a better way of dealing with the question of death. Among Christopher's friends and family that week, Ted said there was never any doubt that there was a true, heartfelt sense that Chris was now with God. For the Jesuit, it was as if God were breaking into the world and bringing people together through that tragic situation. It was for him a vocational affirmation.

Morgan "MG" Ernest is a screenwriter in Los Angeles. MG was excited to connect with his "cousins" Colin and Chris in New Orleans. However, seeing Chris in that condition shook him deeply. It was the first post-EMT tragedy of his life, and it hit a little too close to home. During that week in 2008, MG successfully suppressed his emotions and allowed his background as an EMT to take charge. Two weeks later, it caught up to him. His emotions erupted. One night, he sat up in his bed and cried his eyes out.

He has no doubt Christopher's death and subsequent events had an impact on his life. He was triple major at Tulane preparing for a career in finance. But seeing Chris in the hospital was not the same as losing a grandfather. He ultimately left a safe and promising job with JP Morgan. "Life is not a dress rehearsal," he told me. You never know what the future holds. He says that Christopher's death absolutely formed his decision to follow his true passion for writing and his move to California.

Kevin Abdo is a teacher at a Xaverian Brothers high school in Massachusetts. After graduating from college, he spent a year in South Africa serving the poor and dying. Kevin is an avid runner and assistant cross-country coach. We ran the 2011 Marine Corps Marathon together wearing our Team Chris shirts. The weeks we spent training together were special for us both.

He spent the better part of one evening on the porch of Grace's father's beach house with Matt Nolan. They reminisced about Chris and what losing him meant to them. They toasted their friend; they missed him dearly. As the sun set and the beer tasted cold and good, it reminded them of their friend. Kevin told Matt that he deeply regretted listening to him and not flying to New Orleans when he'd first heard the news about

Chris. Matt confessed that he regretted telling Kevin not to come. But there is no such thing as practice for such events, and we can never go back in time and correct mistakes.

Carolyn Harrell passed away in late 2015. We sent her a letter one year and got an e-mail in response. She included her phone number. We talked on the phone for a while, and she told us that she was surprised to have been diagnosed with liver disease. She'd never drunk alcohol in her life. She told us that she is a Dallas Cowboys fan. We told her Chris rooted for the Washington Redskins. We lost contact after that one phone conversation.

Then I received a phone call from Carolyn's husband, Horace. He called to tell us of her passing only days earlier. He knew that we had sent a few cards and that we were in Arizona, so he just started dialing numbers in the phone directory until he found us.

Carolyn died from complications related to her heart, not her liver. Horace thanked us for the seven and a half years Chris had given his wife. His call was a kind and considerate gesture. I told him I'd like to visit sometime when in Texas on business. He agreed. We'll see where that chapter of the story takes us.

In late 2010 and early 2011, we received cards from Chuck and Arlene. They had received Christopher's corneas and a better quality of life as a result. As of this writing, efforts to meet with them have been unsuccessful, but the cards we received gave us every reason to believe that their appreciation for Chris was as genuine as that of those who received his organs.

Arlene explained that Chris provided her with her second cornea transplant, and her vision was the best it had been in several years. She wanted us to know that Chris was living on and that he was helping Arlene see life in a unique way.

Chuck used similar language in his kind note to us. "I do see the world in a very different way, and I am forever grateful," he wrote. Inside his card was a prayer card of Saint Lucy, patron saint of people suffering from eye disorders. Chuck had received the card at a Mass, and he wanted us to have it. It just so happens that the feast day of Saint Lucy is December 13, Christopher's birthday.

Joe Guillory left LOPA and returned to college to get an engineering degree. He presently works for the Louisiana Department of Wildlife and Fisheries. Joe told me during the research for this book that he remembers Chris's case as well as any in which he had been involved. He was so moved by the sense of community that he saw develop that he tried to persuade his nieces to go to Loyola.

It's complicated getting all the donors lined up and getting everyone moving to the hospital for their transplants. It's a lot of work, and it takes a lot of coordination. There are many people involved in a case such as Christopher's. But the one thing I have learned about all of them is that they genuinely care. They sincerely want to see life succeed over death and health over sickness. The world is a better place with people like Joe Guillory in it. People like Joe give you the distinct impression that as complicated as it is his work is nowhere near more trouble than it's worth.

Brant Langlinais is a certified registered nurse anesthetist in College Station, Texas. For the longest time, the big Cajun had difficulty sleeping. The nights he cared for Chris kept running through his mind. Did he do everything right? Did he do all he could? We wrote Brant a thank-you letter, and his response had us in tears. He and Chris had somehow hit it off and become friends, and our son's death affected Brant deeply.

He did marry his fiancée, and the two have two sons and a daughter. We have remained friends, and when Brant applied to nurse anesthetist school, he asked for a letter of recommendation from us. We were more than happy to do so. It was a special night to be invited to his graduation party. And it was a hoot.

Amy Schullingkamp received a master's from Loyola the same day Colin graduated. We have a photo of the two of them in their caps and gowns and big smiles. Such a different mood than the circumstances that had brought them together. She's a nurse in Alabama.

Dr. Patrick "Gene" Parrino is still performing heart and lung transplants at Ochsner Medical Center in New Orleans. When not saving lives, he enjoys watching his young kids play soccer. I shared with Dr. Parrino what Carl Jackson had told me about his brother having to receive open-heart massage to get Chris's heart started. He got a puzzled look on face. So I asked him, "How often do people die during a heart transplant?" He replied, "Never. We don't let them." He explained how the heart spontaneously begins to beat once blood is introduced, and how they can gently shock the heart to control its rhythm, and besides, the transplant recipient is on the heart-lung machine anyway. The real miracle is in the science.

I asked Dr. Parrino what his job meant to him. He replied that he recognizes that as a society, we've found a way to salvage something from an event that's otherwise an absolute horror. The death of a young person is a terrible thing in and of itself. And at the same time there's someone else equally deserving of life but facing imminent death. To be able to alter that trajectory is most humbling and rewarding.

Joaquin and Sonia Bacardi are grateful for the extra time Jorge's transplant has afforded them with their uncle. They graciously welcomed us into their home and cooperated exten-sively in the research for this project. Their great respect for Chris and appreciation for his sacrifice is apparent whenever we get a chance to visit.

Joaquin and Sonia are people of deep faith. Joaquin retains vivid memories of discussions with Jorge on the topic of reli-gion and spirituality. As I mentioned, those discussions often left Joaquin frustrated with his uncle. But then he watched his uncle go through a life-changing, double-lung transplant. He saw his uncle's faith affirmed in an unexpected way, and he saw Jorge acknowledge that there is a greater purpose for each of us in life, beyond our personal aspirations. His uncle's transfor-mation gave Joaquin great peace.

Sonia Bacardi too witnessed a huge change in Jorge. She witnessed a softening in his demeanor and an openness to reach out to others. She noticed a gentler interaction with people in her uncle. In him, she sees a man with much to offer the world still.

Matt Nolan is now a musician living in Nashville, Tennessee. Except for Jazz Fest, he has little interest in returning to New Orleans. The week Chris died brought him closer to Colin and Jenn and Nick and Kevin Drohan than he could have ever thought possible. He shared with us that during that final Friday morning as we said good-bye to Chris, he'd never felt so confused and shocked and yet safe as he did that moment. Those in the hospital room that night became exceptionally close.

In the weeks that followed, Matt saw his fellow Beggars come as close as ever to fully living up to the ideals of their fraternity charter. But as time moved on, so too did people's priorities. Eventually, the week in March 2008 became a dis-tant memory for some. Especially the younger fraternity brothers. They just didn't get it. For a while, Matt, like many of us, grouped people into two categories—those who had shared the experience in New Orleans and those who didn't or who didn't care to know about it and thus didn't deserve the time of day.

The Abdos and the Nolans are still next-door neighbors in Maryland. And they still miss Chris very much. When Kevin and Matt graduated from college, the two families hosted one big party. Kevin and Matt had been Chris's best friends. Not going was not an option. Gerry Nolan took me aside for a moment. "It's not lost on anyone that Chris should have been here today." He understood how difficult it was for us to be there. He knew even then that college graduation was only the first of life's milestones that would forever be bittersweet. Those families with whom Chris had those refrigerator rights—the Abdos, the Nolans, the Stacks, the Neihouses, the Rolles—are the few places where Chris's name comes up naturally and without awkwardness. That doesn't even happen at gatherings of my own family.

But I have the words to say thank you to our friends who loved Christopher as if he'd been their own son.

Ellie Trant is training to become a psych professor like her father. Every spring for the remainder of her time at Loyola, Ellie organized a College Camp Day in memory of Chris. The event was held on The Fly, a park space not far from the campus. Hotdogs and refreshments. Flag football. Frisbee. Water balloon fights. The proceeds from these events went to the Brain Aneurysm Foundation in Christopher's memory. Ellie told us that the event always made her feel close to her bestie.

After graduation, Ellie moved to Tennessee and began the long climb up the academic ladder. She also met her husband, Joe. We were thrilled when Ellie invited us to her wedding. The ceremony took place in the antebellum chapel of the girls' high school she had attended in Grand Coteau. Ellie walked down the aisle to a fiddle playing "Ashokan Farewell." The whole scene moved me to tears because I just knew that Chris was in that very space with us silently smiling and nodding approval. It appears that he did live up to his promise to Ellie. Remember? His promise to find her a good man.

Christopher's mother, Grace, never asked for the hand she'd been dealt. All she ever really wanted was to be a mother and a wife. She wanted a family. To see her dreams taken away so cruelly was painful to watch. But she carried herself throughout that difficult week and after with grace and dignity. Looking back, while I thought I was working overtime to support everyone else, it was really Grace who was holding us all together.

Besides a family, Grace wanted to be a nurse. She made several attempts at a nursing degree over the years of our marriage. Every time she got into it, something came up that would cause her to place her education on hold. Usually, it was a change in my job at UPS. She finally got on track again during Chris's senior year in high school. He and I joked that we survived that year on frozen chicken nuggets and tater tots while his mom studied. Chris spent a lot more hours than he had to drilling him mom with anatomy and physiology flash cards. She was in her second to final semester when Chris died.

I was amazed that shortly after the funeral, she picked up her books and walked back into the classroom. We were all in school that semester. Colin and John resumed their studies as well. My professor, Nick Palarino, was waiting for me when I got back to Georgetown. I had one paper to write. It was due at the end of the spring semester. One damn paper. Nick told me to take all the time I needed. And I needed until September to finally finish it. Grace resumed a full-time class schedule right after the funeral and graduated on time.

Grace is now a maternity suites nurse at a nearby hospital. She cares for newborn babies and their mothers. It's a role I think she was born to. Her maternal instincts and patience make her a natural for the job. She has taught me so much about how to deal with loss and adversity. She, John, and Colin are my heroes.

Colin Gregory felt a lot of anger at the loss of his little brother. He bottled it up inside. One night shortly after a girlfriend had broken things off, it boiled over. He opened up to some friends that in great measure his anger was rooted in the fact that he and Chris were just starting to become really close. Losing his little brother meant that for the rest of his life something would always be missing. Things had not felt right since Chris died. They never will. Every family gathering will be incomplete. Every happy occasion bittersweet.

Today, Colin lives for his little brother. He figures Chris missed out on a lifetime of experiences. Time spent with friends and family, especially newly arrived nieces and nephews, are moments he cherishes. Because Chris can't share those experiences and Colin cannot experience them with Chris.

John Gregory doesn't talk about his brother's death with his parents. Not even if we bring the subject up. It's an event a lot of people would like to forget. Can't blame them. For Chris's brothers and close friends, it was something horrible that snuck up on them. Chris's death left them with no time to prepare and only hours to say good-bye. So many things were left unsaid. So many dreams unfulfilled. It's human nature to take for granted that family will always be there especially when you're young. After a lifetime short as it was, their little brother was suddenly no more. I pray every day for John and Colin. I pray God will ease their pain and leave them with only warm memories of Chris.

Christopher loved life. He particularly loved waking up and antagonizing his brothers. He reveled in it. As much as it drove their parents crazy, the Gregory boys were at their best when they were strumming on each other's nerves. The world never knew a soul more filled with enthusiasm for the simple act of living than Chris. A big piece of John disappeared when Chris died. Together, they were more than their sum apart. A broken heart doesn't mend so fast for a young man in his twenties.

John and Sarah got married in 2012. We were pleasantly surprised when they invited Jorge and Leslie Bacardi to their wedding, and we were thrilled that the Bacardis came. When I introduced Jorge to my uncle Gil, I beamed with pride and said, "Look at this, he brought Christopher to his brother's wedding!"

In October 2013, John and Sarah had a baby girl, Madeline Joanne. But she's their daughter, not mine. I'll never hear her call me Daddy, but there's so much pleasure in being a grandfather. I'm teaching her to call me Grandpop. But the best she can offer right now is "Pop." Just like somebody else used to call me.

Someday, when she's old enough, I'll tell her all about her Uncle Chris,

acknowledgments

The French historian Pierre Nora, tells us memory and history are antagonists. In attempting to accurately reconstruct the week Christopher died and the events that followed (history), it was necessary to rely on the firsthand recollections of the people who shared those events with us (memory). My goals in writing this book were to document the events of the week Chris died, honor my son's life and sacrifice, and promote the cause of organ donation. All the recipients of Christopher's organs shared their personal experiences with me, and that is what allows me to tell the story as completely as I tried. But I am indebted to many others as well.

That said, special thanks are extended to Mac Jackson and Carolyn Harrell. May you both rest peacefully in the arms of a loving God. To Nic Whitacre and Xavier Major, thank you not only for helping me tell yours and Christopher's stories but also for showing me what real courage looks like. And for Jorge and Leslie Bacardi … there just aren't enough words.

The physicians who performed the transplants generously took the time to educate me on the mechanics of organ transplantation without compromising their obligation to patient confidentiality. From the Mayo Clinic in Jacksonville, thanks to Dr. John Odell and Dr. Cesar Keller. Dr. Patrick E. Parrino, Dr. Hector Ventura, Dr. George Loss, and Dr. Britt Tonnesen of the Ochsner Medical Center in New Orleans, Louisiana. Also from Ochsner, thanks to Anna Hands (who rolled out the red carpet), Renee DiGiovanni, Ashley Whitlow, and Roxana Marin.

Ryan Nelson and Jacqueline Keidel from the Donor Network of Arizona. Libbie Harrison of the Louisiana Organ Procurement Agency. The wink at the end of the book is for Justin.

To Brant Langlinais and Amy Schulingkamp, Christopher's SICU nurses, I will never forget you.

To Barry Fitzpatrick, thanks for proofreading the manuscript. But thanks more for being a part of Christopher's life. To my editor, Marty McHugh, thank you taking this project as seriously as I did.

To everyone else who shared their time, recollections, and tears in telling his story: Kevin Drohan, Morgan Earnest, Matt Nolan, Gerry Nolan, Brian and Mary Abdo, Kevin Abdo, Brian Abdo, Jennifer Mau, Ted Dziak, Ellie Trant Heaton, Ed and Sandi Asher, Joaquin and Sonia Bacardi, Reidulf Maalen, Alex Lightbourne, Carl Jackson, Joe Guillory, Barbara Ann Weeks, Mo Hasson, Michelle DellaPenna, Erica Backes, and Diana Adkins.

Finally, to John and Colin and especially Grace. I don't know why Chris was taken from us so soon. But you have been my strength and hope, and I owe the three of you more than I can ever express.